THE FAILURE OF THEORY

By the same author

H.G.Wells
Authors and Authority: A Study of English Literary
Criticism, 1750–1900
Science Fiction: Its Criticism and Teaching
James Joyce

(as editor)
H.G. Wells: The Critical Heritage
Science Fiction: A Critical Guide
H.G. Wells's Literary Criticism (with Robert M. Philmus)

THE FAILURE OF THEORY

ESSAYS ON CRITICISM AND CONTEMPORARY FICTION

PATRICK PARRINDER

Professor of English
University of Reading

BARNES & NOBLE BOOKS
TOTOWA, NEW JERSEY

First published in the USA 1987 by
BARNES & NOBLE BOOKS
81 Adams Drive, Totowa, New Jersey 07512

Library of Congress Cataloging-in-Publication Data

Parrinder, Patrick.
  The failure of theory.

  Includes index.
  1. Criticism. 2. English fiction—20th century—
History and criticism. I. Title.
PN81.P32 1987   801'.95'0941   86-32048
ISBN 0-389-20716-0

Printed in Great Britain

To
Eric Homberger

Contents

Preface and Acknowledgements

To judge by a good deal of recent writing, the following resolutions would attract majority support at a conference of devotees of literary theory:

1. We are living at a time of 'theoretical revolution' in the humanities.

2. The theorist is no longer a servant of the literary critic. Theory and criticism should not take second place to imaginative writing.

3. All utterances are implicitly theoretical. All theory is political. The task of the theorist is to uncover, and where necessary to denounce, the theoretical-political implications of all discourse whatever.

4. The enemies of theory are politically conservative. Theory is radical, and so are its advocates. Pragmatists are not to be trusted.

5. 'Literature' is now a redundant category. The study of English literature is in a terminal state and ought to wither away.

6. English lecturers, however, ought not to be made redundant.

7. There is not much to be learnt from contemporary novelists, dramatists and poets. The author is dead. Long live the Theorist!

The 'failure of theory' involves the failure of all these propositions except for No. 6. The essays in Part I of the present book develop a critique of theory and of particular theorists. In Chapter 3, 'On Disagreement and the Public Domain', I develop the notion of criticism as disagreement as an alternative to the notion of criticism as the application of pre-existing theories to texts. I then explore the work of Raymond Williams, whom I regard as the major living English critic, but whose significance has been distorted by our current theoretical obsessions. Chapter 6 seeks to understand the self-proclaimed radicalism of the contemporary 'politics of theory' by means of an extended historical parallel. Was not the failure of the now forgotten movement for proletarian literature more momentous, in the long run, than the failure of theory could ever be?

Part II consists of a sequence of essays on contemporary novels and novelists. Once again the prevailing 'theoretical' accounts of these writers and their works are misleading and prejudicial. By disagreeing with the current theoretical pigeon-holing of a B.S.Johnson, a Doris Lessing or a Muriel Spark I have hoped to say something useful about their writing. The positions defended in Part I have also inspired these essays, and they find their fullest embodiment in the concluding chapter on V.S.Naipaul.

While not fully representative of contemporary British fiction, the range of novelists covered in Part II is sufficient to indicate the distinctive stand that our best writers take on the aesthetics and ideology of the modern novel. These are not authors who have been reduced to ghostliness by the much-discussed theory of the 'death of the author' but, on the contrary, vigorous individualists with a continual capacity for surprise. They are the 'chameleon poets', while the literary theorists have too often played the 'virtuous philosophers' of Keats's famous dictum. I can sympathise with the less virtuous sort of reader who would like to turn straight to Part II, but today it seems impossible to practise criticism where it is most needed without first discussing what it is that critics ought to be doing. I believe I am right about what that is, but if readers disagree I can hardly complain. Perhaps they will have made my point for me.

*

Preface and Acknowledgements

Versions of Chapters 5, 8, 9 and 10 first appeared in *Critical Quarterly*. Chapters 2 (ii), 7 and 11 appeared in the *London Review of Books*, *Powys Review*, and *Encounter* respectively. Chapter 4 was first given as a lecture at North East London Polytechnic. I am grateful to the editors of the journals concerned for their support and for permission to reprint. All these pieces have been revised for this volume, and Chapters 1, 2 (i), 3, 6, and 12 have been specially written for *The Failure of Theory* and are appearing here for the first time.

Essential encouragement in the later stages of writing this book was provided by Sue Roe, John Spiers, and Charles Swann. I am grateful to Coral Howells and to Harvester Press's anonymous readers for some timely criticism. Eric Homberger, to whom the book is dedicated, generously shared his knowledge of proletarian literature. I have learnt more than I can easily say from his example over the years, as well as from many other colleagues, and from my wife and children. I owe a great debt to the teaching of Raymond Williams, to the writings of E.P.Thompson, and to the stimulus and comradeship provided by a series of meetings with members of the Cultural Studies team at North East London Polytechnic. They and their students deserve part of the credit (or part of the blame) for provoking some of the disagreements expressed in this book. For its other disagreeable aspects I alone am responsible.

P.P.
November 1986

There are not, indeed, examples wanting in the history of literature of apparent paradoxes that have summoned the public wonder as new and startling truths but which on examination have shrunk into tame and harmless truisms; as the eyes of a cat, seen in the dark, have been mistaken for flames of fire.

Coleridge, *Biographia Literaria*

To Tony, the criticism of literature was a study, a pursuit, a discipline of the highest kind in itself: to me, I told him, the only use of criticism was if it helped people to write better books.

B.S. Johnson, *The Unfortunates*

Good criticism should be written with love, authority, and a wish to improve the world.

Christopher Priest, at a recent academic conference

Part I

1

The Failure of Theory

I

One of the unrecognised precursors of modern literary theory is Edgar Allan Poe. Poe's texts, like those of a number of contemporary thinkers, maintain that it is both possible and necessary to lay bare the theoretical foundations of art and life. In his most grandiose theoretical work, Poe presents his understanding of cosmogony in the form of a revelation. *Eureka* offers itself as an outline of the essence, origin, creation, present condition and destiny of the material and spiritual universe. Anticipating the reunion of critical and creative discourse championed by some recent scholars, Poe declared *Eureka* to be a 'prose poem'.

Before he took the origins and destiny of the universe for his province, Poe had made a remarkable contribution to literary theory. His essay 'The Philosophy of Composition' (1846) claims to set out the process of reasoning which determined the composition of his popular poem 'The Raven'. At first sight 'The Raven' is simply a poem, and by the highest standards not a very good one. T.S. Eliot grumbled that 'if Poe plotted out his poem with such calculation, he might have taken a little more pains over it; the result hardly does credit to the method'.[1] 'The Philosophy of Composition' is the poem embellished with theoretical reflection and with a strain of hard-headed accountancy of which the poem itself seems blissfully ignorant. Once we have read the essay, our reading of the poem can never be the same. 'The Philosophy of Composition' lays bare the devices (as the Russian Formalists put it) by means of which Poe claims to have constructed a Romantic lyrical narrative. Deeply duplicitous in itself, this essay reveals 'The Raven' to be riddled with what are today the highly fashionable literary qualities of duplicity and deception.

'The Philosophy of Composition' anticipates contemporary literary theory in two ways, since it contains both a structuralist (or pseudo-scientific) and a deconstructive (or self-undermining) level of argument. In the role of critical scientist, Poe denies that there is any element of the accidental or the fortuitous in the creative process. Everything in the poem, he argues—or, at least, everything in *this* poem—is the deliberate and logical consequence of its structuration by the poet. But even as it (re)constructs 'The Raven', Poe's essay deconstructs it by showing it to be founded on an irreconcilable contradiction, which is repeated in the analysis itself. Contradiction is so central in 'The Philosophy of Composition' that its scientific argument must be considered to be both playful and fraudulent. The spectre of Poe the master-hoaxer haunts the reading of this essay, as well as that of *Eureka*, 'The Balloon-Hoax', and arguably 'The Raven' itself.

'The Philosophy of Composition' attempts the seemingly impossible task of persuading us that nothing in the composition of 'The Raven' is referable to accident or intuition. On the contrary, 'the work proceeded, step by step, to its completion with the precision and rigid consequence of a mathematical problem'.[2] The writing of 'The Raven' is thus represented as a development in which logic and chronology went hand in hand.[3] As in the writing of a detective story, the 'step by step' process was a progress *backwards*, from the denouement to the situation which produced it and from the proposed emotional effect to its causes. The composition of 'The Raven', we are told, began with a series of purely rational desiderata. The poem was to be of a certain length, it was to be original, and its subject, diction and tone were to work together to convey the greatest possible impression of beauty. 'The Raven', in fact, was to be a machine to produce a particular kind of reader-response. It is unnecessary to rehearse all the ingenious steps in Poe's argument. Suffice it to recall that, once he had concluded that melancholy was the 'most legitimate of all the poetical tones'—that is, the one most conducive to an impression of beauty—Poe found himself led inescapably to the word 'Nevermore', which had the most effective combination of melancholy sound and melancholy sense in the English language. To heighten the impression of beauty still further, 'Nevermore' was to be used repeatedly, as a refrain. As an unmasking of the devices of Romantic sentimental verse, Poe's chain of reasoning still has considerable power. One of the most revealing ways of deploying it today would be to apply it to Tennyson's slightly earlier and much-admired poem 'Mariana'. Tennyson's refrain with its dragging repetition of 'dreary' and 'aweary' challenges the pre-eminence claimed for 'Nevermore' as a signifier for poetic melancholy. Poe, however, claims to have artfully avoided the monotony of repetition (on which Tennyson's poem is based). Far from being the tedious complaint of the lovelorn narrator, 'Nevermore' is the unvarying answer to the highly varied sequence of questions that he puts to his interlocutor, which just happens to be a raven. The idea that the raven is a 'non-reasoning creature capable of speech' (or rather, of one word of human speech) enables Poe, as it were, to rewrite the 'Mariana' type of Romantic lyric with elegant variation.

According to 'The Philosophy of Composition', the raven is finally revealed as an emblem of 'Mournful and Never-Ending Remembrance'. The poem considered as a mathematical problem thus seems to reduce to an allegory; however, since allegory has been rehabilitated by our modern literary theorists this is no longer necessarily a disadvantage. In Poe's terms, however, 'The Raven' transcends allegory by virtue of the fact that the poetic contemplation of mournful and never-ending remembrance constitutes an experience of supreme beauty. 'Beauty' is the unarguable term in Poe's equations. The point that 'Beauty is the sole legitimate province of the poem', its 'atmosphere and essence', stands, so he asserts, 'not in the slightest need of demonstration'. This, as it happens, is the source of the most flagrant contradiction in the subsequent analysis. Poe with his talk of a 'non-reasoning creature capable of speech' is rather silent about the extent to which the atmosphere and essence of 'The Raven' depend upon the raven...the 'bird of ill-omen', fabled to forebode death, and to bring infection and bad luck. Ravens, though only 'ravenous' by virtue of a pun, are undeniably black, clumsy and raucous birds.

Whether or not the raven's ominous croak is translatable into human terms, a speaking raven is grotesque. The element which Poe so carefully leaves out of 'The Philosophy of Compositon' is, of course, the paradoxical status of the grotesque and its relationship to beauty. At the very least, 'The Raven' has entranced its readers by begging the question that George Eliot's Daniel Deronda was later to ask—'Was she beautiful or not beautiful?'—and the matter might be put much more harshly, or raucously, than that. Can we see the raven as a dark angel ('And his eyes have all the seeming of a demon's that is dreaming', Poe's narrator tells us), or is it just a melodramatic stage-property like the raven in Dickens's *Barnaby Rudge*? The question applies not only to the raven but to 'The Raven', since both are weird and odd and come perilously close to ugliness and bathos. The rational logic of 'The Philosophy of Composition' would seem to be flawless were it not for the unexamined grotesque aspect of the poem, which reduces the essay to absurdity.

As Daniel Hoffman has shown, once we begin to suspect 'The Philosophy of Composition' of absurdity the absurdities multiply. Seeking with mathematical precision to write a hundred-line poem, Poe gives us eight lines too many. Since 'Nevermore' is the very first word which presents itself, his quest for the most melancholy word in the language ends almost before it has begun. The ideal pretext for the continual repetition of the same word is, as we have seen, the presence of a non-reasoning creature capable of speech; and again there are only two plausible candidates, the other one being a parrot. The predicament of the poem's narrator, which is also part of the equation for supreme beauty, just happens to be the same as that expressed in most of Poe's other verse. And so on.[4] The beauty of the essay is that its sheer silliness can just as well be taken as a sign of deep wisdom, of a sustained though tacit critique of the rational assumptions it purports to expound. We could say that it simultaneously sets out and debunks (or deconstructs) a theory which could very well have been responsible for the composition of poems in the genre of 'Mariana', if not of 'The Raven'. If it *had* been so responsible, would these poems have been so very different? Moreover, once we have reacted against 'The Philosophy of Composition' in

8

this way we can begin to look more closely at 'The Raven', and to see it as something other than a grotesque, self-dramatising and Gothic rehashing of Tennyson's type of poem (though it is all that as well). In disagreeing with Poe's essay we are forced to formulate what it suppresses and to say just why its parade of scientific reasoning seems so absurd.

'The Philosophy of Composition' was admired by two of the greatest nineteenth-century poets, Baudelaire and Mallarmé. They must have enjoyed its impeccable logic tinged with an almost Swiftian mixture of dementia and self-parody. Because our ways of reading have changed since the *symboliste* period, the failure of Poe's essay to pass muster as a theoretical explanation of 'The Raven' is doubtless more obvious today than it once was. However ingenious as a piece of reasoning, it is silent or obtuse on the issues which interest *us*. To the contemporary theorist the problem would not seem to be Poe's denial of the role of accident and intuition, but rather that the self-knowledge to which he pretends is so evidently of the wrong sort. Supposing that we wanted to consider a poem as a machine, Poe's way of doing this would no longer be ours.

The first thing our contemporary theorist would be likely to note is that everything asserted in 'The Philosophy of Composition' posits an Author, or poetic composer, in total control of his material. The essay takes a wholly instrumental view of language. The magic word 'Nevermore' is simply a component of the design, like a spark-plug or a piston-rod. But we do not need the poststructuralist dogma of the Death of the Author to read 'The Raven' in a way that Poe's essay makes no allowance for. For example, not only is the narrator first shown poring over his books, but throughout the poem he is tormented by a series of problems of interpretation. Where and what is the mysterious tapping? Who is at his chamber door (or is it the window)? What is a raven doing there, why does it speak and what meaning can be attached to its unfailing word? Is it 'outpouring its soul', or is its utterance 'its only stock and stone/Caught from some unhappy master'? (And who might that master be?) Is the bird a figment of the narrator's imagination, or has it prophetic rather than merely projective significance? The final stanza turns the tables on our suspicion that the 'unhappy master' might have been the narrator or the poet all along:

And the Raven, never flitting, still is sitting, *still* is sitting
On the pallid bust of Pallas just above my chamber door;
And his eyes have all the seeming of a demon's that is dreaming,
And the lamp-light o'er him streaming throws his shadow on
                                                    the floor;
And my soul from out that shadow that lies floating on the floor;
                            Shall be lifted—nevermore!

Here the narrator's soul is reduced to part of the shadow cast by
the raven. The raven, we might say, is 'The Raven'; the narrator
is finally no more than a convention, a lay figure overshadowed
by the poem that is being written. Poe's overshadowed narrator
gives a new twist to the old trope of the poet and his daemon.
The narrator is in the raven's power. It is important to notice
that the poem concludes with the mystery of creative
inspiration, which 'The Philosophy of Composition' goes to
such ingenious lengths to argue out of existence. (The essay,
too, closes by quoting the final stanza of the poem, with the
words 'from out that shadow' italicised. But the point which the
quotation is supposed to enforce is that the raven is merely
emblematical of *'Mournful and Never-Ending Remembrance'*.)
    What I have sketched here is by no means a definitive reading
of 'The Raven', but simply a way of dislodging the claims to
rationality and comprehensiveness advanced by 'The Philosophy
of Composition'. We have been considering what is possibly one
of the most brilliant literary-theoretical essays of the nineteenth
century. But as a theory, even a self-deconstructing one, it is
now utterly superseded. It says nothing about the daemon,
nothing about the grotesque, and nothing about the thread of
self-commentary in the poem which makes it possible for us to
read it as a drama of semiotic interpretation. Considered in
these lights, the only use of Poe's theory is to be disagreed with.

II

The point of resurrecting Poe's essay is not at all to insist on the
superiority of contemporary theories and theory-dominated
approaches over earlier approaches to the nature of poetry.
Quite the contrary. Contemporary philosophies of composition

have failed, and are failing thus around us every day, for much the same reasons that Poe's essay failed. The awareness and the self-awareness that they offer is simply too restricted; their claim to be comprehensive is manifestly false. There is a difficulty here, since the failure of theories is the necessary condition for the production of further theories, and there is little or no prospect of theoretical production grinding to a halt. A distinction is generally drawn between particular theories and what is now called Theory, which, like the biologist's Life-Force, thrives on the continual extinction of its components. Theory is all-devouring, consuming theories, anti-theories, and non-theories alike. Polemics against Theory are themselves a species of theory. There is no practice without theory, so there is no escape from Theory. 'Our practice has become, willy-nilly, theoretical', one apologist has recently written.[5] *The Failure of Theory* could, from this standpoint, be condemned as a meaningless expression; all that have failed are particular theories, which are always already failing. It is to escape from this terminological impasse that I have chosen 'The Philosophy of Composition' by Edgar Allan Poe as an emblem for the idea of the failure of theory put forward in this essay. It is emblematic largely because of Poe's dismissal, or apparent dismissal, of the role of intuitive, accidental or unconscious factors in poetry.

Poe claims to have been conscious of everything he put into 'The Raven'. Contemporary theorists, like him, have tried to reconstitute literary criticism on wholly rationalistic lines. Their claim is to be able to analyse the 'unconscious' of the text, and not merely its surface. In both cases the theoretical reading involves a denial of conventional or 'common-sense' points of view (such as the observation that, since Poe took four years to write 'The Raven', its compositional process cannot have been wholly straightforward). Like Poe's essay, today's theoretical readings are often deliberate 'misreadings' which depend on the existence of pre-formed intuitive responses and common-sense assumptions for their impact. They want to turn the conventional assumptions of criticism upside-down. But the concept of theoretical reading has hardened into a dogma, a political ideology, and an endlessly dishonoured cheque drawn on the literary-critical future. The Mechanistic School of critics which we can just about imagine Poe's essay as having been capable of founding—supposing that such academic bandwagons had existed in the nineteenth century—would soon have run out of steam. But open a recent 'New Accents' volume and we find the following: 'A combination of Derridean and Kristevan theory, then, would seem to hold considerable promise for future feminist readings of Woolf'.[6] What the journal *Poetry Nation Review* has called the 'new orthodoxy' in literary theory has spawned innumerable promises of that sort.

My argument would suggest that, to the extent that theorists like Derrida or Barthes or Bloom genuinely command our attention, it is because they are brilliant and self-knowing and devious operators, literary gadflies like the author of 'The Raven'. Though there are some signs of second thoughts within their ranks, the majority of the supporters of literary theory in England and America seem to think of their heroes as being more like Copernicus and Darwin than they are like Edgar Poe. The claim that Theory has brought about a 'Copernican revolution' in literary criticism is frequently heard. This crude attempt to invoke the prestige of the sciences cannot be reconciled with the epistemological and methodological distinctions between the natural and the social sciences, which most contemporary theorists have been willing to endorse. The history of even the most systematic of the social sciences is, as R.G. Collingwood put it, 'the history of a problem more or less constantly changing, whose solution was changing with it'.[7] In the literary field it is not even self-evident that the rhetoric of 'problems' and 'solutions' is the appropriate one. Talk of a Copernican revolution in such a field is in nine cases out of ten just sales talk.

There are of course epochal and revolutional changes in the arts—the kind that make Poe, let us say, a Romantic, and which have enabled some observers to classify current literary theory as one of the belated phenomena of artistic modernism.[8] The evidence that the present age (that is, since 1965) has been one of artistic revolution comparable to that brought about by the modernist movement in the early decades of the century is, I would say, non-existent. At the heart of the creative revolutions of the past there was an alliance between artistic innovation and avant-garde criticism and polemic, even though such alliances

12

were usually strained and short-lived. There is no easy relationship between creative practice and its rationalisation, so that the poet-critics who figure in English literary history have normally been self-divided figures. But without the intimacy between critical and creative discourse which they provided it is arguable that the artistic revolutions we connect with such names as Wordsworth, Coleridge, Pound and Eliot could not have been achieved. In addition, one outcome of both the Romantic and the modernist revolutions was a substantial reconstitution of the canons of classic literature and art. Today these conditions are lacking, and we have a 'theoretical revolution' proclaimed by literary scholars most of whom seem to work in an artistic vacuum.

There have, of course, been efforts to link the new directions in theory with those in imaginative writing. One thinks of Stephen Heath's *The Nouveau Roman* (1972), and of critics such as Tony Tanner, Robert Scholes and Ihab Hassan. Not much has been heard of this sort of argument very recently. The major critical theorists of the present day would rather reinterpret the established classics, from Plato to Virginia Woolf, than discuss contemporary poetry or fiction. The condescending, perhaps self-parodying title of one recent defence of the 'new orthodoxy'—'Why most contemporary poetry is so bad and how post-structuralism may be able to help'—tells its own story.[9]

It could easily be maintained that the 'normal' relationship between creation and criticism is not one of healthy alliance but of mutual antagonism. Bertolt Brecht, in the 1930s, responded to the offers of 'help' put out by his political allies, the commissars of socialist realism, in the following terms: 'They are, to put it bluntly, enemies of production. Production makes them uncomfortable. You never know where you are with production; production is the unforeseeable. You never know what's going to come out ... Every one of their criticisms contains a threat'.[10] This outburst against one school of theorists—Georg Lukács and his henchmen—was noted down by another critic and theorist, Walter Benjamin. Between Benjamin and Brecht there was perhaps the same sort of close and sympathetic (but also devious and tricky) relationship that we have found between the author of 'The Philosophy of

Composition' and the author of 'The Raven'. In both cases the critic or theorist plays a secondary or subordinate role, as expositor, advocate, and archivist of the poet's thoughts. There is an understood hierarchy. Benjamin reports his conversations with Brecht, and not vice versa. Poe's essay is written *after* 'The Raven', and it ends by simply quoting from the poem, which can once again be left to speak for itself. We cannot imagine the poem as quoting the essay. What I would argue is that contemporary literary theory repudiates, and then fails to consider the consequences of repudiating, these long-standing relationships.

The word *theory* derives from Greek *theoros*, a representative sent to observe public celebrations in cities other than his own. The earliest 'theorist' was thus a spectator, an onlooker, at religious rituals and artistic performances. In philosophical language the term *theoria* was subsequently transferred to the contemplation of the cosmos.[11] The etymology of the word *theory* begins, then, with an implicit contradiction. On the one hand, since the Romantics there has been a tendency to treat the masterpieces of the literary canon as if they were themselves 'sacred events'; the literary theorist sometimes seems to act as an onlooker who is capable of understanding these works more completely and of approaching them more reverently than anyone else. On the other hand, theory, as a systematic explanation of phenomena, tends to reduce its objects—whether literary works or the cosmos itself—to the subordinate status of phenomena to be explained. In modern specialised uses, *theory* has come to mean a system based on general principles independent of the data it is used to explain; theory is opposed to the merely empirical *hypothesis*.[12] In Greek philosophy, the realm of theory was that of permanent and universal cosmic principles rather than the world of physical experience. Today's literary theory has mainly been drawn from disciplines such as linguistics, philosophy, Marxism and psychoanalysis which are quite separate from the experience and practice of poetry. Much the same can be said of the earliest poetic theories, those of Plato and Aristotle. The *Republic* took the side of philosophy in its 'ancient quarrel' with poetry, and the *Poetics* tried to redress the balance by conferring philosophical approval on a certain type of tragedy. Some contemporary literary theory resembles the *Poetics* in that, starting from principles wholly independent of art and the 'aesthetic', it nevertheless contrives to pay rational tribute at the altar of great literature. But not all theory has preserved this customary reverence, which in any case is beside the point. The essence of literary theory has been to dispense with merely descriptive and intuitive procedures, since these conventional elements of literary criticism are not independent of the artistic phenomena themselves.

Where established and canonical authors and texts are in question, a vast amount of intuitive and descriptive critical writing already exists. The habitual and 'common-sense' readings of these works are already available. The theorist can rely on their familiarity in the very act of turning them upside-down. With new works it is different. Conventions of reading certainly exist, but they are always provisional since 'You never know what's going to come out'. What comes out is capable of directly challenging existing theory in a way that the inert and academically-packaged art of the past can never do. Theory claims to 'lay bare the devices' and to analyse the 'unconscious' components of literary works and kinds of works. But with contemporary writing the theorist can be left stranded, or proved wrong, and it may be his own devices which are found to be bare.

III

When I am writing, I am aware both of the labour of constructing sentences, paragraphs and arguments, and of the fact that sometimes a potential sentence, paragraph or argument becomes apparent in a split second. Often the 'flash' follows a period of inattention, a lapse of concentration. I will then say that the particular sentence or paragraph or argument just 'came', and poets and writers through the centuries have appealed to the idea of dictation by an external visitant, whether in the form of a muse or a divinity or of T.S.Eliot's impersonal theory of poetry. Critics for their part spoke of the genius, the *je ne sais quoi* or the richness and complexity manifested in literary works and it was understood that not everything in such works could or would be explained; some of it was simply there to be celebrated. Traditionally the unconscious element was synonymous with the creative process, and while art and the study of art often led (in Max Raphael's words) 'from the work to the process of creation',[13] the journey was never completed.

In modern culture the charting and rationalisation of the unconscious has been the task of Freudian theory and its innumerable descendants. Freud's hermeneutic distinction between manifest and latent contents has become the *sine qua non* of textual interpretation. (Marx's critique of ideology has in some ways run parallel to the Freudian unravelling of the unconscious.) The question whether there are inherent limits to the rational unfolding of the unconscious is a current issue to which various commentators have given a polemical and political colouring.[14] There is a tendency to confuse the utopian potential of rational thought in a liberated society with the championship of a narrow version of rationalism by intellectuals and literary professors in the present social order. Whether or not the goal of a perfect theory is an emancipating one, we are faced with the realities and consequences of the failure of theory.

According to Poe's 'Philosophy of Composition', the raven in the poem of that name was an entirely rational device dictated by poetic ingenuity. But the raven, as we have seen, is also the daemon, the non-reasoning agency or faculty which presides over the throes of literary creation. That a philosophy of composition should give birth to a creature of unreason is a characteristic (and reversible) Romantic paradox. In the Romantic imagination it could have frightful consequences, as we know from *Frankenstein*. The paradox of Frankenstein's creature is not unlike that of Poe's raven. As a rational poet searching for the essence of beauty Poe might have been expected to come up with a bird of paradise, but the image he manufactured instead was that of the 'bird of ill-omen'. The raven's famous pronouncement is, in its way, an Open Sesame, but to a Bluebeard's castle rather than to an Aladdin's cave. Of all the words which the recesses of Poe's mind might have hoarded, 'Nevermore' was 'the very first which presented itself'. Eureka! Two years later, in the revolutionary year of 1848, Poe produced an essay which reverses the despondent message of 'The Raven', arguing that, far from being 'Nevermore', every phase and every event in our universe is destined to take place over and over again. Poe wanted his new essay to be made available in a popular edition of fifty thousand copies; in the end five hundred were printed, in return for an advance of fourteen dollars. Fourteen months later, the author of *Eureka* was found drugged and unconscious in the streets of Baltimore. An election was taking place, and Poe had been one of the stooges used to impersonate the voters. He met his death perpetrating a political fraud, in which he was the victim of somebody else's hoax.

2

Two Case-Studies

(i) CATHERINE BELSEY AND CLASSIC REALISM

Catherine Belsey, *Critical Practice* (1980)
As I write, students in universities, colleges and polytechnics are
being instructed in the gospel of critical practice according to
Catherine Belsey.[1]

According to Belsey, literary texts, like the masses, are enslaved
and need to be liberated. The text must be liberated from
'consumerist' criticism, that is, conventional criticism based on
common-sense views of the author, the nature of language, and
the world to which it refers. The force which is about to free them
is the 'Copernican revolution' in the social sciences inaugurated by
Lacan, Althusser, and post-Saussurean linguistics. Once the
tyranny of common sense is ended, criticism will be able to realise
the text's full potential by seeking the 'multiplicity and diversity
of its possible meanings' (p.109). This, in turn, is a step towards
liberating the world. Unfortunately, this panacea for the ills of
capitalism, imperialism and F.R.Leavisism is not what it claims to
be. What *Critical Practice* actually proposes is a new dogmatics of
reading, a theory which is even more arbitrary and more
duplicitous than the theories or practices it seeks to replace.
Unlike the work of an Edgar Allan Poe, Belsey's self-
contradictions are offered in dead earnest. Once admitted, they
cripple her argument.

But hold on a minute.... Is a purely logical critique of
Catherine Belsey likely to be of any value? Isn't self-contradiction
something on which (in advanced literary and theoretical circles) a
writer nowadays can legitimately congratulate herself? No less an

18

adversary than George Steiner has recently argued that 'formal fallacies' do not really cripple the deconstructive language-game; and hence there is no 'adequate logical or epistemological refutation' of deconstructive semiotics.[2] How can a humanist criticism (Steiner would, I think, say a merely humanist criticism) committed to the values of cross-examination dissent from a movement which claims to have succeeded in cross-examining everything? Belsey's book, like a great deal of poststructuralist apologetics, is founded on a rhetoric of 'putting in question'. What she means by a Copernican revolution is that 'humanist assumptions' and the 'propositions of common sense' have been 'put in question'. And assumptions which have been called in question by poststructuralism are, she asserts, 'not only untenable but literally unthinkable' (p.3).

We have a choice here, either to restrict ourselves to the confines of what poststructuralists declare to be thinkable, or to see how far their own arguments are tenable. When a writer habitually invokes rationalistic criteria in the brisk, no-nonsense manner that Belsey displays, there is a licence, indeed a duty, to submit her own exposition to rational analysis. At stake is the validity of cross-examination as a foundation for humanist criticism, since we can only object to Belsey's type of approach if it turns out that there are legitimate and illegitimate ways of conducting a cross-examination. Common sense tells us that asking a question is of no value unless you stay for an answer, and that 'When did you stop beating your wife?' is often an illegitimate way of asking a question; but Belsey considers common sense itself to be questionable. It might be salutary to remember that in France (Belsey's preferred questioners are mostly French) one of the meanings of *mettre quelqu'un à la question* is 'to torture someone'. The tortured are not necessarily the guilty, but their interrogators derive great satisfaction from forcing them to 'confess' to crimes they have not committed.[3]

On the face of it *Critical Practice* is rationalistic to the point of monotony. Doctrines must be abandoned, Belsey states, if they are 'incoherent' or 'non-explanatory'. 'An account of the world which finally proves to be incoherent or non-explanatory is an unsatisfactory foundation for the practice either of reading or of criticism' (pp.3–4). Moreover, doctrines which are 'incoherent, non-explanatory or even self-contradictory' (p.63) serve an ideological function. Belsey follows Althusser in arguing that ideology is a perversion of reasoned argument and that it too can be detected by rationalistic criteria: ideology is 'a set of omissions, gaps rather than lies, smoothing over contradictions, appearing to provide answers to questions which in reality it evades, and masquerading as coherence in the interests of the social relations generated by and necessary to the reproduction of the existing mode of production' (pp.57–8). The task of critic and theorist is at once to unmask ideological thinking and to 'produce new, more coherent discourses which, until their own contradictions are exposed, can lay claim to the status of knowledge' (pp.63–4). Such a knowledge is 'never final, always hypothetical'. 'Its only certainty is the inadequacy of the discourses of ideology' (p.64).

Unfortunately the 'only certainty' of the kind of knowledge Belsey advocates is by her own lights one certainty too many. If all discourses contain contradictions, then all discourses are seen to be ideological once these contradictions are exposed; indeed, they were so all along. Belsey's argument reduces to the proposition that all discourses are ideological, but some are more ideological than others (which is more or less a truism). If this is so, the discourses of ideology *must* be 'adequate' in some sense of that (Arnoldian) term, since they are all we have. The reason why Belsey's reverence for 'calling in question' is not Socratic but pseudo-Socratic is that (unlike some of the deconstructionist masters) she is not willing to pursue the rational consequences of her own attitude of rational scepticism. This can be amply demonstrated. A careful reading of *Critical Practice* will reveal a host of hesitations, qualifications, and momentary qualms belatedly inserted into the argument. (I say 'belatedly' because the objections will usually have occurred to the alert reader some pages before they are acknowledged, and brusquely dispelled, by Belsey herself. Students with examinations to pass in which Belseyite questions are expected to receive Belseyite answers—and I am not joking about such things—customarily overlook these textual hiccups.) Despite her inquisitorial attitude towards other people's pragmatic self-contradictions, Belsey's way of dealing with her own qualms is, precisely, one of 'smoothing over contradictions' in the interests of sustaining her own point of view. She has, she candidly admits, embarked on what is, in a sense, a contradictory undertaking (p.6). She feels she ought to concentrate 'on what post-Saussurean theories have in common rather than what divides them' (p.6). She writes that the pragmatic strategy of drawing on incommensurable theories 'without dwelling on the incompatibilities between them ... seems to me to be admissible if it generates a productive critical practice' (p.55). Finally, her confession that the new concepts are 'still vulnerable, still in many ways precarious' leaves her with no choice but to resort to Boxer's injunction: 'But this only means that there is more work to be done' (p.145). No one could suppose that Belsey's interrogation of more conventional theoretical and critical positions would have been called off in deference to special pleading like that.

Nevertheless, *if* Belsey's approach generated a productive critical practice, we ought to let this pass; and it would be unworthy and irresponsible to spend much time attacking her procedure, if her exposition of the theories of Saussure, Barthes, Lacan and Althusser amounted to a convincing case for the Copernican revolution in literary studies. I do not believe that it does. I shall be concerned here with Belsey's case against 'classic realism'; that is, her assault on received and common-sense notions about the practice of artistic representation. (It should be said that in *Critical Practice* classic realism is described as forming part of a larger and vaguer doctrine called 'expressive realism', which supposedly had its most influential formulation in Ruskin's *Modern Painters*.) In Belsey's view the goal of a 'mimetic' art which has preoccupied writers and painters since the Renaissance has been undermined by recent theoretical work which shows it to have been based on a false—and therefore 'ideological'—notion of art. The falsity of mimesis is said to follow from the discoveries of structural linguistics, so it is to linguistics that we must initially turn.

Structuralism and poststructuralism are based on a rejection of what Husserl described as the 'natural attitude' towards the reality of the 'world existing out there'.[4] According to Husserl (the founder of phenomenology) this 'natural attitude' is inscribed in positivist science. But what consequences flow from the Husserlian rejection of positivism? Where a number of recent writers have drawn on phenomenological insights to undermine the 'natural attitude', Belsey implies that this can be done simply by referring to post-Saussurean linguistics. Contrary to our intuitive perceptions, a language, Saussure insists, is a 'system of differences with no positive terms ... far from providing a set of labels for entities which exist independently in the world, language precedes the existence of independent entities, making the world intelligible by differentiating between concepts' (p.38). The idea that language simply refers to a world of things is refuted by the 'different division of the chain of meaning in different languages' (p.39), examples of which Belsey gives. But these examples will not bear the weight of the theoretical explanation that Belsey, following Hjelmslev, offers for them.

The English word *blue*, we are told, cannot be translated directly into Welsh or Latin since their words *glas* and *glaucus* include shades which English speakers would identify as green or grey. Colour terms, 'like language itself, form a system of differences, readily experienced as natural, given, but in reality constructed by the language itself' (pp.39–40). This explanation is non-explanatory: 'language itself', we are told, is 'in reality' constructed by none other than 'language itself'. By eliminating the phenomenological category of intentionality Belsey has produced a situation in which colour-differences themselves are said to originate—mysteriously and incomprehensibly—within language. The more she tries to clarify her example of colour-terms, the more deeply Belsey mystifies the operations of language. 'It is not that I cannot distinguish between shades of blue but that the language insists on a difference, which readily comes to seem fundamental, *natural*, between blue and green' (p.40), she writes. Far from insisting on anything, 'the language' is indifferent in this matter, since it allows us both to say what Belsey says and to speak in a familiar and common-sense way of a shade as being bluish-green or greenish-blue. Using language I can say, in a manner that is not at all problematical, that certain colour-shades are simply difficult to describe. Language erases differences just as much (or as little) as it 'insists' upon them. We cannot do anything we like with language, but we can do a good deal more than Belsey allows for.

The blue-green example leads Belsey to offer the following

proposition about language: 'The world, which without signification would be experienced as a continuum, is divided up by language into entities which then readily come to be experienced as essentially distinct' (p.40). Following Saussure, Belsey is arguing here for the *priority* of language. The truth is, however, that experience 'without signification' is as empty a notion as signification without experience. The Saussurean assertion that language precedes experience turns a 'common-sense' doctrine (ie. that experience precedes language) on its head; but if the Saussurean assertion were correct we could not hope to proceed via language to objective knowledge of the world. Belsey stops short of this conclusion, since her own statement pretends to convey such a knowledge of the world. The possible way out of this dilemma—which would involve a dialectical argument recognising the double-bind involved in statements of the priority of language over experience, or vice versa—is one she does not take. Instead, Belsey adopts what has been called a conventionalist position, arguing that language is an entirely arbitrary sign-system shaping and controlling our knowledge of the flux of external reality. Like other exponents of the conventionalist view she challenges the truth-claims of all modes of discourse except her own, which is the vehicle of a dogmatic scepticism. In particular, Belsey dismisses the common-sense doctrines she calls 'classic realism' and 'expressive realism', while paying lip-service to the idea of a 'scientific criticism' and thus sneakingly readmitting the possibility of epistemological realism.

In *Pictures of Reality* (1980) Terry Lovell has very concisely pointed out the specious nature of the rational critique of artistic realism mounted by post-Saussurean thinkers. Conventionalist arguments, Lovell maintains,

> cannot be used selectively to undermine the pretensions of an art which claims to 'show things as they really are' without also undermining that goal for *any* 'discourse' including that of science. On the other hand, if the 'real' *is* knowable, then the realist goal is a perfectly proper one for art, and realism in art does not stand self-condemned as ideology. Realism, the goal of showing things as they really are, is only ideological *per se* if *all* attempts to produce knowledge of the real are similarly doomed. There is no stopping

point in the conventionalist critique short of a radical conventionalism which denies the existence of a knowable reality.[5]

Barthes and Derrida may have approached such a radical conventionalism, but Catherine Belsey certainly does not. The standard she invokes when she demands an 'explanatory' discourse, one which transcends the 'inadequacy' of the discourses of ideology, can only be that of a knowable reality. Her privileging of her own thought over the 'ideologies' she opposes is merely an opportunist gesture. Belsey condemns literary realism as a 'guilty' ideological form because—for whatever reasons—she does not like it. She goes so far as to quote Barthes' perceptions that poststructuralism entails the rejection of 'reason, science, law' and of the 'tyranny of lucidity' (pp.135, 145). But the tyranny of *Critical Practice* is precisely that of a presumption to 'reason, science, law' and of a stupefying pseudo-lucidity.

*

Literary realism is a form of narrative which claims to represent the world outside language; but Belsey's consideration of language leads her to conclude that, since the world we experience is already differentiated by language, the aims of realism are 'simply tautological' (p.46). The tautological status of realistic fiction can be circumvented, however, if the novel is 'interrogative' rather than 'declarative' in its approach to reality; that is, it must question the forms of intelligibility within which 'realistic' narratives are generated, by refusing to privilege any of the discourses within the fictional structure (p.92). The contrast of 'interrogative' and 'declarative' texts is a typical ploy of contemporary literary theory. It makes possible a purely rationalistic scale of literary judgments of the 'four legs good, two legs bad' type which can be applied *a priori* without any reference to aesthetic considerations. At the same time, it imposes constraints on the creators of fictional texts which the theorist makes not the slightest attempt to comply with in her own discourse. *Critical Practice*, like most of the texts whose theories it summarises, is a one hundred per cent 'declarative' work. There is no question as to whose discourse is privileged, or as to whether a true perception of the world can be expressed in Belsey's writing. She asserts that theory and criticism must be 'explanatory' but, of course, she knows better than the realistic novelist who has the temerity to be 'knowing' and attempt to explain things. However, no coherent argument is offered in *Critical Practice* as to why what is said of fictional narrative should not be equally applicable to non-fictional discourse. The cross-examination stops sharply at the point where it might have become uncomfortable for the questioner herself.

Far from addressing the distinction between fictional and non-fictional discourses, Belsey relies entirely on the assumption that readers will unthinkingly make this common-sense distinction for themselves. To recall what is at stake here, Karl Marx, no less, recommended Dickens, Charlotte Brontë and their contemporaries as 'The present splendid brotherhood of fiction-writers in England, whose graphic and eloquent pages have issued to the world more political and social truths than have been uttered by all the professional politicians, publicists and moralists put together'.[6] The epistemological basis of the truth-claims made for art in a judgment like this is the same as that made for non-fictional discourses. They are competing in the same race, as it were. A critic who rejects this ought to show some grounds for singling out realism *in fiction* for attack. In fact, critics who consider the idea of a realistic narrative to be tautological almost invariably go on to accuse realist literature of ignoring the 'reality' of language and realist criticism of misrepresenting the 'reality' of texts![7] The critics are licensed to show us what reality is—the novelists, apparently, are not. If this is due to something in the nature of the novel-form, we are not told what it is. The 'defining characteristics' of 'classic realism' put forward by Belsey do not in fact help to distinguish between classic realism and other forms of writing. The formula for classic realism that she offers—'illusionism' plus 'closure' plus a 'hierarchy of discourses which establishes the "truth" of the story' (p.70)—is less an example of scientific criticism than an amateur conjuring trick.

Let us take the elements of Belsey's formula one by one. She expresses the pious hope that the concept of illusionism is self-

explanatory (!), but shows no awareness of the difficulty of
saying what 'the illusion while we read that what is narrated is
"really" and intelligibly happening' (p.51) entails. (She would
need to say what she really means by 'really', for a start.) In the
manner of other poststructuralists Belsey breaks with
conventional definitions of narrative verisimilitude by arguing
that forms such as science fiction and fantasy fiction belong to
the category of 'realist' texts. Is narrative vividness, or the
presentation of a coherent invented world innocent of any sort
of truth-claim, enough to establish fictional realism? Belsey
intends that we should consider (say) *Winnie-the-Pooh* a 'realist'
text but nowhere does she show how a theory of literature based
on structural linguistics could differentiate between a narrative
purporting to describe what is 'really' happening and an
argument purporting to say what is intelligibly the case. The
post-Saussurean concept of 'classic realism', we are told, 'makes
it possible to unite categories which have been divided by the
empiricist assumption that the text reflects the world' (p.51). By
the same token Belsey's loose and taken-for-granted notion of
illusionism makes it possible to unite categories divided by her
own assumption that anything she says about fictions will have
no consequences for the nature of 'non-fictional' discourse.

The other two items in Belsey's formula—closure and a
hierarchy of discourses establishing the 'truth' of the story—are
self-evidently applicable to all modes of discourse. It is needless
to demonstrate this, since Belsey herself has analysed the
strategies of closure and a hierarchy of discourses which
F.R.Leavis's criticism shares with George Eliot's fiction.[8] What
she omitted from this not imperceptive analysis was the fact that
exactly the same strategies were repeated in her own writing.
For Belsey is herself a classic realist, though of course she cannot
face up to the fact. Introducing the discussion of classic realism
in *Critical Practice*, she writes as follows:

> In what follows I have drawn very freely on recent work on film in
> *Screen* magazine, probably one of the most important sources of
> critical theory in Britain at the moment. I have not always
> attributed specific insights and I have not hesitated to adapt others.
> The debate in *Screen* has been more complex and subtle than it is
> possible to indicate in an argument which inevitably modifies and
> abridges much of what it borrows. (pp.69–70)

Here, very properly, Belsey is telling us how 'truth' may be approached through a hierarchy of discourses. There is a similar use of the rhetorical devices she identifies and stigmatises in her opponents' work in her essay on Leavis.[9]

It might be said that, shorn of its polemical intent, the diagnosis of 'classic realism' shows how narratives and arguments 'position' the reader, and then naturalise the means by which positioning is achieved; the result would be a new form of rhetorical analysis.[10] This is a sympathetic objective, but the first casualty, in working out such an approach, must be the category of 'classic realism' itself. (There *is* a difference between, say, Leavis's and Catherine Belsey's ways of positioning the reader, but 'classic realism' cannot tell us what it is.) The critique of the 'natural attitude' can be applied to *all* forms of intelligible discourse. Belsey and critics like her have principally used it to devalue nineteenth-century fiction by associating it with the debased and automatic forms of present-day popular fiction.[11] Very simple, stereotypical texts (advertisements and the detective novel are standard exhibits) are chosen to exemplify the semiotic properties of realistic fiction. The critic then introduces an alternative literature (postmodernism, self-conscious fiction, the nouveau roman or, in the case of Belsey, pre-Enlightenment narrative forms) which is praised for its less-than-total observance of realistic conventions. One may then show that even the works of avowed nineteenth-century realists 'break the limits of classic realism'[12] in certain respects. But naturally this cannot be taken too far. Catherine Belsey nowhere so much as mentions Flaubert, although one might have thought that a theory of the realist novel which failed to pay attention to the phenomenon of Flaubert was not worth much. What is concealed by this argument is that on Belsey's principles *any* major nineteenth-century novel could be shown to 'break the limits of classic realism' by means of familiar and straightforward interpretative moves such as critics of these novels are always making.[13] Nor is this in any way surprising. The three 'defining features'—illusionism, closure and a hierarchy of discourses—all betray the fact that 'classic realism' is not a property of texts but a way of reading them.

And, indeed, some texts ask to be read in that particular way—not least, expository textbooks of critical theory. How do the great nineteenth-century novels ask to be read? Any answer to this question from a non-structuralist position had better be tentative, but a starting-point is provided by Belsey's contrast between closed and open forms and between 'declarative' and 'interrogative' texts. For the wholly open, perpetually interrogative text, in which the author resigned all the prerogatives of formal creation and content-construction to the reader, would also (like John Cage's silent musical composition, which is much discussed though no one has heard it) be a wholly trivial one. And, to the extent that it exists at all for the artist, the choice between writing in a relatively closed or open form is likely to turn on contingent and aesthetic, not *a priori* and rationalistic considerations. In addition, a critical interpretation can challenge our way of reading a narrative and open up what was apparently 'closed'; so that we need an account (as Richard Johnson has put it) of how some readers, including, presumably, the theorists of 'classic realism', can use conventional or 'realist' texts critically.[14]

If we abandon literature's cognitive claims—what Belsey calls 'the theory that literature reflects the *reality* of experience ... in a discourse which enables other individuals to recognise it as true' (p.7)—how else can we explain the existence of an inherited body of literary texts to which readers, critics and teachers return again and again? If literature and criticism were simply charged with enhancing the plurality of meanings we might expect that all literary works (and not merely a sizeable proportion of them) would be superannuated soon after their first appearance. The unconfined multiplicity and diversity of the 'production of meanings' might suffice to replace literature as we know it but it certainly cannot explain the phenomena of the literary tradition. What this quasi-utopia of semiotic anarchy overlooks, I would argue, is the nature of meaning itself. Meanings are not generated *ab nihilo*. They can only come into existence by displacing already existing meanings. A meaning like an electric current can only be generated against a resistance; and once generated it becomes part of the resistance against which further meanings are generated. Where resistance to the production of new meanings is lessened—which is one effect of the current licence to 'misread' literary works—the meanings themselves tend to dwindle in importance. The vocabulary which speaks of new meanings as being 'challenging', 'provocative', 'suggestive' and so on no longer applies.

The notion that all meanings are generated against a resistance helps to explain the power and plausibility of a theoretical rhetoric of 'unmasking', 'exposing contradictions' and 'calling in question'. But, by the same token, it also explains one of the most familiar and recognised features of realistic fiction. When Engels wrote of the 'triumph of Realism' in Balzac's novels in his well-known 1888 letter to Margaret Harkness he drew attention to the keenly ironical and satiric nature of Balzac's portrayal of the French aristocracy. Marx, who was himself no mean satirist, can hardly have overlooked Dickens's savage social criticism when he spoke of the truths to be found in his novels. For Belsey, irony is used by the nineteenth-century novelist to fix the reader in '"knowing" subjectivity', and the fact that a Dickens novel may be 'critical of the world it describes' (p.81) is a strictly secondary matter. But the novel, as everyone knows, began by parodying earlier forms of narrative fiction and has continued to develop, in large measure, by constantly debunking and remaking its conventions and its way of seeing the world. As Harry Levin has argued, the history of realism is not one of flat picturing but of a dialectic of 'fabulation and debunking'. Realism is a synthesis of the 'imposition of reality upon romance' and the 'transposition of reality into romance'.[15] To anyone who has seriously studied the realist tradition Belsey's notion that 'Classic realism cannot foreground contradiction' (p.82) is surely an absurdity.

But we are getting rather close to the source of this whole argument, for realist fiction appears to be the one form of imaginative writing which openly lays claim to the same cognitive horizons as rationalistic literary theory. The debunking of pretence and the unmasking of ideologies was, as Marx and Engels recognised, the province of the nineteenth-century novel long before it became the declared aim of literary criticism. Poststructuralism imposes reality upon romance by 'unmasking' the politics of discourse in nineteenth-century realism and by praising contemporary self-conscious fiction for the realism it shows in abandoning 'realism'. But poststructuralism also transposes reality into romance by implying that the cognitive development of the novel is now played out and that fiction is properly subordinate to theoretical discourse. Thus theory, armed with its own strategies of narrative closure and a hierarchy of discourses, creates the widespread illusion that ('in theory', as we say) 'declarative' fictions are now redundant. Theorists for the most part admire very clever novels which are funny, don't try to make sense of anything, and which debunk any pretensions which 'Literature' may have to making sense of humanity. Not only is this sort of novel pleasantly relaxing after Foucault and Althusser but it evidently poses no challenge to declarative theory.

(ii) THE MYTH OF TERRY EAGLETON

Terry Eagleton, *The Function of Criticism* (1984)
Terry Eagleton's books have been getting shorter recently. It is eight years since he offered to re-situate literary criticism on the 'alternative terrain of scientific knowledge'; three since, self-canonised, he included his name in a list of major Marxist theoreticians of the twentieth century.[1] *The Function of Criticism* is a history of three centuries of English criticism in little more than a hundred pages. Its conceptual basis seems (not for the first time) to have been hastily borrowed for the occasion. The scholarship is cobbled together from the works of others. Since he makes great play with the split between the professional and amateur pretensions of literary critics, it would be tempting to adapt his own style and portray him as the helpless victim of contradictory impulses. Yet in many ways he thrives on contradiction. His struggle against 'bourgeois' criticism has the agility, the opportunism and the sniping provocativeness of a guerrilla campaign. Though his books have grand titles, he has lately abandoned any pretence of working towards a Grand Theory. His recent work has consisted of critical introductions, essays, and theoretical pamphlets like the present one.

Eagleton's reputation as Britain's leading Marxist critic owes little to any philosophical consistency. Politically, it is true, he has held steady while former comrades 'sank into disillusion, veered to ultra-leftism, or collapsed ignominiously into the arms of the bourgeoisie', as he once colourfully put it (*Walter*

Benjamin, p.91). His intellectual veerings and careerings have not affected his socialism. Much of the impact of his work has been due to the adventurism of a critic swiftly assimilating, and memorably responding to, wave after wave of neo-Marxist theory. As major influences, Sartre, Williams, Lukács, Goldmann, Anderson, Althusser, Macherey, Benjamin, Derrida and the feminist movement have followed one another in quick succession. *The Function of Criticism*, hard on the heels of *The Rape of Clarissa* and *Literary Theory: An Introduction*, marks if anything an intensification of this fleet-footed pamphleteer's progress.

Eagleton's launching-pad was the magazine *Slant*, a Catholic Existentialist journal which he helped to found as a Cambridge undergraduate. He was a pupil of Raymond Williams, and his first book *The New Left Church* (1966) was an amalgam of Williams's socialism, of Eliot's and Leavis's literary criticism, and of Catholic apology. 'Papal encyclicals on social themes,' he confided, 'are often full of large rhetorical generalisations ... which it is sometimes difficult to relate to any lived, complex reality' (p.88). Eagleton's own rhetoric leaned very heavily on the concept of 'community', which was offered as a standard of godliness ('the reality of the world since Christ') and of a cultural politics based on Williams's thoroughly secular study of *Culture and Society*.

In *From Culture to Revolution* (1968) Eagleton and Brian Wicker introduced a *Slant* symposium devoted to Williams and his 'richly creative tradition of socialist humanism' (p.3). But at some point in the early 1970s Eagleton became a convert to the materialist Marxism of Louis Althusser, another former Catholic (though to what extent Eagleton has actually renounced the Church it is hard to say—he has preserved a diplomatic silence on the issue). As an Althusserian, Eagleton found it necessary to cast off the 'petty-bourgeois moralism' of his old teacher. *Criticism and Ideology* (1976), which begins with an attack on Williams, is perhaps best read as a belated result of the student revolution at what Althusserians call the 'level of theory'. Literary criticism was now to be scuttled in favour of an anti-humanist 'science of the text' in which the production of art was dialectically reduced to a series of complex quadratic equations. Yet if Eagleton had transvalued his reading of

Williams, Eliot and Leavis, he did not manage to purge himself wholly of their influence. The literary history offered in *Criticism and Ideology* was a tacit rewriting of Leavis's 'great tradition'. The Victorian and modern 'major authors' were all to be found in their accustomed places—Joyce, conventionally enough, was the one addition to the strict Leavisite canon—and Eagleton's contribution was to show them, not as great literary mentors, but as crippled and distorted ideological freaks.

'The guarantor of a scientific criticism,' he wrote, 'is a science of ideological formations.' It was 'only by the assurance of a knowledge of ideology' that a knowledge of literary texts could be claimed (p.96). So far from providing such knowledge, the English tradition of literary criticism had simply mystified the texts it claimed to interpret. The worst mystification of all, of course, was a 'common-sense' reading. 'The function of criticism,' Eagleton proclaimed, 'is to refuse the spontaneous presence of the work' (p.101). (Needless to say, he has now found a rather different function for it.) But there were cracks in the armoured surface of *Criticism and Ideology* through which a more impressionable sensibility could be glimpsed. An English Marxist literary theorist, Eagleton complained, was 'acutely bereft of a tradition ... a tolerated house-guest of Europe, a precocious but parasitic alien' (p.7). What could be more grotesque than an Althusserian literary scientist sounding just like J. Alfred Prufrock?

Eagleton soon disowned the more ludicrous pseudo-scientific pretensions of *Criticism and Ideology*—though he stopped short of a full-scale recantation. *Walter Benjamin: or Towards a Revolutionary Criticism* (1981) was as far removed from a 'science of the text' as one could possibly imagine. The 'revolutionary criticism' was riddling, allusive, post-Derridean, and steeped in Benjamin's baroque and vaguely sinister metaphors. The revolution (or was it the millennium?) would 'blast history apart' (p.xiii); and Eagleton's rather too successful aim was to 'blast Benjamin's work out of its historical continuum' (p.179). The book ended with a weird rhetorical mixture of terrorism and shamefaced neo-humanism. There was a poem, 'Homage to Walter Benjamin', and the affirmation that Benjamin's anti-historicism might be 'quite literally the warrant of our survival' (p.179). It was Matthew Arnold who wrote that

currency and supremacy were assured to good literature by the
'instinct of self-preservation in humanity'; I.A. Richards had
echoed him in describing poetry as being 'capable of saving us'.
Eagleton's new book ends on the same note of orthodox Eng.
Lit. revivalism. Criticism, he says once more, 'might contribute
in a modest way to our very survival'(p.124).

A fairly constant feature of Eagleton's work in these years was
his habit of referring to earlier English critics in exasperated,
contemptuous terms. In *Walter Benjamin*, he compares Eliot's
notion of tradition to a 'large, bulbous amoeba' and a 'grazing
cow' (p.54). The English sections of *Literary Theory* (1983) were
written in a similar knockabout spirit. Eagleton's account of the
growth of English studies leans heavily on research done by
Chris Baldick and published as *The Social Mission of English
Criticism*. Indisputably his own, however, are such *jeux d'esprit*
as the descriptions of the *Scrutiny* project as 'at once hair-
raisingly radical and really rather absurd'(p.34), and of the
founders of Cambridge English (seen as carrying on the First
World War at the level of theory) as, 'on the whole, individuals
who could be absolved from the crime and guilt of having led
working-class Englishmen over the top' (p.30). *The Function of
Criticism* adopts a very different tactic. *Literary Theory*, billed as
an introduction to its subject, ended by pronouncing its
epitaph. *The Function of Criticism* ends, not with fancies of
bomb-blasts or funeral orations, but with a sentence likely to
astonish even the most inveterate Eagleton-watcher: 'The point
of the present essay is to recall criticism to its traditional role,
not to invent some fashionable new function for it' (p.123). We
needn't have worried, however: he doesn't really mean it.

The Function of Criticism is a polemical history, not of
criticism as such, but of the 'critical institution' within which it
acquired what Eagleton recognises as social significance. He
knows, really, that criticism is an ancient discipline beginning
with Aristotle and Classical rhetoric, and concentrating its
expertise on the techniques of literature, drama and oratory. At
least, he knew it when he wrote *Walter Benjamin* (pp.101–5).
But here he must pretend that criticism in England began with
the Enlightenment and the rise of journalism, and converted
itself into a 'species of technological expertise' (p.56) some time
in the early twentieth century. In *The Function of Criticism* the

relations between criticism and the production and consumption of imaginative writing are either ignored, or, where they are not ignored, treated with the utmost banality: thus we are reminded that Dickens required no middle-man between himself and his public, and that Romantic poetry offered a general social critique. Eagleton's 'critical institution' is a continuum stretching from Addison's *Spectator* through the Victorian higher journalism and *Scrutiny* to the present lucubrations of literary theory.

'In the times when art was abundant and healthy,' William Morris once wrote, 'all men were more or less artists.'[2] Modern criticism, Eagleton maintains, came into existence with the establishment of a bourgeois 'public sphere' in which all members of the propertied classes were more or less critics. The concept of a 'public sphere' is derived from Jürgen Habermas, and has been elaborated in Peter Hohendahl's *The Institution of Criticism*, a book from which Eagleton quotes repeatedly. Within the 'public sphere' reasoned debate and informed value-judgment can take place in relative detachment from the imperatives of rank, sect and party. Set up by the bourgeoisie in opposition to the absolutist state, the 'public sphere' slowly disintegrates as its beneficiaries are put on the defensive by the emergence of new social classes. Eagleton admits that this is not a wholly satisfactory concept, but he prefers to deploy it 'flexibly and opportunistically' (p.8), rather than subject it to a rigorous critique.

The decline or disintegration of the bourgeois 'public sphere' inevitably entails the notion of a classical period, or golden age. In this respect, Eagleton's version of the age of Addison is strictly comparable to Leavis's 'organic society', Eliot's 'dissociation of sensibility' and other expressions of literary nostalgia, including the medievalism of William Morris. And since—as with Morris's medievalism—the 'public sphere' is also an intimation of the socialist future, it bears a striking resemblance to the ideas of a common culture and of spiritual 'community' which Eagleton abandoned in the early 1970s.

The notion that a healthy society depends upon a current of criticism emerged in the nineteenth century. In Carlyle's essay on the 'State of German Literature' (1827) we can witness the idea that criticism has a social mission being imported from

Germany to England. Since the word 'criticism', or *Kritik*, features in famous titles by Arnold and Marx, it is not surprising that Eagleton's essay should centre on the Victorian period. Yet the Victorians' self-consciousness about the critical function indicates a criticism already in crisis. The golden age, therefore, must be found somewhat earlier. Where better than the place in which influential Victorians themselves located it—the *Spectator* with its model of a timeless discourse based on the reality of Augustan clubs and coffee-houses?

The evidence Eagleton offers for this 'reality' is, basically, a series of quotes from a venerable collection of Whig historians: Macaulay, Stephen, Beljame, and Legouis and Cazamian. Curiously, he deals only in the most general terms with Addison's *writing*; the main concern of his discussion of the bourgeois 'public sphere' is to define the paradigmatic 'speech act' performed in the coffee-houses—doubtless a proper concern of the critical theorist. Following Hohendahl, he describes this 'ideal discursive sphere' as one in which 'authoritarian, aristocratic art judgments were replaced by a discourse among educated laymen' (p.13). This means, first, that a pretty formidable part must have been played in the literary culture of pre-Restoration England by 'authoritarian, aristocratic art judgments': but it is not a point which the author condescends to argue with us. Secondly, the critical discourse of the coffee-houses was, within limits, egalitarian (Eagleton seems rather more anxious than Addison himself was to show that poets and writers played their part in it). Among the features of an 'ideal discursive sphere', one assumes, are that no voice dominated the others, no one was put down or frozen out of the circle, and nobody had to pay for more than his share of the coffee.

What this theory conceals is that the contemporary testimony as to the quality of coffee-house criticism is often extremely hostile. Where the theoretician perceives an 'ideal discursive sphere', the historian can turn up endless tales of claques and cliques. If this is an egalitarian society, it is one in which the air is thick with accusations of petty dictatorship. Pope's Atticus is accustomed to

> give his little Senate laws,
> And sit attentive to his own applause;

Johnson's Dick Minim occupies the 'chair of criticism' in a 'society elected by himself, where he is heard without contradiction'. Johnson's life of Addison portrays its subject, without any quibbling, as a critical 'instructor'. In Johnson's writing the 'public sphere' is a marketplace in which the different contenders, by fair means and foul, must vie for dominance. A serious historian would have mentioned these scarcely recondite texts, and would have tried to settle the argument between contending myths. Despite his (renewed) professions of admiration for Raymond Williams and E.P. Thompson, Eagleton has not learned from them what it means to be a serious historian.

Beside the Augustan, the three other 'moments' covered in his whistle-stop tour of the critical institution are the Early Victorian and the middle and late twentieth century. Eagleton has interesting things to say about the Victorian period, though not, oddly enough, about the Romantics. Throughout, criticism is viewed in relation to the class struggles of the bourgeoisie, and one of his more curious omissions is its religious dimension. Carlyle's sagelike stance is dismissed as specious transcendentalism, and the devotional concerns never far below the surface in Addison (whose famous *Spectator* papers on *Paradise Lost* were meant to be read on Sundays), and in Johnson, Coleridge and Arnold, are not (I think) mentioned.

With the twentieth century. Eagleton returns to the onslaught on Yale deconstructionism which he began, with considerable verve, in *Walter Benjamin*. Deconstruction 'is able to outflank every existing knowledge to absolutely no effect' (p.103), he points out. (Much the same could have been said, however, of the Althusserian fantasy of a 'science of the text'.) But before this, the scene has been suddenly changed from Victorian journalism to the growth of academic English, and the subsequent fortunes of the 'public sphere' are viewed entirely through the optic of Leavis and *Scrutiny*. Once again, we seem to be faced with history as myth. For what is it but the Marxist Left's obsession with a principled anti-Marxism which has kept the '*Scrutiny* project' and Leavis's social thought at the top of the agenda? It is the tribute of a belated avant-garde to a more powerful, more authoritarian predecessor.

In Eagleton's latest account of *Scrutiny* (for it is not exactly a fresh topic for him) the morass of problems, dilemmas, sutures and contradictions afflicting bourgeois criticism is so agitated as to become a maelstrom. What cannot be concealed, however, is that the Scrutineers failed to be sucked under. In successive sentences we find them running 'headlong into an impasse', and then managing 'this incipient contradiction' with 'some aplomb' (p.83). One minute it is the Charge of the Light Brigade, the next a successful exercise in forward planning. But in a final chapter Eagleton returns to the theme of Raymond Williams's career, and it is like the Lone Ranger riding off into the sunset at the end of a hectic Western.

Williams and his socialist contemporaries, we are told, have addressed themselves to an 'absent counterpublic sphere', based on institutions of popular culture and education which failed to materialise under the 1945 Labour Government. The pathos of Williams's isolation is thrown into relief by the successful realisation of a 'counterpublic sphere' in today's feminist movement (pp.112–18). Eagleton develops a bizarre parallel between Williams and Wordsworth (both Cambridge men, it seems, who 'returned finally to rural environments', which in Williams's case means a weekend cottage). Of course, if Williams is Wordsworth, this has the convenient result that his vivacious, mercurial and Oxonian pupil must be Matthew Arnold (see the latter's 'Memorial Verses'). Hence *The Function of Criticism*?

One reason for Williams's isolation, apparently, is the lack of a popular socialist newspaper in Britain. But as a young man Williams's affiliations were with Eliot and Leavis: had they not been, he could presumably have written for *Tribune*, the *Daily Herald* or the *Daily Worker*. Eagleton's version of Williams's career, in fact, is sheer undergraduate fantasy. (Can it be a coincidence, by the way, that when Eagleton was an undergraduate the New Left used to meet in a Soho coffee-bar?) What is most telling about it is that Eagleton presents 'isolation' and 'withdrawal' in entirely negative terms. For, to the extent that Williams *has* undergone such enforced experiences, he has retrodden the path of virtually every major Marxist intellectual. Marxist theory as we know it is largely the product of intellectuals subjected to exile, internal exile or even imprisonment. Beginning with Marx himself, these thinkers offer noble and sometimes tragic examples of the faith that sustains writers through years of isolation. Eagleton, it seems, has little conception of this. For him, faith means submergence in a believing community. When the 'public' or 'counterpublic sphere' is the model of such a community, it can lead the critic into the position of an intellectual Beau Nash or Beau Brummell, at once the arbiter and the prisoner of fashion.

In *Walter Benjamin* Eagleton wrote that the 'primary task of the "Marxist critic" is to actively participate in and help direct the cultural emancipation of the masses' (p.97). In *The Function of Criticism* his ideal for present-day criticism is not the common pursuit of true judgment but the common pursuit of the overthrow of the bourgeois state. Eliot's not wholly despicable alternative to the 'common pursuit', in *his* essay on 'The Function of Criticism', was a 'Sunday park of contending orators'.[3] One does not go to Eagleton's works for true judgment, by and large, and it is hard to know what contribution he has made to the emancipation of the masses. The best that can be said is that he remains one of the most spectacular orators in the park, and English criticism would be a good deal less entertaining without his pamphlets.

3

On Disagreement and
the Public Domain

Criticism ... must always profess an end in view, which, roughly
speaking, appears to be the elucidation of works of art and the
correction of taste. The critic's task, therefore, appears to be quite
clearly cut out for him; ... But on giving the matter a little
attention, we perceive that criticism, far from being a simple and
orderly field of beneficent activity, from which impostors can be
readily ejected, is no better than a Sunday park of contending and
contentious orators, who have not even arrived at the articulation
of their differences. Here, one would suppose, was a place for quiet
co-operative labour. The critic, one would suppose, if he is to justify
his existence, should endeavour to discipline his personal prejudices
and cranks—tares to which we are all subject—and compose his
differences with as many of his fellows as possible, in the common
pursuit of true judgment.

T.S. Eliot, 'The Function of Criticism'[1]

I

Which of Eliot's two alternatives—the common pursuit and the
Sunday park—best describes the practice of criticism? And which
would be the more desirable state of affairs? Would criticism be
improved if it were a 'simple and orderly field of beneficent
activity, from which impostors could be readily ejected'? Eliot
dealt with these questions with headmasterly simplicity, opting
for a dignified rather than an efficient view of the institution of
criticism. Johnson's appeal to the judgment of posterity and
Arnold's notion of a 'tribunal, free from all suspicion of national
and provincial partiality' lie behind Eliot's view of the critical

function; Leavis, in turn, collected his essays together under the title *The Common Pursuit*. Leavis's protocol for critical arguments—a forthright statement taking the form 'This is so, isn't it?', anticipating the reply 'Yes, but...'—may be put together with Eliot's idea that the critic's task is to 'compose his differences'.

'Difference' is a key concept of poststructuralist thought, which points the way to a possible deconstructionist reading of the passage from Eliot's essay on 'The Function of Criticism'. In Saussure, language itself is a system of differences, so that the 'composition of differences' would appear to mean the opposite of what Eliot intended. Writing is at once a mode of 'composition' and a constant rehearsal and deployment of differences. 'True judgment', involving the ending of difference, would also be the end of critical writing or composition, in the sense of reducing it to silence. The common pursuit of true judgment can never attain its goal, any more than the hounds can catch the electric hare. Neat though such a reversal of Eliot's argument would be, it eliminates the idea of difference as a product not of preordained semiotic conventions but of divergent human initiatives—and is therefore a kind of cheating. To say anything useful about 'difference' in criticism we require, not a theory in which difference and signification are inseparable, but one in which human beings can choose between seeking to agree and begging to differ.

There is, however, some value in the poststructuralist approach, in that it turns the oversimplified formula of the earlier critics—who wrote as if the achievement of unanimity were the be-all of criticism—on its head. A defence of criticism today might be founded not on the composition of differences but on the intellectual and cultural necessity of vigorous disagreement. In Leavis's terms, criticism ought to emphasise the 'but' rather than the 'yes'. Disagreement is what a pluralist culture is all about.

The crucial charge against contemporary literary theory is that it has used a rhetoric of 'challenging' and 'calling in question' to try to stifle debate, rather than (as one might have expected) to foster it. Above all, debate is narrowed and foreclosed by the constantly reiterated belief that art and ideology are inseparable. Criticism, in this view, becomes a party-political battle; 'He who cannot take sides should keep silent' is the slogan of the advocates of the politics of theory.[2] Education, by the same token, becomes indistinguishable from indoctrination. The politics of theory leads to a politics of teaching, supposedly justified by the claim that the educational system is already occupied by the 'dominant ideology'. The basis of this attitude is the theory of contemporary culture as a capitalist conspiracy. Before tackling this it seems advisable to bring disagreement to bear in a rather less heated engagement, and so I shall begin by considering the elegant and provocative arguments of the American theorist Stanley Fish.

Fish, in *Is There a Text in This Class?* (1980), rejects the structuralist 'science of criticism'. His outlook seems on the surface to be an impeccably pluralist one. Criticism, he suggests, is a form of persuasion, not of demonstration. 'The business of criticism ... [is] not to decide between interpretations by subjecting them to the test of disinterested evidence but to establish by political and persuasive means (they are the same thing) the set of interpretive assumptions from the vantage of which the evidence (and the facts and the intentions and everything else) will hereafter be specifiable'.[3] Pluralism here, I shall argue, has thrown the baby (disinterested evidence and the possibility of deciding between interpretations) out with the bathwater. Fish's essay 'Demonstration vs. Persuasion: Two Models of Critical Activity' argues that the 'demonstration' model, in which interpretations are either confirmed or disconfirmed by facts that are independently specified, must be discarded in favour of the political model of persuasion in which 'the facts that one cites are available only because an interpretation (at least, in its general and broad outlines) has already been assumed' (p.365). The goal in a persuasion model, he adds, is one of 'challenging and redefining' the assumptions of criticism itself (pp.366–7). Criticism and the politics of theory are one and the same game.

Some preliminary observations are in order here. Intuitively, Fish's attempt to persuade (or is it to demonstrate to?) the reader that criticism proceeds by persuasion and not by demonstration suggests a fallacy of the excluded middle. New Criticism and structuralism emphasised criticism as a mode of demonstration, and Fish is concerned to turn them on their heads. Might it not be that criticism and other forms of argument employ both methods? Intuitively, also, can it be irrelevant that Fish has established a major reputation as a literary theorist despite the fact that hardly anyone has confessed to finding him wholly persuasive? He is a 'major theorist' in other words, not because people agree with him but because he is provocative and stimulates thought. His success as a theorist is a lucid and exemplary *demonstration*, as it were, of the virtues not of persuasion but of disagreement. By disagreeing with Stanley Fish we confer value on his writings. And yet the defect of Fish's theory is, precisely, that it cannot give a coherent account of the benefits of disagreement. In his model of intellectual argument there is no halfway house between being persuaded by an interpretation, and rejecting the premises on which it is based (which would imply that one found it valueless). Fish's pluralist institution of criticism is not a field of open and productive argument, but a set of closed and mutually competitive cliques.

A third preliminary point is that Fish's belief that criticism is inherently political does not, for him, entail any political consequences. The politics of academic professionalism, as he describes it, is a politics hermetically sealed from the world outside; still more remarkably, it has no appreciable consequences (except in terms of personal aggrandisement) within the academic profession itself. What are the implications of his argument, Fish asks, for literary-critical practice? 'The answer is, none whatsoever' (p.370). The 'general or metacritical belief' that he argues for 'does not in any way affect the belief or set of beliefs (about the nature of literature, the proper mode of critical inquiry, the forms of literary evidence, and so on) which yields the interpretation that now seems to you (or me) to be inescapable and obvious' (p.359). If politics and persuasion are inseparable the argument I have just quoted must itself be construed as a political act. Assuming that Fish is not being disingenuous and pretending that his argument is more politically innocent than it really is, his description of his preferred model of critical activity as being 'political' is a peculiarly empty gesture. Fish, however, is not alone in using the term 'political' as a buzz-word which no longer has any meaningful content.

The main reason for disagreeing with Stanley Fish, in my view, is that his theory is founded on an explicit and thoroughgoing conventionalism. 'Interpretation is not the art of construing but the art of constructing. Interpreters do not decode poems; they make them', he writes (p.327). Indeed, 'all objects are made and not found, and ... they are made by the interpretive strategies we set in motion' (p.331). It only needs the application of Occam's Razor at this point to do away with the need for poets, and, lo and behold, Fish in 'How to Recognize a Poem When You See One' tells us of his decision to make up his own 'poems' for his students to practise interpretation upon. (Not one of these students, apparently, dared to question the assumption that a poem was a poem if Professor Fish said it was a poem.) The same notion of economy rules out 'demonstration' as a possible model of critical procedure. Criticism *cannot* be a demonstration, according to Fish, since the text itself is constructed (not construed), and is *only* constructed by the interpretative assumptions brought to bear on it.

If the text is not simply 'there' (thanks to the poet) but is constructed by the reader, and if—as he also argues—criticism is a process of persuasion in which success is measurable only by the professional rewards won by the most persuasive, then Fish has to answer the objection that this makes criticism a 'supremely cynical activity', a pointless competitive struggle for mastery (p.358). He does this by the device of simply asserting that critics believe what they say. The readings we offer are ones that we know to be correct. In criticism, Fish declares, 'one believes what one believes, and one does so without reservation' (p.361). He cannot say *why*—alone among 'political' pursuits—criticism should depend to this extent on the sincerity of its practitioners. For all his rejection of the 'test of disinterested evidence', he is forced to assume the disinterestedness of the critic's intentions. The success of an interpretation is measurable by the professional rewards it brings but critics do not, apparently, have professional rewards in mind when they advance their interpretations.

What, then, is the basis of successful interpretation? For Fish it cannot be one of knowing the author's intention (a position he shares with the New Critics), or of seeing the literary text 'as in itself it really is'. Nor is interpretation purely the subjective matter of knowing one's own response. An interpretation succeeds because it is persuasive; and critics agree, and interpretations are shared, thanks to the existence of what Fish calls 'interpretive communities' sharing particular sets of assumptions. The idea that criticism at any time is divided into a number of distinct 'interpretive communities' has a certain empirical appeal; there are, notoriously, a number of competing critical schools. Within a given interpretative community we might think that constructive disagreement would be possible; at the same time, the often acrimonious disputes between different communities could be readily reduced to politics and ideology. But having abolished the author and the free-standing text as sources of authority, Fish can (apparently) no longer imagine what it is that members of a particular interpretative community would have to disagree about. They agree with one another—therefore they belong to the same community—and if they disagreed they would, *ipso facto*, belong to different communities. 'Members of the same community will necessarily agree', Fish writes, 'because they will see (and by seeing, make) everything in relation to that community's assumed purposes and goals; and conversely, members of different communities will disagree because from each of their respective positions the other "simply" cannot see what is obviously and inescapably there: This, then, is the explanation for the stability of interpretation among different readers (they belong to the same community)' (p.15). Fish's notion of a community is as simple-minded and empty of content as his notion of politics. Real communities are not institutions or groups whose members 'will necessarily agree'.

Disagreement in Fish's system, like the splintering of the Protestant sects, exists only because we have all fallen away from the potential of forming one big interpretative community. Instead of worshipping at the one altar, each community constructs its own little tabernacle. The doctrine of the 'authority of interpretive communities' makes sense with regard to religious sects; equally, it reveals the necessity of defining criticism in terms of productive disagreement, not of agreement. The expectation of productive disagreement requires that we perceive the same objects to disagree about—only we perceive and interpret them differently. Because they are the same objects, we can learn from other people's ways of construing (not constructing) them. Disagreement is essential to this particular form of the learning process—which is why we speak of liberal *education*, as against political and religious *indoctrination*. A critical argument, whether it persuades or fails to persuade, has a demonstrative value for its readers; which is why one can speak with genuine gratitude of arguments which, though ingenious, are hopelessly unpersuasive.

Doubtless there was disagreement in plenty at the Mermaid Tavern. Tradition has it that Shakespeare and Ben Jonson were drinking companions, even though (on Fish's principles) the members of the Friday Street Club must have constituted several distinct 'interpretive communities'. Where the modern institution of criticism has the advantage over the 'nimble words' spoken at the Mermaid is in its public function. Criticism presupposes a wider forum than the tavern or, for that matter, than the 'classroom' and the 'academy' to which contemporary theorists such as Fish would confine it. In proposing a model of criticism as disagreement it is necessary to specify the context within which disagreement takes place.

II

The contrast between 'demonstration' and 'persuasion' models is at least as old as Aristotle. Fish's main innovation, it could be argued, is his resolute anti-Aristotelianism. Aristotle distinguishes between matters of merely popular and approximate debate, and those to which a rational procedure of scientific demonstration can be applied. But the Greek tradition offers a third alternative, that of the 'dialectic' championed by Plato and Socrates. Aristotle had a low opinion of his predecessors' dialogical method, classifying it as, at best, a part of 'eristic' or the art of non-scientific disputation.[4] But in the nineteenth and twentieth centuries the 'Socratic method' and the notions of dialogue and dialectic have become indispensable, in their various forms, to our ideas of knowledge and its dissemination (at least in the humanities and social sciences). All versions of the notion of dialectic offer a position, or positions,

45

for 'disagreement' to occupy. In what follows I shall, however, restrict myself to the idea of the 'Socratic method' within a liberal and pluralist university system.

The Socratic method is one of cross-examination. Convinced that he was wise only in his awareness of his own ignorance, the Socrates of historical tradition stood in the agora cross-examining other men about what *they* knew. This is the foundation of Socrates' reputation as an educator. But the Socrates who appears as protagonist in the Platonic dialogues often seems to conduct a one-sided debate, with his interlocutor as no more than a sounding-board for his own thoughts. Walter Pater, for one, interpreted the Platonic dialectic as a method of argument 'primarily with one's self'.[5] Nevertheless, Socrates' habit of cross-examining the received ideas of his young and impressionable followers led to his trial and conviction for corrupting Athenian youth. His *Apology* or speech in his own defence at his trial has made him into the eternal prototype of the critical intellectual. On the other hand, Plato's Spartan ideas about the education of the Guardians, as developed in the *Republic* by the figure of Socrates, have become a byword for political authoritarianism. Between these rival myths of Socrates there is, it might seem, no philosophical middle ground possible.

Matthew Arnold, the major influence on the modern Anglo-American tradition of humane studies, tried to wrestle with these contradictions. Arnold believed fervently in 'disinterestedness' and the 'free play of the mind' as the necessary conditions for critical thought. The Socrates of the *Apology* embodies these notions. Socrates tells of his failure to derive any personal profit from his calling, and of his renunciation of any political role in order to survive as a free intelligence. His mission is to act as the 'gadfly which God has attached to the state'.[6] He adds that the true reward for his activities would be a state endowment, but this is said, gadfly-fashion, in front of the judges who are trying him for a capital offence. In many ways the Arnold of the 1865 *Essays in Criticism* set out to play a Socratic role, and in *Culture and Anarchy* —a book nowadays routinely denounced for its authoritarianism—he invokes the historical Socrates. 'Socrates has drunk his hemlock and is dead; but in his own breast does not every man carry about with him a possible Socrates, in that

46

power of a disinterested play of consciousness upon his stock notions and habits, of which this wise and admirable man gave all through his lifetime the great example, and which was the secret of his incomparable influence?'[7] It is this side of Arnold's thought that we must emphasise if we are not simply to hand him over to the conservatives.

Arnold, of course, was reacting both against the free-enterprise bourgeois culture of his own time and against the rise of the working class. Therefore he argued that the critic's disinterestedness and mental freeplay should always be circumscribed by 'urbanity' and 'tact'. Thanks to these qualities the critic could be absolved of the suspicion of subverting youth—Arnold was a school inspector. Urbanity and tact were, in Arnold's view, the qualities most needed to improve the tone and temper of public debate. Today they still find their most natural home in the place where Arnold first encountered them, the liberal university.

The purpose of urbanity and tact is to soften disagreement. Within an academic system they help to reconcile intellectual debate with the 'common pursuit' of teaching and learning. One reason why literary theorists have come to overlook disagreement may be that gladiatorial combat between intellectual rivals is rarely part of the teaching process. Academic freedom normally entails that rival interpretations are taught side by side, in different classrooms, leaving it for students to make sense of and try to resolve the differences between them. This in turn has led to the suspicion that the disagreements which get voiced within the 'academy' are only theatrical and superficial; educational pluralism then comes to be seen as a mask for a 'form of cultural dictatorship'[8] which seeks its ideological justification in a particular definition of the interests of students.

The power-relations of teaching, however, are more subtle than this. The aim of most educational systems is not one of direct domination but of the transfer of power and authority, in something like its present structures, from one generation to the next. Students at the higher levels of education are therefore by definition a privileged group. This is the basis of the assumption of practical equality between teachers and taught on which the 'Socratic' style of teaching relies. The liberal ethos entails that every student should be treated with a mixture of authority (the teacher 'supervises' the learning process) and the deference due to an equal and a potential successor.

What this rather chummy and clubbable account of the pupil-teacher relationship cannot allow for is not so much the extension of democracy—the Arnoldian ethos carries within it its own implicit democracy—as the further implications of Arnold's cry: 'but in his own breast does not every man carry about with him a possible Socrates?' We could not replace the idea of 'a possible Socrates', in this sentence, with 'a possible Matthew Arnold'. Arnold at his best gave a superb display of critical penetration armed with urbanity and tact; but Socrates bore witness with his life to the belief that disinterestedness and the free play of the mind were the supreme qualities. Socrates stands for the heroism of the dissenting intellectual, and his *Apology*, unlike Arnold's apologias, is wholly unapologetic. Socrates is a nay-sayer who is fully prepared to find himself in a minority of one; Arnold believes that, if only you can find the right tone, your readers will be persuaded to agree with you.

In the Socratic model of cross-examination, the crucial element, I would suggest, is the cross-examiner's propensity to disagree with his interlocutor. Without the potential for disagreement there would be no cross-examination. Disagreement often carries a personal risk. Where Arnold is most valuable is in reminding us that disagreement is judged, among other things, by its quality of disinterestedness. If it is objected that no one is disinterested, the point may be put in the following way. In the long run the successful fulfilment of the critical function is dependent on the critic's personal role in society, and his ability to embody the mission he speaks for. (Arnold, of course, possessed this ability.) Literary theory cannot account for the extent to which the impact of the 'great' critic or theorist—a Leavis, a Lukács, a Benjamin or a Barthes—relies upon the force of heroic or tragic personal example.

Far more than a Leavis or a Barthes, a 'possible Socrates' would be an uncomfortable and perhaps a highly unwelcome figure in modern universities. This I believe is why the liberal interpreters of the Socratic method, such as Arnold and Pater, have stressed the extent to which the Socratic cross-examination—'that power of a disinterested play of consciousness upon his stock notions and habits'—should be turned in upon itself. It is as if they could not admit that Socrates' unyielding public stance, his refusal to temper his beliefs and (in the end) to sue for pardon, was essential to the critical function. Having disagreed, they may have thought, he should have urbanely and tactfully swallowed his disagreements and sought to compose his differences. His obduracy and stubbornness were not, so to speak, dialectical. But Socrates took his hemlock and died, and it was Plato who both composed the Socratic dialogues and taught at the Academy.

III

Teaching is at once private and public activity; private in that it involves the teacher in a greater or lesser degree of personal relationship with the pupils, and public in that it prepares them by publicly recognised and regulated means to participate in the division of labour. Criticism, equally, has a private dimension, but comes to fruition only in the various forms of public argument. In the last hundred years both teaching and criticism have been profoundly affected by changes in the public controls under which they operate. The growth of state education, corporate publishing and the communications industry have influenced the kinds of public disagreement that are possible. These developments, if nothing else, would force us to abandon either the hypothetical 'interpretive community' or the liberal humanist's 'continuous discourse with one's self'[9] as adequate models of intellectual life.

What is appealing about the sociology of Jürgen Habermas is that it offers a general theory of the fate of criticism in the corporate societies of the late twentieth century. In Terry Eagleton's case, a particular reading of Habermas and his follower, Peter Uwe Hohendahl, has led to the conclusion that an adequate 'public sphere' for criticism no longer exists. In its place, Eagleton urges the creation of a radical 'counter-public sphere'—in effect, a politicised and de-professionalised version of Fish's 'interpretive community'. In order to establish whether criticism as disagreement would be better off in such a context, we need to go behind Eagleton's work to his German mentors. And here there is an immediate source of embarrassment: Habermas' concept of *die Öffentlichkeit* has been rendered by his translators as 'the public sphere', and the term has caught on. But 'the public sphere' is in every respect inferior to the familiar phrase 'the public domain' as a rendering of Habermas' concept. The ideas of transparency, openness to scrutiny, and an absence of secrecy are of the essence of *die Öffentlichkeit*. Like the idea of the public domain, it entails the notion of legally guaranteed freedoms of speech, publication and assembly. Habermas himself has defined the concept as follows (I have substituted the words 'public domain' for 'public sphere' in this extract):

> By the 'public domain' we mean first of all a realm of our social life in which something approaching public opinion can be formed. Access is guaranteed to all citizens. A portion of the public domain comes into being in every conversation in which private individuals assemble to form a public body.... Citizens behave as a public body when they confer in unrestricted fashion—that is, with the guarantee of freedom of assembly and association and the freedom to express and publish their opinions—about matters of general interest.[10]

Habermas' concern with the structural change of the public domain (*Strukturwandel der Öffentlichkeit*, 1962), in the movement from feudal to bourgeois society and ultimately to democratic socialism, is reminiscent of Raymond Williams's attempts to trace the growth of a democratic culture in *The Long Revolution* (1961). Indeed, one can attribute some of the main divergences between the early Habermas and the early Williams to the different intellectual needs and historical experiences of Germany and England.

For Habermas, the first modern constitutions with their catalogues of fundamental rights legitimised the public domain as, so to speak, a buffer zone between state authority and individual privacy. Clubs, societies, public assemblies, the press and the book market sought that freedom from state regulation which would enable them to function as forums for open debate and a reasoned exchange of views. The extension of democracy and the spread of literacy implied that participation in the freedoms of the public domain would be extended to all citizens. But in the twentieth century the growth of corporatism and mass communications entailed a 'refeudalisation' of the public domain, as large organisations strove for political compromises with the state and with each other, excluding the public domain wherever possible.[11] In the emergent 'social welfare state mass democracy' the political public domain had, Habermas believed, been irreparably weakened. It could only be restored by a 'rational reorganization of social and political power' under the 'mutual control of rival organizations committed to the public domain in their internal structure as well as in their relations with the state and each other' (p.55). In the West Germany of the 1960s this doctrine impressed the student leaders of the New Left; in Britain in the 1980s, however, it could equally serve to support the Thatcher government's trade union reforms.

Before showing how the concept of the public domain applies to literary criticism it is necessary to allude to its origins in the work of the Frankfurt Institute for Social Research and in the historical experiences to which their theory of culture was a response. The rise of Fascism, as a form of neo-feudal state constructed out of the raw material of mass democracy, has left its mark on any analysis of the supposed 'refeudalisation' of modern society. Fascism succeeded in expelling the Frankfurt school from the public domain by the simple expedient of silencing its members, along with the rest of the liberal, socialist and Jewish intelligentsia, and forcing them to flee the country. The suppression of all political and intellectual opposition by the Nazis effectively shattered the public domain, leaving the way open for the regime to impose a fabricated culture and to manipulate the masses from above. For Adorno, Horkheimer and the other members of the Frankfurt school, Fascism and Nazism were not historical aberrations but the logical extension of monopoly capitalism. This meant that the process of refeudalisation must be traceable in other 'late-capitalist' social formations, such as that of the post-war Federal Republic. Like other NATO countries, Federal Germany was seen to be dominated by media monopolies, multinational corporations, and the institutions of the Atlantic Alliance; to these it added welfare-state policies, restrictions on civil liberties (notably the *Berufsverbot* law curtailing academic freedom) and a political democracy which would not mature until the 1970s and 1980s. The partition of the old Germany by the 'iron curtain' of the two opposing power-blocs also helped to give Habermas' thesis of the 'decline of the bourgeois public domain'[12] a resonance it might not have possessed in a nation like Britain, where social divisions were at once more deeply ingrained, and less likely to be perceived as a threat to national survival.

Habermas, as the successor to the Frankfurt school, supplemented his theory of the 'refeudalisation' of late-capitalist society with something approaching a conspiracy theory of bourgeois 'high culture'. The Frankfurt school had tended to view art, criticism, and 'bourgeois' philosophy in the twentieth century as being 'one-dimensional' rather than genuinely 'critical' in nature, and hence as serving to apologise for the status quo. This conspiracy theory of high culture is the effective legitimising force behind the current neo-Marxist (or more strictly pseudo-Marxist) notion that teaching and criticism are necessarily forms of ideological warfare. The politicisation of literature and art is, indeed, the theme of a rather wide spectrum of documents from the anti-Fascist 1930s, many of which have enjoyed a remarkable new lease of life in the last two decades. The Frankfurt school's own expulsion from, and subsequent readmission into, the public domain is nowhere more dramatic than in the case of Herbert Marcuse's essay 'The Affirmative Character of Culture' (1937)—an essay which does not seem to have appeared in English until 1968, when Marcuse was acclaimed as the guru of the 'campus revolution' in the United States. Marcuse's essay is a classic statement of cultural conspiracy-theory. High culture, in his view, functioned as part of the apparatus of bourgeois repression by virtue of its fundamentally idealist nature. Culture devalued the 'factual world of the everyday struggle for existence' by affirming a 'universally obligatory, eternally better and more valuable world' realised in cultural objects and in the activity of intellectually and artistically sensitive individuals.[13] 'Affirmative' culture constituted an 'abstract internal community', a 'realm of cultural solidarity' placed 'high above factual antitheses'; and the progression from Arnoldian disinterestedness to the 'abstract external community' of race and *Volk*, of the Nuremberg rallies and the concentration camps, struck Marcuse as a natural and inevitable process (p.125). Marcuse's tactic is to exclude disagreement and contradiction from his characterisation of the 'community' of affirmative culture; culture with its solidarity and superior status differs fundamentally from the Habermasian public domain in which criticism 'opens itself to debate' and 'invites contradiction'.[14] And yet Marcuse's view of culture, indeed his whole 'critical theory', are themselves disfigured by a massive contradiction. His 1937 essay is the prototype of all those recent theoretical works in which the pretensions of intelligence and culture to Olympian authority are denounced by a cultivated intellectual in a tone of still more peremptory Olympian authority.

In the 1930s culture was said by Marcuse and others to be on the side of the Nazis; in post-war Germany, however, it was denounced for being in league with 'consumerism', mass entertainment, the 'consciousness industry'. One of the forerunners of this argument is Bertolt Brecht, who had complained that criticism had become a 'culinary' art serving the purpose of 'announcing entertainment' and of sending the public to the theatres.[15] Habermas and Hohendahl echo this diagnosis: criticism is no longer rational discourse but consumption.[16] However, this particular complaint is scarcely a new one. The perception that reviewing and journalism had become contaminated by the values of the market lay behind F.R.Leavis's attacks in the 1930s on the Auden group and the metropolitan literary world. Eighty years before that we find Leavis's precursors, such as Mill and Newman, proclaiming the necessity of a liberal education to offset the venality and confusion of the periodical press. Following the historical trail backwards we come to Balzac's exposure of literary prostitution in *Lost Illusions*, and then to the legend and the reality of Grub Street. The accusation that the press is corrupt and that writers are for hire is as old as the public domain itself. The 'consciousness industry' thesis presents the theory of the universal reduction of criticism to advertising and puffery (or else to irrelevance) in a new but not necessarily more plausible form. (As always, it makes a silent exception in favour of the critic or theorist who accuses the others.) Nevertheless, certain developments of the 1960s such as the placing of defence research contracts suggested that the disinterestedness of university studies, to which Mill, Newman, and even Leavis had appealed, could no longer be taken for granted. The public domain may, indeed must, include universities, but we can no longer be sure that the existence of large corporate institutions bearing the name of universities guarantees the survival of a public domain. This must, as always, be fought for.

In his 1965 inaugural lecture on 'Knowledge and Human Interests', Habermas reconsidered the ideal of a 'non-authoritarian and universally practiced dialogue' which had earlier prompted his inquiry into the history of the public domain. Such a free, disinterested and 'Socratic' dialogue is, he argued, only attainable within an emancipated society in which *Mündigkeit* (translated as 'autonomy and responsibility', but literally meaning 'maturity' or 'adulthood') characterises the human condition. Full social emancipation is incompatible with the capitalist system, but philosophy, or what he called 'pure theory', has ignored this temporal limitation:

> The ontological illusion of pure theory behind which knowledge-constitutive interests become invisible promotes the fiction that Socratic dialogue is possible everywhere and at any time. From the beginning philosophy has presumed that the autonomy and responsibility posited with the structure of language are not only anticipated but real.... Only when philosophy discovers in the dialectical course of history the traces of violence that deform repeated attempts at dialogue and recurrently close off the path to unconstrained communication does it further the process whose suspension it otherwise legitimates: mankind's evolution towards autonomy and responsibility.[17]

This is itself philosophy in the grand and gloomy German tradition. The dream of a forthcoming cultural and political revolution, which Habermas shares with his 1930s mentors, is expressed in a peculiarly uninspiring form. It seems to be a philosophical category, no more. Such a passage legitimates the antithetical fiction, or counter-fiction, that Socratic dialogue is possible nowhere and at no foreseeable time. I believe that the proper response to it is to do what we can to *make* Socratic dialogue possible in our present (immature) social order, and that the way to do so is to strive for disinterestedness and to practise disagreement with the dominant ideas. We shall then find that dialogue and a public domain are not merely remote aspirations but conditions that we assume (in however imperfect and fragmented a form) if we are to engage in critical argument at all. In the literary field, for example, the public domain is implicit in the notion of a 'text' as something we can isolate, fix, pin down and scrutinise. Texts come to be seen in this way as a result of being divorced from their immediate conditions of production and circulated extensively; if the text were merely for private consumption, the circulation of critical opinions about it, also in the public domain, would soon come to a halt.[18] Criticism, in other words, is a form of writing which can only address itself to a shared reality. But criticism to be effective has to find its way into the public domain. As disagreement it is forced to compete for a hearing, and to dislodge or displace existing meanings in order to get one.

It is in the nature of any actual public domain that it is never felt to be extensive enough by its participants; its membership, and the amount of expression it allows, will always fall short of their maximum potential. No writer would deplore an increase in readership, and no speaker believes he has quite enough listeners. While someone is being read or being listened to, others must wait their turn in silence. The structure of the public domain which allows for maximum participation is that of a proliferation of smaller units such as clubs, societies, professions, journals, and pressure-groups, each with an explicitly sectional appeal. Many participants in the public domain are content to address and to belong to such small groups. But against this image of the public domain as a network of small cells must be set the development of agencies of cultural homogenisation—broadcasting, television, mass-market newspapers, state propaganda, political parties—which seek to reunify the various audiences and (to the extent that they speak with one voice) to impose a dominant ideology.

If culture is a conspiracy then the means of expression in the public domain are entirely controlled by the dominant ideology. The argument for cultural separatism, whether in the name of socialism, feminism, or other forms of 'counter-culture', is that only by a voluntary withdrawal from, or refusal to enter, the public domain can the dominant ideology be overcome. In Germany, Negt and Kluge have interpreted Habermas' analysis

of contemporary culture as pointing to the need for a
'proletarian counter-public sphere.'[19] (The 'proletarian counter-
public sphere' is a successor to the 1930s ideal of proletarian
literature, to be discussed in Chapter 6). A separatist 'counter-
public sphere' needs to be distinguished from the various
coteries, campaigns, specialities, and minority voices which
already exist, since the latter form part of the public domain and
make a crucial contribution to its vitality. A counter-culture is
not so much a multiplication of small groups as their bringing-
together under the banner of disaffection and withdrawal. But
either this is a temporary and tactical expedient, or the need to
protect the 'counter-public sphere' from contamination by the
existing public domain is likely to lead to a closing of the doors
to outsiders and the enforcement of a greater or lesser degree of
unanimity within the group. Like the setting up of a utopian
community or of a religious sect, the 'counter-public sphere' can
only be achieved at the price of 'self-exclusion from forms of
communication directed at society as a whole'.[20] The resulting
interpretative community is then virtually a mirror-image of the
'affirmative culture' described by Marcuse: a culture within
which there was no disagreement, based on the 'segregation
from civilization of an independent realm of value that is also
considered superior to civilization'. Its decisive characteristic is
the 'assertion of a universally obligatory, eternally better and
more valuable world'—in this case, the world of 'socialist' or
'feminist' or other counter-cultural values—which must be
'unconditionally affirmed' (Marcuse, p.95).

The argument between cultural participation and counter-
cultural separatism turns, I would suggest, on the issue of
disagreement. Neither the public domain as at present
constituted, nor the various proposals for a separatist culture,
are wholly favourable to disagreement. In the public domain
there is at least a formal commitment to the values of
disagreement and of the pluralist society in the legal guarantees
of freedom of speech, publication and assembly. Conventional
practices such as parliamentary debates, the public inquiry,
'questions from the floor' and 'letters to the editor' embody a
recognition of the principle of disagreement, though it is hard to
sustain much faith in such easily manipulated outlets. With
radio and, especially, television as they function today public

disagreement is virtually impossible. At most it takes the form of retrospective controversies conducted in other media, such as the newspapers and Parliament. The limits placed on disagreement within small, like-minded groups are almost equally restrictive. Radical communities and associations are notoriously fissiparous since any serious disagreement is liable to shatter the group. One cannot disagree fundamentally with a fellow-member without calling their right or one's own right of membership into question.

Disagreement, however, ought to be profound—as profound as were Socrates' disagreements with the Sophists, and Shakespeare's with Ben Jonson. For disagreements to be profound they must be capable of being fully and rigorously worked out. This is perhaps why some of the seminal thinkers of the twentieth century have been noted both for their participation in a specific group or movement, and for a subsequent (voluntary or involuntary) withdrawal from it. Neither the belonging to an 'interpretive community' nor the 'continuous discourse with one's self', pursued in conditions of scholarly retirement, are enough. Disagreement can only be completed within the public domain. If the public domain is a noisy and argumentative place, that is almost certainly a sign of cultural vigour. T.S. Eliot vented his dislike for the idea of criticism as a 'Sunday park', and the author of the *Republic* would doubtless have expelled the unruly orators from the gates of his ideal city. Socrates, however, would have felt at home there. He believed it was his mission to cross-examine the ideas on offer at the Athenian equivalent of Speakers' Corner.

4

Culture and Society in the 1980s

Raymond Williams's *Culture and Society 1780–1950* came out nearly thirty years ago. It must be one of the most widely-read studies of cultural history ever written. Often, it is true, such a reading is highly selective, the result of its having earned a place on so many student booklists: one is told to take on board Williams on 'The Romantic Artist', 'The Industrial Novels', 'Art and Society', or on individual thinkers such as Tawney, Morris, Cobbett or Mill. And there is much to be said for this. Not only is the book as a whole hard going for the uninitiated, but what one owes most to it are some unforgettable quotations, generous and incisive perceptions, an alertness of commentary, a tone of thought. But something crucial is also missed if, as I suspect, the introduction and conclusion are the least frequented chapters of *Culture and Society* today.

It is not only that *Culture and Society* is a political book, though its politics is what we must finally come to. Nor is it simply that the introduction and conclusion both offer theoretical statements. The book's beginning and ending cannot be dispensed with if, following Williams's own favourite interpretative principle, we are to try to understand *Culture and Society* as a product of its time. We can sharpen our sense of its time-conditioned quality by remembering that, though published in 1958, its concluding chapter was written in late 1956, during the decisive weeks of the Soviet invasion of Hungary and the British invasion of Suez.[1]

Here is how *Culture and Society* begins:

In the last decades of the eighteenth century, and in the first half of the nineteenth century, a number of words, which are now of capital importance, came for the first time into common English use, or, where they had already been generally used in the language, acquired new and important meanings. There is in fact a general pattern of change in these words, and this can be used as a special kind of map by which it is possible to look again at those wider changes of life and thought to which the changes in language evidently refer.

Five words are the key points from which this map can be drawn. They are *industry, democracy, class, art,* and *culture.*[2]

What Williams says so firmly here is, firstly, that cultural change is critically reflected in changes in words, and, secondly, that a particular set of words possesses structural importance. In effect, he was systematising an approach which had been more haphazardly developed in earlier twentieth-century English studies. Logan Pearsall Smith, for example, wrote in *Words and Idioms* (1925) of 'those subtle changes in men's feelings, and in their ways of looking at the world, which are so important and yet so elusive, and which can perhaps be most definitely traced in the emergence of new terms, or in a change in the meaning of old ones'.[3] The examples he took were words such as *romantic* and *sentimental.* William Empson in *The Structure of Complex Words* (1951) tried to deflect attention from the 'official verbal machinery' of a historical period to its unconscious presuppositions, as revealed in colloquial phrases and witticisms;[4] and *his* examples were words such as *fool, honest,* and *dog.* It is easy to feel that *Culture and Society* has the advantage of 'playing it straight', so to speak, as against the learned buffoonery of Empson's inimitable essay on 'The English Dog', but the issue is not quite as simple as that. We can see this from an experience Williams recounts as being formative in the conception of *Culture and Society.*

In 1945, after serving in the Army, Williams returned to Cambridge to resume his university studies. The intellectual climate that he found there after four years' absence was 'new and strange'; a strangeness that he and another ex-Army friend summed up for themselves in the observation that '"the fact is, they just don't speak the same language"'. One word that he found he was hearing much more often was the word *culture.*[5] Being confronted by an unfamiliar vocabulary is a characteristic experience of modern society, and, as Williams is well aware, it runs much deeper than the coming and going of undergraduate intellectual fashions, which is presumably what he encountered in 1945. He had negotiated more difficult linguistic transitions than this one, no doubt, as he moved to university from a working-class family and a provincial grammar school, and then became an Army officer. Such crossings of linguistic boundaries are recorded in Williams's own novels and, of course, in much earlier English fiction. A passage from George Eliot will help us to consider Williams's way—in *Culture and Society* and its successor, *Keywords* (1976)—of constructing the 'map' of changes in social life and thought from verbal markers.

Early in *Middlemarch* we see the family of Mr Vincy, the self-made manufacturer, at breakfast. Mr Vincy has already breakfasted and gone off to business; and his industrious habits are contrasted with the genteel indolence of his son Fred, who comes down late and scandalises his sister Rosamond by ordering up a grilled bone. Fred has been sent to Cambridge, and has failed his degree. Before he makes his appearance Rosamond, who has been to a finishing school, is explaining to her mother that no young man in Middlemarch is good enough for her:

'But I shall not marry any Middlemarch young man.'

'So it seems, my love, for you have as good as refused the pick of them; and if there's better to be had, I'm sure there's no girl better deserves it.'

'Excuse me, mamma—I wish you would not say, "the pick of them."'

'Why, what else are they?'

'I mean, mamma, it is rather a vulgar expression.'

'Very likely, my dear; I never was a good speaker. What should I say?'

'The best of them.'

'Why, that seems just as plain and common. If I had had time to think, I should have said, "the most superior young men." But with your education you must know.'

'What must Rosy know, mother?' said Mr Fred, who had slid in unobserved through the half-open door while the ladies were bending over their work, and now going up to the fire stood with his back towards it, warming the soles of his slippers.

'Whether it's right to say "superior young men,"' said Mrs Vincy ringing the bell.

'Oh, there are so many superior teas and sugars now. Superior is getting to be shopkeepers' slang.'

'Are you beginning to dislike slang, then?' said Rosamond, with mild gravity.

'Only the wrong sort. All choice of words is slang. It marks a class.'

'There is correct English: that is not slang.'

'I beg your pardon: correct English is the slang of prigs who write history and essays.'...

'Dear me, how amusing it is to hear young people talk!' said Mrs Vincy, with cheerful admiration. (Ch.11)

Or, as poor Mrs Vincy (an innkeeper's daughter) might have permitted herself to think, 'the fact is, they just don't speak the same language'.

What are the 'keywords' in this extract from *Middlemarch*? The speakers focus, first of all, on two colloquialisms: 'the pick of', and 'superior'. Each of the protagonists is manoeuvering for position, trying to determine the use of these expressions. To do so they use a second series of terms, which betray their anxieties about social class: 'vulgar', 'plain and common', 'shopkeepers', 'prigs'. But then there is another disputed word in the passage, the word 'slang' which gives rise to an argument of genuine substance, and indeed of a continuing urgency: either 'all choice of words is slang', or there is slang and there is correct English. The word *slang* does not have a complex semantic history like Williams's markers, but it does denote a concept of considerable importance, and, moreover, it belongs (unlike *industry* and *democracy*) to the category of metadiscursive words, words used to reflect on the speech-acts of the mind itself. Fred's assertion that 'all choice of words is slang' is, in its way, the key to the justification of the whole project of *Culture and Society*. But *slang* appears neither in the book itself, nor among the 110 terms discussed in *Keywords*, the 'Vocabulary of Culture and Society' which grew out of a planned appendix to the earlier volume.[6]

The word that does appear both as one of Williams's keywords and in the *Middlemarch* passage is *class*. When Fred observes that all choice of words 'marks a class', he is using *class* in a sense not found before the beginning of the Industrial Revolution (*KW*, p. 51). (The same is true of the use of *slang*.)

However, the *word* class is not problematic for Fred and his family—or not on this occasion—whatever position it may hold in a generalised and abstracted 'structure of meanings'. This example perhaps suggests the intellectualist basis of Williams's method, its reliance on keywords whose principal characteristic is that they stand for key concepts.

We cannot assume that the history of a word and the history of its concept are the same history. To do so is to adopt a version of the conventionalist argument that reality is determined by our 'ways of seeing', so that our language, instead of being shaped by our thought, effectively patrols the limits of the thinkable. But we are capable of making raids on the inarticulate, and new thoughts may be expressed long before they come to inhabit what strikes us as their appropriate language. Quentin Skinner has pointed out, for example, that the concept of originality in art is older than the use of the term *originality* to denote it. The most that can be said, according to Skinner, is that the development of a consistent, corresponding vocabulary is a sure sign that a group or society has entered into self-conscious possession of the new concept.[7]

Williams might well agree with this, since in his view the change in the meaning of a word signifies not conceptual change in the narrow sense but a 'wide and general movement in thought and feeling' (*C & S* p. 17). That is, the 'structure of meanings' of a word such as *culture* or *class* encodes particular 'structures of feeling'. It is these 'structures of feeling' which, for the Williams of *Culture and Society* and *The Long Revolution*, are the peculiar province of the critic and cultural historian. Williams's concept of 'structure of feeling' justifies his concern with specific texts of social theory rather than with 'abstracted problems'. For Williams these texts are 'statements by individuals', 'personally verified' utterances (p.18). Nevertheless, within these texts the sort of language which encodes feelings most tellingly is the language of abstracted social analysis rather than the kind of language on which George Eliot focussed. Williams's life's work can almost be read as a series of examinations of words such as *culture, masses, community, consumer, tragedy, modernisation*, and others, including his recent inquisitions into *de-industrialisation* and *post-industrial society*.[8] The abstraction involved in this process (and notoriously reflected in some of Williams's prose) must be understood as qualifying a habitual rhetorical emphasis on 'actual language', 'real history', 'lived reality', 'felt experience'.

One of Williams's prime reasons for singling out his keywords has always been to expose their unthinking cant use in contemporary debate. In Cambridge in 1945-6 we must suppose that Williams was alive not just to the semantic confusions of the word *culture* but to its habitual association with the idea of privilege: culture as the possession of the 'cultured' minority. Culture in this sense was inherently opposed to the concept of the 'masses', to whom, at best, it might one day be 'extended' or transmitted. *Culture* in the excluding sense was not only found in the obvious places, such as F.R. Leavis's pamphlet *Mass Civilisation and Minority Culture*; it also pervaded socialist thinking on the topic. Communist governments invariably set up Ministries of Culture charged with spreading the inherited 'bourgeois' culture to the proletariat, while the cultural thought of the major Labour Party theorist treated in *Culture and Society*—R.H. Tawney—was, as Williams saw it, crippled by the unresolved contradiction between the need to promote a genuinely popular culture and to preserve existing standards of excellence. The conclusion to *Culture and Society* sought a way out of this impasse by presenting working-class attitudes and values as an integral and necessary part of the 'common culture' of the future.

Though for Williams the idea of a common culture is a political and moral ideal, it is also inscribed in the word *culture*, as part of its structure of meanings. Moreover, the fate of *culture* is tied up with that of the other keywords *industry, democracy, class* and *art*. What are the connections between these words, or rather between their concepts? A classical liberal might argue that industry and class, as social factors, demand a political response—democracy. Art and culture may respond to any or all of these, but they are principally the unrestricted expression of the free individual. For the 'romantic conservative' thinkers of the early nineteenth century, however, art and culture and class embodied an older, more permanent and more Christian scheme of values; they were a 'rock of defence of human nature' steadfastly opposed to industry and democracy. A third system, Marxism, views democracy, art and culture as parts of a superstructure raised on the determining base of industry and class. Williams rejects both the conservative and the crude Marxist articulations while accepting, and transvaluing, the systematic linkage which they propose between the five terms. In particular, he interprets the opposition to industrialism voiced by the romantic conservatives from Burke to Ruskin as pointing the way to a socialist opposition to capitalism. Such an interpretation of romantic conservatism was not, of course, unprecedented. Bernard Shaw claimed that Ruskin and the Dickens of *Hard Times* had converted him to socialism, while Marx praised the insights of such 'reactionary' thinkers and novelists as Carlyle, Balzac and Disraeli. The dialectical process of learning from one's enemies is epitomised, within the tradition Williams surveys, by John Stuart Mill's essay on Coleridge: it was Mill who wrote that 'even if a Conservative philosophy were an absurdity, it is well calculated to drive out a hundred absurdities worse than itself' (*C & S*, p. 224). Nevertheless, for Williams's argument the pivotal figure who crossed the 'river of fire' separating romantic conservatism from revolutionary socialism was William Morris. Without Morris's thought Williams's whole interpretation of the 'culture and society' tradition as a source of socialist thought would have been much less plausible.

Williams's selective method and his reconstruction of the meanings of the word *culture* enable him largely to bypass liberal individualism. The use of *culture* to mean the accomplishments of a cultivated individual was prevalent before the Industrial Revolution; in the period covered by *Culture and Society*, however, 'The development of the idea [of culture] has, throughout, been a criticism of what has been called the bourgeois idea of society' (p. 314). Three principal new meanings of *culture* are the bearers of this criticism: culture as denoting a range of highly-valued moral and intellectual activities, culture as a term constituting these activities as a 'court of appeal' or source of judgment over life as a whole, and, finally, culture in the collective or anthropological sense as denoting a whole way of life (pp. 17–18). Culture as a court of appeal—the Arnoldian sense—is characteristic of romantic conservatism; but to the extent that it is seen as the inheritor of a whole way of life in the past (the 'organic society' from Burke to Leavis) it may be said to anticipate the collectivist idea of culture. Socialists and romantic conservatives are at one in the recognition that 'The forces which have changed and are still changing our world are indeed industry and democracy' (p. 321). The difference is that, for the prophet of a socialist culture, industry and democracy are positive values pointing to the future.

In the conclusion to *Culture and Society* Williams approaches the idea of a common culture by examining concepts such as 'the masses', 'communication' and 'community'. His debunking of the cant use of *mass* and *masses*—as in *mass culture, mass communications, mass media*—is one of the finest examples of his ability to identify and challenge dominant 'structures of feeling'. The description of the working community as 'the masses', he argues, is lineally descended from the earlier notion of the 'mob'. The masses, by definition, are seen from above. We do not think of ourselves, or people we know, as part of the masses; the masses are the crowd, the people we do not know:

> To other people, we also are masses. Masses are other people.
> There are in fact no masses; there are only ways of seeing people as masses.... The fact is, surely, that a way of seeing other people which has become characteristic of our kind of society, has been capitalized for the purposes of political or cultural exploitation. What we see, neutrally, is other people, many others, people unknown to us. In practice, we mass them, and interpret them, according to some convenient formula. (p. 289)

The problem, as with several other passages in the concluding chapter, is to know whether to read this as moral exhortation or as scientific description. Williams appears to be saying that seeing the masses as masses is one of several possible ways of seeing, and that it may have a limited, practical use; but, paradoxically, there is also a 'neutral' way of seeing, according to which the masses are simply people. If 'in fact' there are no masses, our pragmatic decision to interpret them as masses would seem to be both morally and scientifically false.

When I first puzzled over this passage in the late 1960s, I tried the experiment of reversing its terms: 'There are in fact no people; there are only ways of seeing masses as people'. In my innocence, such a statement seemed pure fantasy, the projection of a sociological vision into the realms of nightmare. Then I discovered Louis Althusser. The theory of interpellation in Althusser's 'Ideology and Ideological State Apparatuses' was the nightmare made flesh. For Williams, 'I do not think of my relatives, friends, neighbours, colleagues, acquaintances, as masses; we none of us can or do' (p.289). But for Althusser it is merely bourgeois humanist ideology which constrains our thinking in this way. Ideology interpellates (or 'hails') us as individuals; snared by this illusion of individuality, we become self-willed and independent-minded subjects of the bourgeois state rather than blissfully anonymous units in the communist masses. At the moral level it is hard to imagine anything more antipathetic to the Williams of *Culture and Society* than Althusserian thought; but once it has been dogmatically asserted that one 'way of seeing' is true and the other false it is all too easy for the terms to be reversed.

In truth, the opposition is a misleading one. Masses exist, just as people exist. It is simply a question of the appropriate scale. By excluding this middle position Williams more or less inadvertently endorses the conventionalist doctrine according to which there are no masses or people independent of our 'ways of seeing' them. The conclusion to *Culture and Society*, as we shall see, derives some of its rhetorical force from the conventionalist assertion that the key to the achievement of a common culture is a correct understanding of the word *culture*. In Williams's next book, *The Long Revolution*, he cited contemporary scientific theories of perception as authority for the belief that 'our way of seeing things is literally our way of living'[9]—a striking endorsement of conventionalism. At the same time, Williams continued to appeal to experience (his own experience, largely) as the source of correct vision; and this could only be taken to imply that certain modes of experience, and ways of living, were *morally* better than others. Behind his assault on the habit of seeing other people as 'masses', for example, is the traditional injunction to do as you would be done by. We might even say that Williams's outspoken preference for 'people' over 'the masses' bespeaks a mixture of prudence, conscientiousness and respect for the individual characteristic of Protestant morality, and enshrined, above all, in nineteenth-century English fiction. The conclusion that 'there are no masses' echoes the process of social education undergone by the heroines of novels such as *Daniel Deronda* and *North and South*.

To be fair, Williams rejects the idea of the masses not simply because it groups people together but because it does so in order to dominate them from above. The common culture he foresees also groups people together, but voluntarily, through the collective identity offered by a 'whole way of life'. It is in working-class culture that he finds the basis for this collective identity: working-class culture, however, which 'is not proletarian art, or council houses, or a particular use of language; it is, rather, the basic collective idea, and the institutions, manners, habits of thought, and intentions which proceed from this' (p.313). The institutions are principally those of the labour movement, while the 'basic collective idea' of solidarity is shown to be superior to the middle-class ethics of individual opportunity and of service to the community. The relative merits of solidarity and self-help, and of solidarity and service, are even more bitterly debated in England in the 1980s than they were in the 1950s; in addition, the service and self-help ethics can no longer be seen as benignly complementing one another. Where we might disagree with *Culture and Society* today is not in the definition of these competing ethics—the terms of the dispute have changed very little—but with its emphasis on the development of a single culture, rather than a plurality of cultures, and with Williams's very Morrisian insistence that the ethics of a culture are founded in the workplace. Among Williams's immediate predecessors Leavis had (perhaps unthinkingly) suggested that a culture could be judged by its purely literary achievements, whilst Eliot's more ecumenical definition boiled down, as Williams observed, to 'sport, food and a little art—a characteristic observation of English leisure' (p.230). Williams rejected these minority versions of culture, and rejected also the crude Marxist generalisations about bourgeois and proletarian culture. Nevertheless, his own analysis of cultural ethics is clearly founded both on a class analysis of society, and on the assumption that men's deepest cultural identity stems from their relationship to the mode of (industrial) production.

Before examining these difficulties in Williams's idea of a common culture in more detail, we need to notice the tone of the peroration to *Culture and Society*. Here, tacitly echoing the Carlyle of 'Signs of the Times', Williams urges his readers to act to bring about a new culture by means of a philosophical apocalypse, or a change in generally accepted ways of seeing. In passages like these the conventionalist tone of his thought is coloured by a tincture of 1950s existentialism:

> To rid oneself of the illusion of the objective existence of 'the masses', and to move towards a more actual and more active conception of human beings and relationships, is in fact to realize a new freedom. Where this can be experienced, the whole substance of one's thinking is transformed. (p.321)

> We are coming increasingly to realize that our vocabulary, the language we use to inquire into and negotiate our actions, is no secondary factor, but a practical and radical element in itself. To take a meaning from experience, and to try to make it active, is in fact our process of growth.... The human crisis is always a crisis of understanding: what we genuinely understand we can do. (pp.323–4).

The rhetoric is uplifting, but just as the voluntaristic excesses of Parisian existentialism led to a reaction in favour of mechanical structuralism, so Williams's moralism left too many of his followers in the English cultural studies movement defenceless against the intellectual *rigor mortis* of Althusserianism.[10] For better and worse Williams's analysis of the meanings of culture issues finally in the linguistic construction of a cultural utopia. His 'common culture' is an absolute moral aspiration, but it is also already implicitly present in our society, embodied in ways of seeing that are said to come naturally and neutrally to everyone, and embedded in the very fabric of the language we use. The main struggle that Williams puts before his readers is to understand a 'structure of meanings', since those meanings are what a culture consists of. To reinterpret our culture, on the conventionalist hypothesis, is tantamount to changing it. Like other utopias, Williams's common culture is organic and monolithic as well as being somewhat easily brought about. It is organic since it builds on the meanings and experiences of the recorded past, by a process which is 'at once the idea of a natural growth and that of its tending' (p.323). It is monolithic because, though he occasionally pays lip-service to cultural diversity, Williams's emphasis falls entirely on 'community' and 'culture' in the singular. And while the utopianism of his vision continues to inspire respect, the vision of a monolithic culture founded on the ethic of solidarity has, I think, been superseded by events.

We might ask whether the very considerable cultural changes which have taken place in Britain since 1956 amount to the emergence of a common culture, in Williams's sense. The argument would go on for a considerable time, and perhaps could never be settled at all since there are no agreed criteria for a common culture. The only firm criterion to arise from the conclusion to *Culture and Society* is that to have a common culture we would have to *think* that we had one! Williams himself clearly does not think this—possibly on the Marxist grounds to be set out below—but it would be interesting to know to what extent he still stands by a common culture as an ideal. For the greatest failure of his conclusion, to my mind, is its failure either to predict or to offer grounds for valuing the proliferation of cultures in what we are accustomed to refer to as a multicultural society. In present-day society we are less aware of the dichotomy of 'mass civilisation and minority culture' than of the profusion of assertive 'minority cultures' and communities based, very often, not on the workplace but on a shared ethnic, religious, political, regional, generational, or even sexual identity. It may be argued that Williams's model of a single common culture speaks more to the experience of a nation accustomed to the rigours of war and National Service than it does to one which has enjoyed forty years' insulation from military aggression. Indeed, Williams's own biography can be cited as an illustration of the cultural pluralism of the later twentieth century. In his later work he has increasingly stressed his ethnic identity and his political allegiances, describing himself for example no longer as an English writer but as a 'Welsh European'.[11] Not only is the 'national community' of Wales something very different from the community extolled in *Culture and Society*; 'Wales' and 'Welshness' are in reality simply one of the plural cultures of Britain and (in a much weaker sense) of Europe. To be sure, Wales today has a jealously-guarded culture with a strong sense of solidarity uniting many of its members. But that is only to be expected. Everything is unique about such cultures except the quality of uniqueness itself.

A Marxist might say that the plurality of ethnic, national,

religious and other cultures in today's advanced societies, however vividly experienced, is ultimately an ideological delusion (part of the bourgeois strategy of 'divide and rule') concealing the general subjection of labour to the ruling class and the hegemonic dominance of the culture of the state. The only 'real' communities, therefore, are those of capital and labour. Marxists have frequently argued that communal identities based on anything except the experience of the workplace are manifestations of false consciousness. Nor are they always wrong in this. What would be quite illegitimate, however, would be to combine a Marxist suspicion of cultural identities as possible manifestations of false consciousness with an unqualified endorsement of the ethic of solidarity. Solidarity is fundamentally tenacious and local, based on immediately identifiable shared interests. (Marxists, however, are inclined to use the language of solidarity as a disguise for middle-class humanitarianism.) The feeling and experience of solidarity are evidently aroused by religious, national, ethnic and other forms of identity just as much as by class and the division of labour. Today feminism, mass unemployment and new forms of technology are severely shaking our notions of wage-labour and the workplace as the necessary prototypes of communal experience. What is needed is a new understanding of the relationship of the plurality of lived cultures to the 'common culture' composed (and imposed) by the confused mixture of nation-states, administrative areas, and economic, military, linguistic and intellectual polities in and under which we live. To the extent that it is a moral understanding of culture and community that we seek, flexibility, mutual tolerance, and recognition of cultural plurality and the assurance of minority rights will be quite as important as the ethics of solidarity.

All this from the point of view of 1987: but what of 1956? It is perhaps only to be expected that, rather than looking forward to our time, Williams's utopian common culture now seems a powerful exercise in *looking back*—to 1945, and to 1940, to go no further. 'We lack a genuinely common experience, save in certain rare and dangerous moments of crisis... we shall not survive without it' (p.304). A veiled reference, surely, to the 'Dunkirk spirit' of which we were to hear so much when Labour came back to power in the mid-1960s? Finally I will suggest that the utopianism of *Culture and Society* can now be read as a tacit reply to a writer central to English socialist thought whose books dominate the literature of the 1940s, just as Churchill, Attlee and Bevan dominate its politics. George Orwell, with whose legacy Williams has engaged in a lifelong struggle, had a vision of English culture which was organic, monolithic, and (at the end of his life) profoundly and distressingly dystopian. Where for Orwell England appeared as a 'family with the wrong members in control',[12] for the Williams of *Culture and Society* it is a native language and literary tradition with the wrong meanings in control; in each case there is a strong sense of cohesion and a feeling that putting things right may be only a matter of time. Nevertheless, in *Nineteen Eighty-Four* Orwell not only reduced English socialism to 'Ingsoc' and the rank and file of the army of labour to moronic proles; he imagined a common language and culture brutalised to the point where there was nothing left but 'Newspeak'. Orwell is the last of the individual writers considered in *Culture and Society*, and Williams concludes by observing that Orwell's dystopia reveals 'how the instincts of humanity can break down under pressure into an inhuman paradox; how a great and human tradition can seem at times, to all of us, to disintegrate into a caustic dust' (p.284). It is as if Williams had sought to regenerate humanism from these ashes by imagining a cultural utopia reflecting the instincts embodied in the vocabulary of an intellectual and literary tradition—a tradition moreover, which had grown out of, and had influenced, everyday speech. As with *Nineteen Eighty-Four*, to read *Culture and Society* is to enter at least temporarily into the intellectual community it describes, and to revalue, where Orwell's Newspeak had mordantly devalued, the human content of that community's language. Like Orwell, Williams finds in language not only a structure of feelings but the measure of a future—a future which is no less memorable for being no longer ours.

5

Utopia and Negativity in
Raymond Williams

'Within each of these areas, in increasingly interesting ways, developments are occurring which belong to the convergence...'

'These profoundly alternative directions are still, I believe, a matter of complex dispute...'

'What, then, is "English Literacy"...?'[1]

Who was writing, or (as he has sometimes put it) *what* was writing these fragments from a recent lecture? The style is complex and highly distinctive; it is not difficult to recognise the accents. An assertive, even prophetic note is half hidden by a fog of judicious abstractions. For all his diffident, even disinterested, air we can sense that the author has a controlling vision to impart. His rhetoric of connections and interacting forces has an affirmative, not just descriptive purpose. Yet what abides is the form of the question—'What, then, is "English Literacy"?'—rather than the intricacies of the answer. One of Williams's greatest contributions to literary and cultural debate has been his ability to transform the terms of its questions.

Raymond Williams has been the pre-eminent representative, in his own generation, of the Cambridge English school. Very likely he is the last in that particular line of succession. Much of his work in the last two decades—on tragedy, on the English novel, on the pastoral and country-house tradition, and even on Marxist literary theory—demonstrably began in the context of inbred Cambridge debates. Most of the issues he had tackled until very recently had been broached by Eliot, Richards, Leavis and *Scrutiny* before him.

Like these (usually antagonistic) predecessors, he is a prolific writer who has found a wide, multi-disciplinary and not necessarily 'academic' audience. He has a deserved reputation as an educationalist and a pioneer of cultural and media studies. Like Leavis, his role has been that of a cultural missionary whose books offer both a record of his intellectual development and the cumulative outline of a course of studies. He has also combined theory and criticism with political activity and the writing of novels. Allowing for an evident difference in stature, parallels can be drawn between his very English career and that of Sartre in France. Leavis's editorship of *Scrutiny*, and Sartre's of *Les temps modernes*, have their counterparts in Williams's long (though less intimate) association with *New Left Review*. There is at least one other crucial affiliation in his work. The finest commentary on Williams to date—apart from those published under the *New Left Review* imprint—is J.P. Ward's excellent monograph in a series on 'Writers of Wales'.[2]

Williams, then, is a very versatile figure; despite taking early retirement from his Cambridge chair he remains a member of the English Faculty; and he is still very much in his prime, with a new discipline (that of cultural sociology) to advocate, a new novel, *People of the Black Mountains*, which has still to be published, and doubtless further books in preparation. Nevertheless I believe it is still appropriate to view him, centrally, as a writer on English language and literature. He began as a self-proclaimed literary critic—the author of a primer on *Reading and Criticism* (1950), and co-editor of a short-lived journal called *The Critic*—however chary of the term he later became. In *Reading and Criticism* he was a straightforward advocate of 'practical criticism'. At the same time, he protested his independence both of Leavis and of the established critical profession. The grounds of this dissent, it was to become clear, were his loyalty to working-class values, and his socialism (these are by no means the same thing). Leavis's attitude to the working classes had been very much that proclaimed—as part of a socialist creed—by George Bernard Shaw: 'an intense desire to abolish them and replace them by sensible people' (*C & S* p.182). Williams's genuine levelling beliefs were expressed in the title of an early autobiographical essay, 'Culture is ordinary' (1958). But socialism and working-class loyalties do not in themselves differentiate him from the category of 'Left-

Leavisites', to which he has sometimes been assigned. It is the dialectic of utopia and negativity in his work which gives it its peculiar intentness.

In everything he has written Williams has opposed the Spenglerian cultural pessimism—so marked in Eliot and Leavis—which came to dominate English literature and criticism after the Second World War. In book after book he scorns the conventional account of social and literary forms as being degenerate or in decline. At first this was a very lonely campaign, but in the long run it has won him hundreds of thousands of readers. In *Culture and Society* (1958) and *The Long Revolution* (1961) he argued that democracy was the necessary condition of a genuine culture. *Communications* (1962) and *Television* (1974) discussed the expressive and liberating potentials of the electronic media. *Modern Tragedy* (1966) was a riposte to George Steiner's *The Death of Tragedy*. *The Country and the City* (1973) countered nostalgia for the 'organic community' with the argument that more real community was possible in the modern village than at any time in the past.

It would be a fundamental mistake to confuse Williams's optimism with liberal complacency. When he turned to the actual judgment of contemporary (capitalist) society he had more in common with Eliot and Leavis than with most of their detractors. But he found present culture unsatisfactory, not by comparison with an idealised past, but from the perspective of a possible future. Nor was the future merely a rhetorical device, as it has too often been in socialist criticism. Williams has never felt bound by the orthodox Marxist prohibition of utopian thought. The results are to be seen in his attempt to define a 'new socialist order' at the end of *Politics and Letters* (1979), in his advocacy of 'new forms of cooperative effort' to overcome division of labour in *The Country and the City*, and—most famously—in the model of a common culture that he developed in *Culture and Society* and *The Long Revolution*. Williams's utopian constructions can naturally be criticised on the grounds of their thinness, their vagueness, and their abstraction. (It is a pity he has not yet written a utopian novel.) Their significance, however, lies in the attempt. His model of culture as a communications system or forum of ongoing debate is something that is not found in other utopian thinkers. And, writing nearly a century after Morris, Bellamy and Wells, and amid a host of Marxist and Marxising voices, he is our only utopian critic.

Consonant with Williams's utopianism is the patient, emollient tone he has cultivated even in the most controversial arguments. This has often been seen as a weakness. In 1961 E.P. Thompson described his puzzled reaction to the absence of 'anger, indignation, or even malice' in Williams's writing (*NLR* 9). Thompson and Williams are the twin leaders of the Old Guard of the intellectual Left in Britain; but where Thompson has magnificently indulged (and occasionally over-indulged) his anger, Williams has tended to muffle his. His reasonableness finds expression in a rhetoric of openness and 'good faith' (sometimes, it is true, a way of protesting his own sincerity). His concern with 'connections' and 'convergences' makes a sharp contrast with the hairsplitting acerbity not only of the critical profession but of many professed revolutionaries.

But to regard Williams simply as an emollient, utopian mind would be a caricature. Were it not for the deep, negative energies of his thought he would never have been heard of. At its most public level his negativity is a recognition of the obstacles the twentieth century presents to the utopian spirit. These obstacles—an all but crushing historical inheritance—are named by him in such general terms as violence, alienation, robbery and fraud. Violence and fraud are present in all actually existing forms of socialism—was it some inchoate realisation of this that helped to terminate his brief membership of the Communist Party (1939-41)?—and this has led him to speak movingly of the inevitable links between revolution and tragedy. Negativity in Williams, however, is very much more than an awareness of the recalcitrance of society and politics. It is the very dynamic of his intellectual development.

Where Leavis named his enemies, and then belaboured them, Williams is noted for what J.P. Ward terms the 'cryptic, imputing strain' of his arguments.[3] Although it is not quite true that 'there are no good or bad men in Mr Williams's history',[4] the bad are invariably classes of men, not individuals. Reading him one learns to decode many instances of disguised polemic, and also to recognise the instances when—with equal vigilance, and possibly greater vigour—he is tacitly belabouring himself. A good deal of his negativity is turned inwards. As a striking example, *Politics and Letters*—a thick volume of interviews conducted by the *New Left Review* editors—manifests a process of avowed and extraordinarily detailed self-criticism to which it is hard to imagine many of Williams's contemporaries submitting. His whole career, however, has been one of self-criticism and re-orientation. Time and again, his reasonable tone represents a balance between opposite and discordant impulses. (Taxed with being unduly sympathetic towards Carlyle in *Culture and Society*, he told the *New Left Review* team that 'I too wrote my essay on Carlyle as a fascist when I was an undergraduate'.[5]) Of course, this balancing process is sanctioned by academic and literary tradition. What is unusual in Williams's case is the extent to which a sense of personality—of 'self-composition'— is invested in it.

Traditionally, the separation of the spheres of 'person' and 'family' from those of knowledge and theory has been a condition of entering intellectual life. Schools and universities work to enforce such a separation, which is understood in the very concepts of 'intellectual discipline' and 'profession'. Even the work of the artist involves this separation, since it is part of his role to break through inhibitions which constrain us in the family circle and even in private. It is surprising to what an extent the separation has held. Many people have written autobiographies, but very few have introduced the accidents of their personal history into professional work at the most formal level. Williams has gone further than most in this respect, and his main predecessors are romantic and post-romantic writers affiliated to the 'culture and society' tradition he himself has outlined. The brief, though eloquent, personal testaments to be found in his criticism make it almost, at times, a kind of *Biographia Literaria*. It would be easy to write picturesquely about this side of his work—the boy from the Welsh borders, the long struggle to reconcile the values of 'home' and 'Cambridge', and so on. More important is to recognise the autobiographical impulse in his work as a highly unusual and formative strategy. It is a way of asserting direct experience as the court in which art and theory are judged; of affirming the deep unity of a culture riven by surface splits and specialisations; and, perhaps most importantly, of refusing the concepts and challenging the ready-made categories that the intellectual world holds out to the unwary.

If autobiography is a form of empiricism—a touchstone to be invoked in the course of a relentless criticism of concepts—then it must also be said that the attempt to be 'true to experience' has, at times, distorted his judgment. Eager acceptance of a particular set of values and attitudes has been followed by vehement yet unstable rejection; it has not always been possible to achieve the illusion of balance. Among Williams's sticking-points have been attitudes to Cambridge, to literary criticism, to George Orwell, to Marxism and (it might be argued) to Welsh and English patriotism. When he returned to Marxism in the 1970s, having treated it with scant respect in the preceding years, he wrote of 'for the first time in my life ... belonging to a sphere and dimension of *work* in which I could feel at home' (*M & L*, pp.4–5). Similar sentiments have accompanied his intellectual rapprochement with Wales. The other conflicts are still un-resolved. Williams has written brilliantly and prominently on Orwell, yet always with an undercurrent of strong irritation.[6] In the late 1970s he was saying that 'I cannot read him now' (*P & L*, p.392). By 1984, when there was an explosion of media interest in Orwell, he was reading him again.[7] The ambivalence Williams has so often voiced towards Cambridge is very common among undergraduates and junior lecturers there; much less so, one would imagine, among its professors. The most vexed of his self-conflicts has been that over literary criticism.

Criticism, ironically enough, is itself a practice shot through with negativity. In *Keywords* (1976) Williams suggests that the word's connotations of 'judgment' and 'taste' should be weighed against the 'continuing sense of criticism as fault-finding' (p.76). Even in his early practical-criticism primer he was already measuring his distance from the 'critical profession', which he portrayed as 'almost ... the last-hope profession for the unplace-able son' (*R & C*, p.21). His rejection of Leavisism, a personal crisis lasting several years, was completed by the time of *Culture and Society*; this, however, was followed in the 1960s and 1970s by what he has called his rejection of literary criticism. The concepts of 'literature' and 'criticism', he wrote in *Marxism and Literature* (1977), are 'forms of a class specialisation and control of a general social practice' (p.49). One product of such a 'class specialisation', he has suggested, is the critical habit of 'unconscious ventriloquism', bred by 'undue immersion in a writer' (*P & L*, p.252). He is, of course, criticising his own habits here. And since he had also reached the conclusion that the 'dominance of literary criticism in English culture' was now over (*P & L*, p.85)—even though, from another point of view, that culture might be described as 'rotten with criticism' (p.240)—his anathema was made to seem at once virtuous and opportune.

We shall come back to the problem of Williams's 'rejection of literary criticism'. It was the result of applying the (critical) principle of negativity not to literary works but to criticism itself, or rather to the concept of criticism. His response was of rejection, not of redefinition. And such a process of rejection, firstly of *readings* and secondly of *concepts*, forms the gathering dynamic of his work over the last twenty-five years. Of *Culture and Society* he has said: 'I knew perfectly well who I was writing against: Eliot, Leavis and the whole of the cultural conservatism that had formed around them—the people who had pre-empted the culture and literature of this country. In that sense the book was informed by a very specific national consciousness' (*P & L*, p.112). This is an illuminating comment on a book usually seen as wholly positive in spirit: a classic survey, as it were, of a tradition of thought which was manifestly there and waiting to be described. The tradition as a continuous process was not there—it was Williams's achievement to discern and discover it—and to do so was to reject other emphases, other definitions of literature and culture that were on offer. The book *does* construct a 'specific national consciousness', as we can see from its conclusion, and also from its successor *The Long Revolution* with its long essay on 'Britain in the 1960s'. More recently the very idea that literary study can yield up a valid notion of the national consciousness—a definition of 'Englishness'—has drawn his ire (*NLR* 129). Now he rejects the concept, though it is hard to see how (save by withdrawing into the redoubt of his 'Welshness') he can consistently do so.

The authority of Williams's rereadings and redefinitions is seen at its clearest in his more 'literary' books: *Drama from Ibsen to Eliot* (1952), *Culture and Society*, *Modern Tragedy*, *The Country and the City*, and some lesser works. Most of them are exercises in tradition-building. As we move through the sequence, the element of negative polemics becomes much more overt. *Modern Tragedy*, though a fragmented and uneven work, opens with a brilliantly incisive demolition of attempts to separate the literary and the everyday uses of the word 'tragedy'. The book is divided between literary and intellectual history. The famous 'Tragedy and revolution' chapter, for example, is a cogent piece of moral and political thinking at some distance from 'Cambridge criticism'. Yet the same book contains not only a fine contrast of Tolstoy and Lawrence but the text of Williams's play 'Koba'. *The Country and the City* is more integrated but, again, it deliberately straddles the fields of 'social, literary and intellectual history' (p.3). Chapters which read like a literary anthology are interspersed with chapters of polemical metahistory. The result is an admirable, if often controversial, interrogation of the texts as 'representations of history—including ... misrepresentations' (*P & L*, p.304). In assessing such genres as the pastoral poem and the country-house novel as sources of knowledge Williams is, naturally, subject to the limitations of historical documentation, and of his own intuitions. Sometimes, as when he offers to describe the 'tone' of a period, there is a patent elision of the historical and the literary. The 'real life of the country' (p.62) is necessarily elusive once we treat it as anything more than a negative litmus-test to show up the falsity of literary fictions. The methodological problems of *The Country and the City* are considerable, and have been pondered at length in Williams's more theoretical works. But as the record of a wise, committed, socially-responsible reading of literature it will stand comparison both with the works of British Marxist historians such as Thompson and Christopher Hill and with the best of *Scrutiny*.

In what sense is the literary imagination a cognitive faculty? What are the connections between literary criticism and cultural history? Williams at first inherited the Leavisian position on these matters; this in turn goes back to Eliot and Hulme. T.E. Hulme, whose ideas were being expounded in university extension lectures by Eliot as early as 1916, was an eclectic figure who linked the social history of style (derived from the German art historians) with the concept of ideology that he found in Georges Sorel. Hulme and Eliot saw each period as distinguished by a particular 'ideology', a particular 'sensibility', and a corresponding 'style' or means of artistic expression. The difficult term here is, of course, the middle one. Ideological awareness and artistic expression are given to the few, but the mediating concept, 'sensibility', is the property of the many. Sensibility is at some level the reflection of ideology or (as Hulme sometimes called it) *Weltanschauung*. It is also what predisposes an audience to appreciate a new form of art. Sensibility became a deeply mystified concept; in Cambridge twenty-five years ago one still heard endless versions (including Williams's) of its 'dissociation'. Eliot's view of the link between literary form and the experience of the writers' contemporaries is most clearly developed in his essays on drama. His discussions of Elizabethan conventions and the 'Senecan attitude' were directly relevant to Williams's interests. Where Eliot saw these literary patterns as reflecting a 'sensibility', Williams was to cite them as evidence for a 'structure of feeling'.

There are some points of convergence between Eliot and Williams. Eliot had launched the *Criterion*, Williams the *Critic*. In addition, Eliot had written on contemporary theatre, the Russian ballet, and the music-hall as well as on Elizabethan drama. His 'Dialogue on dramatic poetry' (1928) was paralleled by Williams's 'Dialogue on actors' (1947). In 1948 Eliot published *Notes Towards the Definition of Culture*; soon Williams, too, was looking into the semantics of the word. Williams's concept of 'structures of feeling' was first used in a subsequent essay, 'Film and the dramatic tradition' (1954), to describe the relationship of dramatic conventions to the 'living experience' of their period. Williams has not so much refined as wrestled with this concept over the years. It is easier to say what the reasons for this were than what its success is. He has continually sought a political basis for literary criticism which avoids any crude reading-off of the work's ideology or political tendency. Yet the 'structure of feeling', however much it appealed to the sense of complexity and felt experience, was largely an enabling device to allow him to discuss textual ideologies.[8] The end-product was to relate the literary work to the needs and experiences of a particular class at a particular time. During the 1970s Williams discovered the Gramscian concept of 'hegemony'—an attempt (as he saw it) to describe class domination not as exercised through a particular ideology, but by 'a saturation of the whole process of living' (*M & L*, p.110). In *Marxism and Literature* he transfers to 'hegemony' much of the enthusiasm and much of the rhetoric formerly associated with 'structure of feeling' (which he presents, a few pages later, in hesitant and lack-lustre fashion). Still more recently he has published an introduction to cultural sociology in which both concepts are conspicuously hushed up (though I take a cryptic dismissal of 'paper bridges or even more airy constructions' (*C*, p.144) to be a reference to 'structure of feeling'). In this book, *Culture* (1981), the mediating concept is now the internal and external 'social relations of forms' (p.178). In future we might see Williams's negativity brought to bear on this concept, too.

We must now look at the desperate paradox of *Marxism and Literature*—the book in which Williams announced his reaffiliation to Marxism ('I have had the sense, for the first time in my life, of belonging to a sphere and dimension of *work* in which I could feel at home') and yet, to my mind, the book in which his clearing of the ground is least offset by positive construction. The exposure of clichés and rejection of cant concepts had been one of the most liberating achievements of his earlier work (see Chapter 4 above). 'Keywords' were a key to the 'structure of feeling'. But in *Marxism and Literature* Williams tried to use them to open the lock of Marxist aesthetics.

At a quick count, no fewer than nineteen of the terms indexed in *Keywords* also receive extended historical discussion in *Marxism and Literature*. Virtually every chapter begins with the historical semantics of a particular term of debate. Many chapters end with the rueful dismissal of the same concepts (among them 'literature' and 'ideology'—and why not 'Marxism' too?) since they are judged to raise more problems than they solve. It is a profoundly nominalistic exercise, timely and even courageous in its scepticism about 'ideology', 'base', 'superstructure', 'determination', 'mediation' and the rest, but mystifying in its positive thrust. Towards the conclusion the chapters end with unfulfilled exhortations to attend to the 'precise material articulations' of particular works; yet the book offers no clear framework, only vague directions and a radical doubt as to how this is to be done. The questions why people write and read, what is the function of literary judgment and why some artists are more important than others remain largely unanswered, and the final section on 'Literary theory' is the weakest in the book. I am not alone in my dissatisfaction here. The *New Left Review* team also seemed deeply disturbed by the venture (*P & L*, pp.324–58).

A less bleak impression, it is true, is conveyed by *Culture* and by the two retrospective essay-collections *Problems in Materialism and Culture* (1980) and *Writing in Society* (1984). But Williams's tendency to reduce theory to lexicography in his Marxist work should not be passed over. It reflects the impact of semiotics on a critic who had always taken 'communication' as his basic cultural model. In *Culture*, he defines his subject as a 'realised signifying system' (p.207). Here is the 'linguistic model' with a vengeance. We may ask how readily musicians, sculptors, architects, and even poets would recognise their activity in this description—and how readily they should do so. 'Signifying system' can be interpreted in a number of ways, and Williams of all people is qualified to give it a complex and subtle articulation. Yet he has moved some way from his earlier emphasis on lived experience. Is Williams's 'cultural materialism' a genuine new discipline, or is it merely symptomatic of the mad rush to theorise literary studies in the past few years? In some ways it seems like a very obvious response to Terry Eagleton's injunction (delivered at the close of a blistering attack on Williams's work) that 'criticism must break with its ideological pre-history, situating itself outside the space of the text on the alternative terrain of scientific knowledge'.[9]

In *Culture* for the first time Williams outlines a whole landscape of European sociology. His explicit field is cultural studies, not literary theory (though he repeats the analysis of dramatic forms which had figured so prominently in his previous work). In his discussion of the relations between drama and society Williams continues the process of self-criticism and self-consuming theory, as we have seen. The process, which has deep roots in his own work, now shows signs of becoming the dominant procedure of literary studies everywhere. The reductiveness of much current theory, its overweening ambitiousness and vanity, and the incommensurability of different theories cannot be laid at Williams's door. But its disposability is something in which he does seem complicit. The 'theoretical line' changes as often as the Party line once did, and nearly as often as fashionable hemlines. Williams's negativity, his criticism of concepts, has become part of the general deconstructive tendency.

Thus it is symptomatic that in the 1970s he did not redefine literary criticism (say, along continental lines, as 'critical discourse' or 'literary history'). Instead, he 'rejected' it. As a personal decision this is understandable, though it leaves open the question whether he has any literary disciples or a 'school'. The contrast with Leavis in this respect is extreme (and perhaps not unhealthy). Williams's influence has too often been felt as encouragement to deconstruct literary criticism, including his own, and to replace it with prepackaged chunks of European theory. Where criticism still flourishes—not least (overtly or covertly) in a good deal of Marxist and feminist work—we may find a more positive legacy. Williams differs from almost all the literary theorists in that he does not accept the formalist dogma of an 'aesthetic' category or of specifically literary uses of language. He sees a continuum between literary and non-literary language. Thus, while the literary imagination is subject to ideological distortion it is also a cognitive faculty, a source of 'recognitions' (C, pp.128-9). Cognitive status is not reserved (as in all too many contemporary accounts) for theory alone. It is sad that Williams has gone on the defensive about this, that he saw fit to describe himself in *Politics and Letters* (p.304) as 'still realist enough' to hold certain expectations of poetry and novels. The apologetic tone is quite inappropriate. His best work is all based on the assertion of literature's actual or potential cognitive power. How do such cognitions affect our own lives and perceptions? Consider him on the private car:

> It is impossible to read the early descriptions of crowded modern streets—the people as isolated atoms, flowing this way and that; a common stream of separated identities and directions—without seeing, past them, this mode of relationship embodied in the modern car: private, enclosed, an individual vehicle in a pressing and merely aggregated common flow; certain underlying conventions of external control but within them the passing of rapid signals of warning, avoidance, concession, irritation, as we pursue our ultimately separate ways but in a common mode. (C & C, p.296)

The reference is to *literary* descriptions of crowded streets— to Wordsworth and Dickens—and also to a perception that Williams had earlier expressed in fictional form, in *Second Generation* (1964). We could easily deconstruct the passage, with its familiar accents of the complex, the convergent, the thwarted community. Yet the accents are struggling to understand and explain—even to hint at a utopian potential against which this society should be judged. Williams concludes *The Country and the City* by saying that his reading has 'brought me to the point where I can offer its meanings, its implications and its connections to others' (p.306). It took, he says, a long time to reach that point. Isn't that what writing on literature should be about?

6

Revolutionising the Canon: From Proletarian Literature to Literary Theory

I

'Is this your "art"?' Victorian ethnographers are reputed to have asked, when confronted by the decorated earthenware and bone necklaces of some savage tribe. If it was, they wanted to take possession of it. Labelling a text a 'work of literature' is a similarly practical assertion of our cultural values. When someone denies these values, we are apt to be told that the culture is in crisis and that an 'attack on literature', conducted by 'terrorist-critics', is taking place.[1] But the search for an uncontroversial definition of literature—one which could only be attacked by self-confessed madmen or terrorists—is doomed to disappointment.

Of course, if we are to say what criticism, or writing on literature, should be about, we must have some notion of what literature is. Both the necessity and the limitations of formal definitions of literature were apparent to the pioneering school of twentieth-century literary theorists, the Russian formalists. Roman Jakobson argued that the object of the scientific study of literature was 'literariness', a characteristic of literary texts which could be isolated by technical linguistic analysis.[2] In England and America the New Criticism took a parallel course, defining poetry in terms of poetic language or the 'poetic experience'.[3] But another strain in formalist poetics, headed by Tynjanov's article 'On Literary Evolution', held that literature was not a fixed category but a fluid system of functions differentiating the literary from the non-literary. The system and its composition was subject to change, so that the existence of the

85

distinction between literary and non-literary texts was its only permanent feature.[4] This view, according to which the category of literature is constituted by changing social conventions, seems to be borne out (following Raymond Williams's principles) by the history of the term itself. 'Literature', in the sense of a body of writing, has been traced back to Latin texts of the second century AD in which pagan *litteratura* is contrasted with Christian *scriptura*.[5] We may deduce that 'literature' arises out of the distinction between sacred and secular writings in the Western tradition. It is always a value-laden term, usually with a positive valuation implying secular learning, artistic expression, and writings distinguished by wisdom and beauty. That the same word may also carry a negative valuation ('mere *literature*') should in no way be disturbing. The negative valuation implies a distinction between literature (as commentaries, or writings-about) and a revelation of some sort. Evangelical booksellers, for example, sell Bibles and 'devotional literature'. Political parties distribute 'campaign literature'; the implicit contrast—as at a public meeting with its 'literature-stall'—is between written propaganda and the voice and presence of the party leaders. The young James Joyce declared 'literature', the realm of 'accidental manners and humours', to be inferior to drama, the realm of 'underlying laws'.[6] The essential point is that, whether positively or negatively weighted, 'literature' is used in contexts which imply a hierarchy of values.

The last two hundred years have witnessed the gathering momentum of literature as an institution. This coincides with the spread of literacy and the decay in the authority and prestige of religious revelation since the Enlightenment. As literature took the place of religion in intellectual life it came to be seen as the embodiment not only of learning and beauty, but of creative power, the mystique of the nation and the national language, and of moral and emotional ideals. 'The language of poetry naturally falls in with the language of power', Hazlitt wrote.[7] But was it not rather that literary language, in the modern world (and in some earlier civilisations too) was *made* to fall in with power? The Tudor court could plan to produce a strong Navy, but not to produce a Shakespeare. And whilst Shakespeare's modern reputation is the outcome of many factors besides the accident of genius, it owes little or nothing to considerations of social orthodoxy or political expediency. But something very comparable can be said of other constituents of modern culture, such as the scientific community, private industry, and popular journalism. It is precisely their formal independence which makes them such potentially valuable sources of ideological support. Shakespeare's works became an instrument of socialisation throughout the English-speaking world. He is, as Orwell said of Dickens, worth stealing or at least co-opting.[8]

Poets and scholars who deplore the political uses of literature characteristically seek to purify the concept, by defining a cordoned-off area in which literary values alone apply. This area is either the literary canon or the field generated by whatever principle is said to produce the literary canon. But political and other extra-literary considerations cannot be excluded from literary discussion so long as the canon remains changeable and fluid; and a fixed canon is, conversely, a dead one. For this reason the fiercest literary debates are never restricted to theoretical issues but concern the composition of the canon and its hierarchy of values. In our own time fantasy, science fiction, black writing, women's writing, film, television and (I shall argue) literary theory all challenge traditional identifications of the 'best' literature and of the reasons why it is worth reading, studying and imitating. Such debates do not merely affect the fringes of the canon, even if there is no immediate threat to the status of Shakespeare and Homer. At the very least they are bound to affect the ways in which Shakespeare and Homer are read.

The literary canon is not only a collection of works. It is a system, in which the works themselves become intelligible as parts of larger units (genres) and also as wholes consisting of smaller units (elements of works). The hierarchical nature of the canon entails the existence at any one time of what the formalists called a 'dominant' grouping of genres, works and elements of works—the 'dominant' being, in terms of the metaphor consistently used by the formalists, those placed in the foreground.[9] The champions of any new mode of writing invariably seek to bring it into the foreground. Their demand is for a controlling, not a subordinate place in the hierarchy. Other genres, works, and elements must make way. In this context, the liberal and permissive tendency to find room for the new mode—but in a suitably humble and marginal position—is no more than a holding tactic. The terms on which new modes of writing demand entry into the canon are terms on which—as I.A. Richards said of his reinterpretation of Coleridge—'the order of our universes will have been changed'.[10] At their most extreme, the militant proponents of a new form seek to make a 'tabula rasa' of the works of the past. It is for this reason that in the twentieth century an attitude of revolutionary nihilism, such as the futurists and Dadaists displayed, came to be regarded as the sine qua non of a self-respecting avant-garde. At the same time, one cannot seek both to dominate a hierarchy and to sweep it out of existence; some form of compromise between these two aims eventually has to be found. Every new literary movement, if it is to be a *literary* movement, must find some supporting point in the canon as it already exists. In practice, avant-gardes often break apart under the strain of the conflict between the proponents of a tabula rasa and those who favour the critical assimilation of the 'heritage' of the past.[11] There are numerous historical examples of the dilemmas raised by such radical challenges to the literary canon. Wordsworth's 1800 preface to *Lyrical Ballads*, and his and Coleridge's later revisions of the doctrines of the preface, are particularly interesting in this respect. In recent years the most vociferously radical challenge to the literary canon has been posed, not by any new mode of creative practice, but by literary theory. To understand the 'theory' boom as a historical phenomenon it will be necessary to analyse its relationships to earlier twentieth-century literary movements.

Some of these movements are not far to seek, being movements of avant-garde criticism and theory: the New Criticism, the Russian formalists. The object of this chapter is to probe a very different relationship, outlining a history which—however well served by specialist scholarship—has been undeservedly (and in some cases deliberately) overlooked. For it goes without saying that present-day theorists are not the first group to have attempted to politicise literature, or to have privileged its supposed ideological dimensions over the other elements of writing and literary technique. When we look for the lineal ancestor of the 'politics of theory' we find, not just a movement which embodied a genuinely revolutionary impulse, but one whose fate (both political and intellectual) was exemplary in the highest degree. We can understand more about why contemporary theory is failing, and must fail us, and what we may hope to salvage from that failure, by considering a single unsung precursor: the debate about proletarian literature in the 1920s and 1930s.

II

The concept of proletarian literature implies that valuable writings and sources of writing have been condemned to lead an invisible existence, suppressed and ignored by the established canon. At the same time, it is a prescriptive concept, suggesting that new writers, by the force and historical logic of their achievements, have the task of visibly creating a new canon. It is not just a question of rescuing the contents of 'literary backyards',[12] but of capturing the commanding heights of the literary system. To enter fully into the vision of proletarian literature was to affirm that literature (to adapt Terry Eagleton's prognosis for criticism and theory) was about to break with its ideological prehistory, and to resituate itself on an alternative terrain. The 'alternative terrain', moreover, was not the terrain of an intellectual theory, but of a class in the forefront of social revolution. Perhaps that is why proletarian literature had so little impact in the universities, and why in England it took an academic critic as unorthodox as William Empson to treat it seriously, to measure its claims against those of the received canon, and to incorporate it—however marginally and provisionally—into the canon as a version of pastoral. (Besides which, Empson's essay on 'Proletarian Literature'[13] was in fact written not in England but in Japan.) Although it was often seen as the preserve of anti-academics and 'terrorist-critics', proletarian literature had some significant effects upon literary criticism. We shall see this in the work of Empson—who used it as the starting-point for a re-examination of English literary tradition—and in the work of another idiosyncratic critical genius, the Marxist aesthetician Max Raphael, whose far-reaching revaluation of European art is based on the premise that the whole historical tradition of the West should be viewed as a prehistory, a prologue to what is to come. I stress the writings of Empson and Raphael in this chapter because, as critics, they seem to me to be the true revisionaries, the inheritors and arbiters of the vision of proletarian literature. Their significance is completed by the fact that, knowingly or unknowingly, they wrote at a time when the proletarian literature movement was already doomed to failure. Movements which live by politicising art must also die according to the dictates of power and necessity. The correct verdict at an inquest on proletarian literature would probably be one of death by political assassination.

The origins of the concept of proletarian literature lie in the writings of nineteenth-century cultural critics, including John Ruskin and William Morris, who looked to the rebirth of an 'art of the people' expressing man's 'joy in labour' and contrasting with what they saw as the effete, refined and morbidly alienated art of the modern bourgeoisie. Such an art expresses communal feelings and experiences and is not to be confused with the work of individual artists who have risen from plebeian origins. Ruskin located the art of the people in the spirit of craftsman-ship which he rediscovered in medieval Gothic architecture; Morris, following Ruskin, projected this spirit into his vision of a future communist society. Ruskin's contemporaries Marx and Engels stated, in a famous passage of *The German Ideology*, that 'In a communist society there are no painters but at most people who engage in painting among other activities'.[14] Late nineteenth-century realistic and naturalistic artists endorsed the principle that the proletariat should be represented in literature, though the doctrines of naturalism portrayed the writer as a scientific specialist. A more systematic and more politically-inspired concept of proletarian literature was advocated by the Proletcult movement, which arose during the prelude to the Russian Revolution in 1917. The message of the Proletcult spread gradually to the West. In 1921 Mike Gold [Irwin Granich] produced his manifesto 'Towards Proletarian Art' in New York, and in the same year the English writers Eden and Cedar Paul published their book *Proletcult*, linking the Soviet developments to the Ruskin-Morris tradition and the movement for workers' education.[15] By the time that the writings of Gold and the Pauls appeared, the original Proletcult had already been suppressed; however, its successor, the Proletarian Writers' Movement (RAPP) was to dominate Soviet cultural life in the late 1920s and early 1930s. Victor Serge's articles and pamphlets, published in Paris, gave a lively and topical account of communist literary debates from a position sympathetic to RAPP.[16] By 1930 Mike Gold was able to come out with the plausible (if doubtless exaggerated) claim that 'thousands of books and articles on the theories of proletarian literature have been published in Soviet Russia, in Germany, Japan, China, France, England, and other countries'.[17] We cannot doubt that there was a spontaneous movement of support for proletarian literature, reflecting the aspirations of ordinary people in the Soviet Union and elsewhere. But this 'greatest and most universal of literary schools'[18] had become an instrument of bureaucratic struggles within the Soviet elite long before Stalin moved to suppress it in 1932.

To Lenin (never the most enthusiastic supporter of proletarian literature, as it happens) is credited the doctrine that a 'cultural revolution' is an essential component of political revolutions.[19] The political seizure of power creates the conditions in which cultural revolution has to occur if the new proletarian order is to be consolidated. In 1917 the most immediate questions facing the Proletcult militants were those of educational policy. Should the existing Tsarist school system be allowed to continue? On the Marxian principle of 'Who educates the educators?' the setting up of proletarian educational institutions would have to go hand in hand with the construction of other aspects of proletarian culture, including its own class literature. The Proletcult militants believed that such a literature was possible and necessary, and that hegemony belonged to it as a historic right.[20]

In 1920 Lenin forced the Proletcult congress to pass a resolution affirming that 'a proletarian culture could arise only on the basis of the "bourgeois" thought and culture which already existed'.[21] Trotsky's *Literature and Revolution* (1924) include a spirited attack on the Proletcult (as also on its diametrical opposite, the formalist school of literary theorists), based on premises resembling those of traditional humanism. Literature for Trotsky is a criticism of life and therefore cannot remain indifferent to the 'convulsions of our epoch'; but literature is also the expression of intellectuals, who can 'sing' the peasant and the proletariat but cannot, short of the achievement of a fully socialist culture, merge into those classes.[22] Culture is the accumulation of centuries—Trotsky, like Ruskin but for very different purposes, cites the construction of the Gothic cathedrals—and a proletarian culture cannot be created by 'laboratory methods' such as the setting up of a Socialist Academy (pp.186, 193).[23] The period of transition leading via the 'dictatorship of the proletariat' to a fully socialist culture will be a short one, and the emerging culture will be 'human' (ie. classless) rather than proletarian (pp.185–6). An essential part of the building of socialist culture is the 'systematic, planful, and, of course, critical imparting to the backward masses of the essential elements of the culture which already exists' (p.193).

After *Literature and Revolution* came out there was a good deal of quibbling over the expected length of the 'transitional period' to full socialism. Bukharin and Serge were among those who argued that the transition would take several decades, during which there was time to develop a proletarian culture.[24] In 1933 Max Raphael compared proletarian writers to the early Christian artists, suggesting that it would take many *centuries* for the new art to reach full maturity.[25] Raphael's argument that proletarian art 'does consciously what bourgeois art does unconsciously: it serves a political cause' (p.42) could, however, be taken as a retrospective justification of the politically tendentious art advocated by the RAPP spokesmen—retrospective because in 1932 Stalin had settled the argument by dissolving RAPP and abolishing the official distinction between 'proletarian' writers and 'fellow-travellers' (Soviet loyalist writers of bourgeois origin). All writers supporting the programme of the Communist Party were now designated as 'socialist', or 'Soviet', writers. The culture of the USSR was officially declared to be a 'socialist' phenomenon;[26] in fact, it had been brought under centralised bureaucratic control and the various competing factions were swiftly and brutally silenced. In 1934, at the first congress of the Soviet Writers' Union (the new organisation for writers), socialist realism took the place of proletarian literature as the literary doctrine and slogan of the world communist movement.

Socialist realism and proletarian literature: each of these concepts embodies the tension between the appropriation of an earlier cultural heritage, and the revolutionary dream of a tabula rasa. Socialist realism, as defined by Lukács and others, involved a critical takeover bid for one of the primary artistic achievements of bourgeois culture. Scott, Balzac and Tolstoy became the prescribed models for twentieth-century communist writers. The new form of official culture soon became a byword for artistic conservatism. The RAPP theorists had rejected the socialist-realist tenet that literature should cater for the new proletarian reader with positive 'heroes' capable of inspiring and guiding him.[27] Nevertheless, RAPP stood for the politicisation of culture and pioneered the view that literature should reflect, not the empirical interests of the working class, but the interests of the communist dictatorship: 'literature' was to be imposed by the Party, and by 'tearing off the masks' of bourgeois society it could reveal to the workers their own 'real' interests.

Most of the RAPP leadership were not, in fact, of proletarian origin; and in any case they were engaged (and were to be defeated) in the struggle to determine the literary policy of the Soviet ruling elite. In the West, proletarian literature remained an adversary, 'fighting culture',[28] and had a genuine success in tapping the energies of individual working-class writers, many of whom were also communist militants. In England and America the movement lingered on until the outbreak of the Second World War. In the United States, especially, there were remarkable attempts to foster a radical 'people's literature', beginning with the campaign run by *New Masses* magazine in the late 1920s. The short-lived John Reed Clubs with their discussion groups, writers' workshops and magazines soliciting contributions from 'worker-correspondents' set out to constitute an alternative cultural network like that advocated by today's feminist movement. *New Masses* attempted, a shade hypocritically, to rely on the writing of working men and women rather than of professional writers with radical sympathies.[29] Those attached to the movement were, for the most part, fairly gently awakened to the realities of Communist Party control.[30]

Western writers tended to relate proletarian literature, not to nineteenth-century realism (though Walt Whitman was claimed as a precursor[31]) but to more primitive literary and artistic forms. In the United States Mike Gold looked to the new movement to bring about a mystical reconciliation between the solitary writer and the group life: the 'boy in the tenement' struggling to be a writer would come to know the instinct of human solidarity experienced by the masses who remained 'primitive and clean'.[32] Gold's version of literary primitivism was most revealingly expounded in a vision of the future communist culture of New York, which he published in the *Liberator* in March 1922. The scenario is loosely based on classical Greece. It is the spring festival in AD 2400, and 'All day in a hundred amphitheatres of the city, there have been tragedies and comedies, followed by prize-fights, wrestling contests, foot races, poetry readings and song recitals'. ('They have baseball games, too,' Gold adds.) When night falls the hundredfold tragedies and comedies give place to the performance of a single drama, with hundreds of thousands of actors, played on 'immense fields in different parts of the city'; the drama being that of socialist revolution, with a 'hymn of life' concluding the representation of humanity's deliverance from the eons of oppression.[33]

Gold's fantasy of an ideal proletarian art belongs to the genre of utopian visions of the artistic future; indeed, for all its Cecil B. de Mille quality it is by no means to be despised in that proverbially dull company. Evidently it relies on a particular understanding of, and attraction towards, ancient ('primitive') art; it is as if this art, and not that of the bourgeois period, would in the end constitute the usable past. The reason for this is the dream of the tabula rasa which is an element in all revolutionary theories of culture.

Edmund Wilson, in an essay on 'Marxism and Literature' (1938), is the most revered Anglo-American critic to have endorsed this socialist dream:

> It is society itself, says Trotsky, which under communism becomes the work of art ... the human imagination has already come to conceive the possibility of re-creating human society; and how can we doubt that, as it acquires the power, it must emerge from what will seem by comparison the revolutionary 'underground' of art as we have always known it up to now and deal with the materials of actual life in ways which we cannot now even foresee? This is to speak in terms of centuries, of ages; but, in practising and prizing literature, we must not be unaware of the first efforts of the human spirit to transcend literature itself.[34]

Eden and Cedar Paul had foreseen a comparable efflorescence once the social revolution had released the creative forces 'slumbering in the proletariat' (*Proletcult*, p.22). Max Raphael in *Prehistoric Cave Paintings* (1945) made the astounding suggestion that, of all arts, it was that of the Old Stone Age which was most immediately relevant to the visionary tasks of socialist construction:

> The paleolithic paintings remind us that our present subjection to forces other than nature is purely transitory; these works are a symbol of our future freedom. Today, mankind, amidst enormous sacrifices and suffering is, with imperfect awareness, striving for a future in the eyes of which all our history will sink to the level of 'prehistory'. Paleolithic man was carrying on a comparable struggle. Thus the art most distant from us becomes the nearest; the art most alien to us becomes the closest.[35]

Apocalyptic pronouncements such as these must be counted among the legacies of the movement for proletarian literature. Sharply contrasted with them is the well-known view of Empson's *Some Versions of Pastoral* that the proletarian art produced by his contemporaries was a covert form of the old-established literary genre of the pastoral. Empson's starting-point, which was that 'in England [proletarian art] has never been a genre with settled principles, and such as there is of it, that I have seen, is bad', (p.11) would be hard to deny with the benefit of hindsight. One might even say that his empirical approach stands up well beside the approach of writers for whom the vision of proletarian and socialist art was an excuse to indulge in rhetorical utopianism. Nevertheless, Empson readily conceded that it was 'important to try and decide what the term ought to mean' (p.11). He was not alone among his contemporaries in being stung by the idea of proletarian literature into some of his most far-reaching critical reflections.

Empson, at the time when 'Proletarian Literature' was written and published, certainly belonged on the political Left. But his essay, done in his inimitably personal style, is an assertion of the necessity of literary criticism independent of politics. Politics and economics 'do not provide an aesthetic theory', he eventually concludes (p.25). Instead, he uses literary-critical arguments to 'tear off the mask' of proletarian literature and reveal it as a false ideology. He can only do this, needless to say, by having recourse to assumptions which themselves require to be defended. His argument stands or falls by the assertion that the purpose of literature is to express 'permanent truths' (p.12), and that such truths are already widely reflected in bourgeois writing. Moreover they represent an aspect of bourgeois writing which Marxist critics appear to have a vested interest in not drawing to their readers' attention—a point driven home by his famous analysis of a stanza of Gray's *Elegy*. The 'poetic statements of human waste and limitation' are, for Empson, non-political because they are 'true in any society' (pp.22, 12).

Empson's procedure in *Some Versions of Pastoral* is remorselessly intuitive—a fact on which he preens himself to the point of self-parody. Far from writing a 'solid piece of sociology', he has followed the same 'trick of thought' through a 'historical series' (p.25); here both 'trick of thought' and 'historical series' exude a studied vagueness. Empson does not analyse a term, but 'worries its meaning' (p.13). His examples of the pastoral genre are all taken from English literature (proletarian art, like the class and Party it served, was international) and he confesses to a bias towards the 'surprising rather than the normal' cases (p.25). Pastoral as compared with proletarian literature is a 'queerer business, but I think permanent and not dependent on a system of class exploitation' (p.13). There is something comically English, and bourgeois, about the spectacle of Empson using English literature to furnish examples of a form of writing 'not dependent on a system of class exploitation'.

On the other hand, proletarian literature helps Empson to bring into focus the subtleties of the pastoral idea, and to trace its wide ramifications in English writing. Pastoral literature is 'about' but not 'by' or 'for' the people; it is felt to imply a beautiful (though ultimately condescending) relationship between rich and poor. In a bourgeois society, Empson implies, the pastoral idea survives by going underground, so that cults of the criminal and the child take the place of the proverbial shepherd. Proletarian literature offers a further subterfuge for pastoral ideas, by means of its cult of the mythical worker. Empson imagines that the pure doctrine of proletarian art requires that the artist must be at one with the worker; but the reintegration of artist and worker is impossible, 'not for political reasons, but because the artist never is at one with any public' (p.19). The limitation of this view is that Empson, with his comfortable stress on the continuities of post-medieval literature, never really puts it to the test. The nearest that he comes to the notion of a possible 'art of the people' is with the Elizabethan dramatists, who had to satisfy 'both groundlings and courtly critics' (p.58). Empson does not need to take the hegemonic pretensions of proletarian literature seriously because its claims to bring about a cultural tabula rasa are for him entirely specious. Communism in *Some Versions of Pastoral* is more a source of intellectual excitement than an imminent political prospect or threat. His attitude of benevolent detachment is echoed in the poem 'Just a Smack at Auden', with its caricature of English fellow-travelling literary intellectuals:

> What was said by Marx, boys, what did he perpend?...
> Waiting for the end, boys, waiting for the end.[36]

Empson's poetry has its own forms of despair, and of political hope; but in his criticism, with its revaluation of the pastoral genre, he had improvised a curiously effective bottom-of-the-garden air-raid shelter against the apocalypse foreseen by his contemporaries.

Proletarian literature is strictly a class-based form—the 'propaganda of a factory-working class which feels its interests opposed to the factory-owners'[37]—but the term was used more generally to refer to 'folk-literature' and, as both Empson and Max Raphael saw, it raises very general questions about the relationships of art to its audience and of the artist to the people whose experience he supposedly articulates. Herbert Read, who was a friend of both men, described Raphael's *Proudhon, Marx, Picasso* (1933) as 'the most convincing application of the Marxist method I have ever read', and its author as 'a pioneer whose seminal significance will only be realized in the future'.[38] Yet, where Empson is read by every serious student of English, Raphael's art-historical works have remained virtually unknown in the English-speaking world. His life, like that of his contemporary Walter Benjamin, was nomadic, and after his enforced departure from Berlin in 1932 his institutional links were tenuous in the extreme. His slender list of published works spans the whole range of Western art, from paleolithic cave paintings and ancient Egyptian pottery to Monet, Cézanne and Picasso. He died in 1952 at the age of 63, leaving behind a mass of unpublished manuscripts.[39]

Although there are few explicit references to proletarian art in Raphael's writings, his studies in the sociology of art are concerned with two of the crucial underlying issues raised by the Proletcult and its successors. The first is the sociological genesis of art—to what extent it is to be construed as the expression of an individual, or a class, or of some other collective entity—and the second is the relationship of its past to its future development. *Proudhon, Marx, Picasso* begins with a lengthy attack on Proudhon's theories, justified by the assertion that the artistic doctrines professed by Western communist intellectuals in the early 1930s were Proudhonian rather than Marxist in origin. Proudhon viewed the arts as 'emanations from a supra-individual "collective force"' (p.37)—a point of view which led, so Raphael thought, to a 'fantasy Communism', based on the mystification of the artist's relationship to the proletariat. This theme is continued in the second essay, 'The Marxist Theory of Art', where Raphael stresses the significance of the 'problem of folk poetry' for Marxist aesthetics (p.99). Marx had raised, without (in Raphael's view) satisfactorily explaining, the phenomenon of 'unequal development' whereby an art-form such as the Homeric epic may be brought to perfection at a relatively early and primitive stage of the development of human society. Raphael puts Marx's discussion in its context by pointing to two influential bourgeois attempts to explain the excellence of Homer: F.A. Wolf's theory of collective authorship, according to which the 'Homeric' poems were the work of a multitude of individual poets assembled together by an 'editor', and the theory of 'folk poetry' which (like Proudhon's sociology of art) attributes the Homeric poems to the genius of a whole people: 'This theory, which eliminated the role of the individual entirely, asserted that society itself was the creator of the spiritual product' (p.100). If there was folk poetry in the past, one might reasonably assume that a similar form of collective creation would characterise the art of the communist future. But Raphael invokes such theories only to dismiss them. They had proved attractive, he suggests, because nineteenth-century philologists were unable to imagine that such a monumental achievement as the Homeric cycle had been within the range of an individual poet nurtured in a 'primitive', pre-civilised society. Marx had wrestled with the same problem from another perspective, as he sought to explain the 'eternal charm' of ancient Greek art. Since Marx had written, the paleolithic cave paintings of France and Northern Spain had been discovered—a form of art far more ancient than the Greek, which also, apparently, possessed an eternal charm. Raphael, convinced that both the Greek epic and the paleolithic paintings should be attributed to individual artists of genius, set out to reassess the concepts of social development and of the artist's relationship to the people which Marx and his followers had somewhat uncritically taken over from bourgeois sociology and aesthetics.

In his *Introduction to the Critique of Political Economy* Marx asks why, since Greek art and literature are the productions of an early stage of historical development, they continue to give aesthetic pleasure and to prevail as a norm which in some respects has still to be surpassed. Raphael shows how Marx's answer to this—that Greek art possesses the charm of infancy and that the Greeks were not 'ill-bred' or 'precocious' but 'normal' children—differs from those given by his predecessors, Kant, Herder and Hegel. He then proceeds to demolish Marx's answer on the grounds that it is not Marxist enough. Firstly, for Raphael, it would be necessary to study the historical circumstances of the series of renaissances in European art which have erected certain aspects of Greek civilisation into a norm—Raphael here refuses any notion of an eternal charm—and, secondly, the idea that the Greeks represent a stage of human 'infancy' is no longer tenable. Neither Greek drama nor Greek epic can be considered as 'primitive' art-forms. They are not only mature and complex in themselves, but are the outcome of a process of civilised advance which was already ancient at the time of Homer.[40]

Raphael's assault on the myth of an 'infantile' stage of society is carried to still more startling lengths in his book on prehistoric cave paintings. The existence of these paintings poses an even sharper challenge than that of Homer to Marxist and other historicist theories of art. Whereas the normative status of Greek classicism had accumulated over two millennia, paleolithic cave painting and sculpture were utterly lost until brought to light by a series of chance discoveries in the late nineteenth and early twentieth centuries. Yet this art won instant recognition for its qualities of naturalistic draughtsmanship and monumental composition, which were felt to be worthy of the great masters of Western art. As with the Homeric poems, these qualities were generally attributed to the whole society, or to a whole caste of witchdoctors or wizards, rather than to the genius of individual artists. At the same time the mysterious simplicity of cave art was such that it was found virtually impossible to interpret.

Unlike nearly all forms of modern native and primitive art, the paleolithic paintings were, or appeared to be, naturalistic rather than symbolic representations. Roger Fry, one of the first English critics to tackle the problems of prehistoric and primitive art, contrasted the paleolithic and Bushman drawings with the clumsy figures portrayed on early Greek vases. For him, the naturalistic drawings were self-evidently the products of a lower, not a higher, stage of artistic development. Fry squared this circle by distinguishing between perceptual and conceptual art, the former belonging to a pre-intellectual stage of civilisation. The Stone Age paintings could then be seen as ritual representations—or even as aids to field identification—of animals to be killed in the hunt. Spurred by economic necessity, the ordinary prehistoric tribesmen had viewed their animal prey with an uncluttered clarity of hand and eye which, in more advanced societies, all but the most exceptional of specialised artists had lost.[41]

Max Raphael's interpretation of paleolithic cave paintings can never be proved, and for that reason it will always be questioned, and attempts to revive it possibly ridiculed; but he is the only major art critic to have devoted a substantial portion of his career to studying the paintings, and as far as I know his is the only imaginatively satisfying interpretation of them yet to have been produced. Raphael's approach to the problem of the paleolithic was that of a Marxist for whom, as he wrote in his 1933 essay on Picasso, 'the mere fact that there is a proletariat conscious of its class and struggling for it ... already today deeply influences the subconscious of the intellectual worker.

The need for a new, integral work of art adapted to a new social order, makes itself felt in all his creations' (*PMP*, p.145). He begins *Prehistoric Cave Paintings*—in line with his critique of Marx—by dismissing any analogy with children's art or with the art of the stagnant primitive societies which still survive. The cave-paintings, it is true, date from a period when man had just emerged from a 'purely zoological existence' (p.2); but this means that the paleolithic peoples were 'history-making peoples *par excellence*; they were in the throes of a continuous process of transformation because they squarely confronted the obstacles and dangers of their environment and tried to master them' (p.3). All the fundamental categories of human existence were present in this early stage—the idea of an 'absolute origin' of the human race is no more than a metaphysical hypothesis—and, as a result, the force of the paintings derives from their expression of a complex and symbolic vision of human life which, in Raphael's view, can be judged by the same standards as the tragedies of Aeschylus or the art of today.

The paintings had a magic function—'the belief that if an image of an object was hit, the original object was hit, too' (p.7)—but, according to Raphael, its use in hunting magic cannot account for the monumental character of paleolithic art. This consideration leads him to the hypothesis that the magnificently naturalistic representations of deer, mammoths, bisons and bulls are not 'really' pictures of animals at all.... Instead, they are to be understood as totemic representations of tribes and tribal structures, in a culture in which the undisguised portrayal of the human figure was prohibited (just as the Jews were forbidden to make an image of God). To trace the full ramifications of this daring argument is not my purpose here. But for Raphael 'representation implies difference': in this case not merely the difference between man and animal, or between hunter and prey, but between the individual artist and the tribal community that he symbolically depicts (p.10). Paleolithic art is the work of privileged individuals able to express the 'wishes and interests of the ruling classes which possessed the spiritual and material tools and weapons' (p.50) in their society; so much for Marx's theory of 'primitive communism'. Moreover, 'The paleolithic artists of the late Magdalenian period were quite familiar with all the innermost recesses of the human soul' (p.11).

Raphael, it will be clear, is no more capable than Empson or Marx had been of dispensing with permanent, transhistorical categories. In his discussion of Marx's *Introduction to the Critique of Political Economy* he attributed the superiority of Greek art to its 'dialectical' rather than 'dogmatic' character (*PMP*, p.106). Paleolithic painting, too, attains a dialectical unity which for Raphael is open to formal compositional analysis; for example, he considers why it is that the proportions of the Golden Section appear in cave paintings (*Prehistoric Cave Paintings*, p.28). Beyond this, Raphael invokes the transhistorical categories of the individual artist and the human soul, together with those of structural linguistics in which 'representation implies difference'.[42] To this extent the effect of his book is to appropriate prehistoric art and to make sense of it as part of our cultural heritage. The result of doing this, however, is to revolutionise our ideas of art history and of art itself and, by implication, to overturn the existing artistic canon. To fully understand Old Stone Age paintings, he suggests, is to have insight into an art which has yet to be born: this is the art of that other history-making people, the modern proletariat. If 'the art most alien to us becomes the closest' it is because 'these works are a symbol of our future freedom'.

Like the proletarian literary ideal, the perspective opened up by *Prehistoric Cave Paintings* is one of a tabula rasa in which the tradition of Western easel-painting would be displaced, though not of course wholly dismissed. It would no longer seem that the modern European pictorial tradition constituted, as John Berger has put it, a history of 'change without end'.[43] The subsequent course of the twentieth century has yet to live up to Raphael's prophecy. Paleolithic art, it may be, no longer exerts the magnetic attraction it held for Raphael and some members of his generation.[44] It is as if we have grown too world-weary, too introspective, too obsessed with our own immediate past to respond to a form of art speaking across the millennia to bear witness to a new dawning of human consciousness.

Empson and Raphael, both supremely gifted and scholarly critics, were also socialists for whom the difficult theoretical choice between accepting the heritage of the past and endorsing the hegemonic claims of a new revolutionary art was, in the last resort, a matter and a test of faith. For Empson the 'queer forces' and 'trick of thought' which characterised human ingenuity could be illustrated in their rich profusion among the byways of the English literary past. For Raphael, however—in the concluding words of *Prehistoric Cave Paintings*—'What's past is prologue': the art of the past was valuable as a guide and symbol for the future. Both critics emphasised the ways in which art goes beyond the ideologies it conveys. Empson's quatrain from Gray was at once an expression of bourgeois individualism and a statement of a permanent truth. Raphael argued in *Prehistoric Cave Paintings* that 'the artist's ability is less subjected to society than his will'. By his creative effort he 'rises above his time' (p.12). It is for this reason that 'the work of art holds man's creative powers in a crystalline suspension from which it can again be transformed into living energies' (*DOA*, p.187), and that 'questions of artistic value and sociological function must be kept strictly separated' (*PMP*, p.61). The most he will permit himself, in responding to the creative power of the prehistoric cave paintings, is the inference that such works must have sprung from a 'social interaction rich in contrasts' rather than from an 'unbridgeable gulf' between the people and the ruling elite of hunters and magicians whose outlook the paintings represent (pp.12-13). On this point Empson and Raphael, in many ways so different, may be seen to converge. Both viewed proletarian literature and art as a necessary attempt, however premature or potentially misguided, to heal the social and cultural divisions of their time and to recover a beautiful relationship between the artist and his public—a relationship based on genuine mutual respect, if not on equality, and which had been foreshadowed in the richest examples of the art of the past.

III

Today the feelings once attached to proletarian literature are by no means dead. Black writing and women's writing come nearest to being the unconscious heirs of this movement. What passes for socialist literary theory is another matter. With the exception of one or two diehard defenders of socialist realism, the traditional goals of a Marxist theory—those of liberating the working class and ending mass alienation—are no more than empty, formal elements of an intellectual critique. (How does it come about that a political orientation which once fuelled 'proletarian literature' now impels its adherents so remorselessly towards scientism and esoteric theory? That would be a long story, one which would show how repeatedly and how cynically Marxism, as a political system and an intellectual creed, has betrayed the proletariat whose interests it claims to advance.) Of the various contemporary new genres it is theory itself which most openly aspires to hegemony over the whole literary system. Oddly enough, its claims are grounded in the glamour of an abstract rationalism. Where other new literary forms offer to speak for the contemporary needs of an emerging culture or for hitherto tabooed areas of experience and oppressed groups of people, theory asserts a merely intellectual priority, as a meta-discourse on the traditional models of theology, philosophy and ideology.

The liberal and pragmatic argument that theory is useful and deserves recognition to the extent that it aids literary inter-pretation falls far short of the demands of theory itself. For this reason there is an element of inglorious and futile compromise in assigning theory to an optional or subordinate part of the syllabus, or in treating it as the 'servant of a servant'.[45] Theory not only aspires to mastery over interpretation and commentary; it chal-lenges the customary pre-eminence of imaginative works in the traditional genres. Its complexity, and the complexity of lyrical, epic and dramatic works are of very different sorts. Theory in its current manifestations sets out to shame the works of the traditional canon and their accretions of commentary into silence—and then to speak for them, assimilating their concerns to its own. The literary map with its familiar reference-points then seems to be changing before our eyes. And, indeed, canons do change, though few readers have been able to anticipate these changes with any certainty or accuracy. The reason for this lies in the unforeseeability of literary production itself. There is in theory no reason why theory should not become the 'dominant' of the new literary system, standing at the head of a new value-hierarchy and dictating to its subordinates in the way that, to its advocates, proletarian literature once seemed destined to do. Equally, since the penalty of ignoring the lessons of history is to be condemned to repeat them, it is entirely possible that the future-that-never-materialised of the Proletcult and its successors is about to be repeated—the first time as tragedy, the second time as farce. For who but the theoreticians themselves would weep over the demise of 'literary theory'? The failure of theory need not be accompanied by literary suppression or political defeat, still less by martyrdom. It is, after all, simply the passing of a form of scholasticism. The brave new world of the theoreticist canon—a new pedagogics and a new pantheon in which (say) Derrida takes the place of T.S. Eliot, Lacan of Lawrence, Althusser of George Orwell—is not one which can release creative energies or make the slightest contribution to liberating the world's dispossessed. Proletarian literature, in short, had politically serious objectives; literary theory does not. Moreover, 'If the notion of a canon in itself is untouched, then new critical approaches by themselves cannot deconstruct the concept "Literature"'.[46] Changing the canon is the key to changing the literary system. A canon is the consensus of the answers we should give if the proverbial Martian ethnographer, or for that matter the ghosts of William Empson or Max Raphael, were to turn up and ask, not 'What is literature?' but 'What is *your* literature?' And in answering that question we become not theorists but literary critics.

Part II

7

The Age of Fantasy

In May 1907 a periodical was launched in London with the title of the *New Age*. Edited by A.R. Orage, it lasted until 1922 and played a key role in public discussion of the arts during what we now regard as the great age of literary modernism. Modernism, as a period and an international style, receded a long time ago. We have entered another new age—an age as yet unnamed. 'Postmodernism', the fashionable term of the 1970s, shares the logical shortcomings of its predecessor (for what are we to say of a modernism no longer modern?) and is, besides, little more than a chronological conception. I wish to propose an alternative description of the characteristic style of our age: a description based on Fantasy.

Fantasy, a word with a long history, has recently emerged as the name of a loosely-conceived literary mode or genre. This application is of commercial origin (as in the *Magazine of Fantasy and Science Fiction*) and almost certainly reflects the disappearance of any authorised belief in the supernatural. The philosopher Herbert Spencer once claimed that barbarism and superstition, having been eradicated by advancing civilisation, take on a new kind of social utility as the subjects of pleasing tales.[1] This was certainly true of beliefs about witches, monsters, ghosts, wizards, devils and the like. When science and material progress made it impossible for these to be taken seriously they found a home in popular literature, from penny dreadfuls to the more sophisticated nineteenth-century romances. Romance had its ardent and self-conscious defenders—notably Robert Louis Stevenson—but their attempt to return to simple and timeless verities of narrative involved, all too obviously, a preference for childlike over adult reading experiences. In adult fiction, dominated by the conventions of realism, apparently supernatural events were assigned to the area of the 'paranormal' which could always be explained away in terms of psychic delusion.

The present 'return of the fantastic', as it has been called, takes two forms. Interest in the occult as a source of knowledge has never died out, but its manifestations such as theosophy, witch-craft, transcendental meditation and other forms of exotic religion have been more overt in the last two decades than at any previous time in the twentieth century. So have its more frivolous corollaries such as the cult of UFOs, drug-taking, and popular astrology. (The language of star-signs is now indulged in as an almost universal superstition by people under forty.) Occult beliefs and practices were certainly part of the mental furniture of writers in previous generations, though more of poets than of novelists. A newer development is the commercial exploitation of formerly private dreams and fantasies, which has spread from advertising to pornography, satire, and other forms of mass enter-tainment. Billion-dollar horror and science-fiction movies satisfy a double taste for wish-fulfilment and for a mild dose of the occult; and these ingredients are abstracted and served up in isolation from character and story-line, in a manner that would have been incomprehensible to classic Hollywood.

Fantasy, as a psychological concept, is intimately bound up with desire. An Age of Fantasy is necessarily one which has seen great changes in public attitudes to desire and its alleviation. In *The Culture of Narcissism*, Christopher Lasch observes a general abandonment of ideals of historical continuity and social improve-ment in American life.[2] Their place has been taken by narcissistic forms of self-assertion, as if the individual and his or her desires were the only tangible reality. Similar if less far-reaching changes have occurred in British culture, at a literary as well as a popular level. Terms like 'sincerity', 'maturity', 'decency', and 'humanity', once the cornerstones of a critical vocabulary, have now fallen into disuse. An essay like George Orwell's examination of seaside post-cards could no longer be written today. In 1941 the people who bought seaside postcards and those who read about them in the pages of *Horizon* belonged to two different worlds. Today we should have to say that, at most, they represent alternative—but ultimately interchangeable—lifestyles. No doubt this cultural leavening is a gain, of a sort. Yet the spread of the word 'lifestyle' itself illustrates the extent to which our classless, consumerised culture takes for granted the inevitability of narcissism.

So far I have said nothing about contemporary fiction. Its tendency is so overwhelmingly towards the fantastic that detailed exemplification would be superfluous. What is more urgent is to formulate an appropriate critical response. In fiction, as in culture more generally, the symptoms may be interpreted as those of decadence. Yet the concept of an Age of Fantasy implies that wholesale resistance would be futile. Whatever our inherited liberal, progressive, materialist, or just common-sense prejudices may say about it, a new age can only grow out of the decadence of an old one. Some literary critics and theorists are already committed to ideals of hedonism and textual 'freeplay'—in other words, to a critical power-struggle without standards. The majority have welcomed some of the new manifestations of fantasy while trying hard to draw boundaries and limit its encroachments. (Perhaps that is the function of criticism when faced with any new movement.) The way that they try to limit it is by privileging one mode of fantasy at the expense of the others.

We have been taught to regard fantasy as self-indulgent, wish-fulfilling, escapist. We ourselves live in a society which pampers the majority with material goods and fulfils many of the wishes which tormented previous ages. Among these wishes is the desire for vicarious participation in a life of tragedy, nobility, heroism, and significant passion. This desire is met at a sophisticated level by the widespread availability of the literary classics, and at a cruder level by popular fiction, cinema and television. The heroic heroes and villainous villains of popular fiction are felt to be 'escapist'; yet if what they offer is identification with modes of experience beyond our everyday lives, then it is something we all need. For this reason, criteria must be found according to which some escapes are more acceptable than others—whether on grounds of ethics, politics, psychology, aesthetics, or even linguistics. Hence most of the confusion in books about fantasy. Some would confer a privileged status on science fiction and utopian writing; others, on the Gothic; others on writers of allegorical fantasy such as C.S. Lewis or Tolkien. There is a school which advocates the so-called 'pure fantastic', in which the text is left open to either a supernatural or a psychological explanation of the events. Finally, there are propagandists for experimental modes of literary fantasy such as the 'New Wave', the *nouveau* and *nouveau nouveau roman*, and postmodernism.

Much of this theory and criticism is not only ideology-laden but is an outcome of the urge to censor and to legislate. Literary critics are not alone in this, since groups such as educationalists, feminists, and anti-racialist campaigners have recently attempted to discredit some of the traditional modes of children's fantasy. At best, the critic may take us a little beyond the insights of his or her particular blindness. A case in point is Christine Brooke-Rose's study *A Rhetoric of the Unreal* (1981). Brooke-Rose endorses Tzvetan Todorov's notion of the 'pure fantastic', a logical category which perhaps works better in French than it does in English. Her analyses favour the 'complexity' and 'subtlety' of postmodernist writing as against the fully-presented unreal worlds of narrative romance, or what she calls 'the marvellous'. Support for certain literary movements and tendencies against others is perhaps what even the most rigorously abstract analytical approach comes down to—since, in this area, distinctions which seem logical and compelling from one point of view may be more or less nebulous from another. (For example Brooke-Rose concedes that a single explanatory sentence at the end of a story might transfer it from the 'pure fantastic' to the despised category of the marvellous, or vice versa.)[3] Nevertheless, this is an unusually stimulating book of its kind, which joins a general assessment of present-day fantasy to abstruse applications of critical techniques (no less than a hundred pages on *The Turn of the Screw*).

Brooke-Rose concludes, more or less, with the proviso that 'ultimately all fiction is realistic' (p.388). This sentiment has a tried appeal to anyone whose intellectual formation took place before the Age of Fantasy became epidemic. Can we go on using 'realism', the name of a style or mode, as the inevitable synonym for an art of instruction or truth-telling? There may be good reason to expect a 'return of the realistic' some time in the future, but it will not be yet. When it comes, it may have to learn from the strategy of the Victorian novelists, who fed off the Gothic romances while simultaneously disowning them. 'In those days I was young', Jane Eyre informs us, 'and all sorts of fancies bright and dark tenanted my mind; the memories of nursery stories were there amongst other rubbish' (Ch.12). Charlotte Brontë's realism depends upon the construction of a fictional Jane Eyre whose mind was once tenanted by fantastic rubbish, but is so no longer. The story tells of her young (and rubbishy) days, and tails off smartly when they are over. Is *Jane Eyre* 'ultimately realistic', or ultimately fantastic? It is a question of our point of view.

A return to fantasy is just as capable of revitalising fiction as is a return to realism. English fiction, especially, stands to gain from it. British novelists do not figure very prominently within the international canon of postmodernist fiction, a fact that has been noted with much wringing of hands. They are, however, in the forefront of twentieth-century fantasy. It seems to me that it is the general revival of fantastic narrative, rather than the modernist fiction of Proust, Faulkner and Joyce (*Finnegans Wake* as ever is a special case) which provides the work of the postmodernists such as Pynchon, Vonnegut, Brautigan, Barth and Barthelme with their most useful context. At their best, English fantasy writers do not ask to be judged by the criteria of experimentalism, nor by those of ability to produce a pleasing story. (There are always plenty of new writers who can meet this traditional, and fundamental, need.) They should be judged by their ability to use fantasy reflexively, in that, while inviting us to identify with the alien and exotic, they are able to probe unsuspected facets of our own individual and collective identity.

In contrast to the thickly-ramifying realistic novel, fantasy fictions are often episodic and short. By their nature, they invite reduplication. The danger, seen in such brilliant writers as J.G. Ballard and Angela Carter, is perhaps that of remaining bound by a too-easily identifiable set of themes and variations. Often these are of psychic origin, despite Todorov's view (apparently endorsed by Brooke-Rose) that the 'pure fantastic' began to decline once its themes were taken over by psychoanalysis. There is good reason for the continuance of psychic fantasy, even from a point of view which endorses the claims of science in general, and the pretensions of psychoanalysis in particular. The mental troubles for which people seek psychoanalytic help themselves seem to be changing over time. (Lasch quotes expert evidence for the belief that narcissistic disorders have now taken the place of the classical neuroses analysed by Freud.)[4] Writers may also choose to probe the connections between popular fiction and entertainment and narcissistic fantasy. '"You're nothing but the furious invention of my virgin nights"', says heroine to hero at the end of Carter's *Heroes and Villains*,[5] while Ballard used to speak of 'inner-space fiction'.

Fantasy fiction is concerned with our social existence, as well as with our inner disorders and psychological states. In the realistic novel there is, among other things, a tradition of social commentary, of cultural and material concern with Carlyle's 'Condition-of-England Question'. Social identity, however, is constituted as much by legend and mythology—whether inherited or contemporary, in Roland Barthes' sense—as it is by their cultural and material foundations. The costume-drama of past and future, in which exotic settings serve as a backcloth for essentially contemporary characters with contemporary problems, is presumably no more than a vehicle for the narcissism described by Lasch. Nevertheless, themes of historical legend and future destiny may be used to enrich our sense of who we are and to remind us of continuity. Such themes include the post-disaster novel which—according to one contemporary—every English novelist has to write. Survival may be regarded either as a hope for the future or as a fact about the present; and survival, as we see in the Arthurian romances and the Robin Hood legends, is as much a matter of imagination and belief as it is of 'realism'. In an Age of Fantasy the 'Condition-of-England Question' and its associated social commentary in the novel might well be replaced by the question of the 'matter of Britain'. [1982]

8

Pilgrim's Progress:
The Novels of B.S. Johnson

What is it that makes an experimental novelist? There are many possible motivations, but among them must always be the desire for self-projection in a more total, more arresting form than that available to more conventional writers. Self-projection has usually been a risky business, and until recently the threat of ostracism hanging over the experimental writer was very real. Now it is so no longer. The upsurge of experimental art in the 1960s revealed that experimentation had become a recognised form of publicity-seeking. This is the background to B.S. Johnson's career. Johnson was never shy of self-advertisement—one remembers the advance publicity for his novel-in-a-box, *The Unfortunates* (1969)—but the show he put on was as much one of anxiety and vulnerability as of virtuosity. It was uncomfortably typical of Johnson that the 'random order' effect in *The Unfortunates* should seem superfluous in a novel of painfully literal honesty, that his one popular success with *Christie Malry's Own Double-Entry* (1973) should be achieved in apparent contravention of his own principles, and finally that his most ambitious artistic project, the *Matrix* trilogy, should be curtailed in 1973 by his suicide. It was as if Johnson had reintroduced the risk into experimental writing by publicly setting himself tasks which were in fact impossible.

One should beware of arguing that any artist deliberately courted failure. And yet while artistic failure is commonplace, a record of ostentatious 'failures' like Johnson's must surely be rather rare. During his lifetime, he was most commonly seen as a brilliant writer thrashing around in a trap of his own making. I shared this view, but have subsequently come to feel that there was method and not artlessness in Johnson's constant disappointment of the reader's, and his own, expectations. Reread in sequence, his novels can be seen to exemplify a peculiarly British form of self-punishment. Johnson's imagination is of the manic-depressive type, the mania resulting in bold experimentation and extravagant comedy, and the depression in the gloomy, morose self-examination of his more intimate novels such as *The Unfortunates* and *Trawl* (1966). This in itself is not so very remarkable; if they did no more than project a personality, Johnson's novels, though certainly arresting, would hardly stand out as unique. What makes these novels significant is that they are shaped in accordance with a conscious aesthetic, and this aesthetic, I shall argue, has a deep historical correspondence with the particular kind of personality-structure that Johnson's writings reveal.

'Telling stories is telling lies ... I am not interested in telling lies in my own novels.'[1] This thesis which Johnson nailed to the door of his house of fiction provoked a barrage of refutation from critics, even the most sympathetic. It was denounced as an expression of hostility to art and a deliberate shackling of the imagination. It was seen as a denial of its author's own gifts and a pernicious example to others. This sort of misunderstanding may have been inevitable, since Johnson was at once a vociferous member of the avant-garde and an extreme individualist. But Johnson's version of the eighth commandment was devised for his own purposes, not for the general reformation of contemporary fiction. In arguing this, I wish to stress a point that I do not think any previous critic of Johnson has made—that his objection to 'telling stories', so far from being revolutionary, is the traditional objection of English Puritanism. Thus Johnson's originality was not a matter of mere innovation; it was that his innovations, together with other aspects of his art, reveal how far the Puritan tradition survives as a means of making sense of the contemporary world.

A classic statement of the traditional Puritan attitude to fiction can be found in Edmund Gosse's memoir *Father and Son*. Gosse's mother was a prolific writer of missionary tracts and yet she had, her son recounts, 'a remarkable, I confess to me still somewhat unaccountable impression, that to "tell a story", that is, to compose fictitious narrative of any kind, was a sin'.

116

That this conviction was not held without spiritual struggle is witnessed by a passage from his mother's 'secret diary', which he then proceeds to quote:

> When I was a very little child, I used to amuse myself and my brothers with inventing stories, such as I read. Having, as I suppose, naturally a restless mind and busy imagination, this soon became the chief pleasure of my life. Unfortunately, my brothers were always fond of encouraging this propensity, and I found in Taylor, my maid, a still greater tempter. I had not known there was any harm in it, until Miss Shore [a Calvinist governess], finding it out, lectured me severely, and told me it was wicked. From that time forth I considered that to invent a story of any kind was a sin. But the desire to do so was too deeply rooted in my affections to be resisted in my own strength [she was at that time nine years of age], and unfortunately I knew neither my corruption nor my weakness, nor did I know where to gain strength. The longing to invent stories grew with violence; everything I heard or read became food for my distemper. The simplicity of truth was not sufficient for me; I must needs embroider imagination upon it, and the folly, vanity, and wickedness which disgraced my heart are more than I am able to express. Even now [at the age of twenty-nine], tho' watched, prayed and striven against, that is still the sin that most easily besets me. It has hindered my prayers and prevented my improvement, and therefore has humbled me very much.[2]

Gosse describes this confession as 'a very painful instance of the repression of an instinct', but there is surely more to be said than this. While his mother may have been a thwarted novelist she did, after all, become a professional writer and, still more interestingly, she kept a secret diary. Diary-keeping was earlier a frequent habit among seventeenth-century Puritans, and various critics have used this material to throw some light on the rise of the novel. The psychology of Puritan fanaticism exposed in a book like *Father and Son* reveals why such a connection may exist. The last sentence quoted above shows the writer telling a story about herself, and anyone believing that God's book contains a decree concerning their own salvation has a powerful motive for diary-writing. As long as he remains armed against the mirages and deceptions presented by the world, the private story which the Puritan knows in his conscience must be the true one. This certainly may be the source of the hallucinatory vividness available to a writer like Defoe. On the other hand, the more strictly religious the writer's temperament the more wary he is likely to be of the inauthentic, external fictions that surround him. At the heart of English Puritan culture is *The Pilgrim's Progress* with its image of the quest for righteousness as a constant and perilous confrontation with the phantoms and illusions met by the wayside. Only by exploding innumerable fictions does the steadfast pilgrim arrive at the truth.

Why, then, does the devout Puritan's diary have to be kept secret? The answer, evidently, is that it is a record of the individual's shortcomings, of the temptations which surround him and which only constant vigilance enables him to repulse. Where the ideal of conduct he sets himself is strictly unattainable, the relentless scrutiny which a Puritan brings to his actions and thoughts may be viewed as a mechanism for the production of guilt. The kind of inner conflict to which this could give rise does not in fact figure very largely in *Father and Son*. Gosse's mother is allowed a saint-like perfection (she died when he was seven), and his own strong imaginative impulses undergo a natural, though clandestine, development, so that his eventual breach with his father is the expression of a healthy and not a stunted personality. Gosse's narrative recounts all this with an air of serenity which the reader might suspect of itself being 'fictitious'. In some ways the record of the father might have been more interesting than that of the coolly detached and self-assured son.

B.S. Johnson was an aggressively anti-religious writer. Whatever its roots may have been in his personal experience his anticlericalism speaks of a far more austere, more vulnerably religious temperament than Gosse's. The resentful, irritated tone of his comments on religion is typified by the opening sentence of an early short story: 'God got on Henry's wick.'[3] Christie Malry, the hero of Johnson's penultimate novel, tries to prosecute his parish church under the Trade Descriptions Act—after all, they claim to have 'the answer to all problems, personal, political and international' (p.16)—and eventually has to be cautioned by his girlfriend for his 'obsession with knocking religion' (p.101). Christie, an urban guerrilla, is an inverted Christ-figure, and so is Haakon, the scapegoat hero of Johnson's play *You're Human Like the Rest of Them* (1964). The play ends with Haakon's parable of locusts and lizards: the futile resistance of the locusts

118

which are being fed to lizards in a cage is seen as the only protest open to man in the face of a vindictive deity:

> The only thing a locust could do was
> To make itself an awkward thing to eat
> By sticking out its arms and legs and wings
> To make itself an awkward thing to kill
> So shall I: I have to die, but by God
> I'm not going to pretend I like it
> I shall make myself so bloody awkward! (pp.230-1)

Anti-Christian attitudes like these play a regular and certainly not a very profound role in Johnson's writings. But it is within the context of an acknowledged anti-religious obsession that Johnson will be seen to exemplify some underlying patterns of the Puritan intelligence.

When faced with the assertion that 'Telling stories is telling lies', most people's response is to fall back on the doctrine of free creative expression. The Platonic demand for the moral justification of imagination may be met either by asserting the mental freedom is an absolute good, or by arguing that wherever fiction is used to enforce some wider truth, the means of creative fabrication are justified by that end. It was this common rationalisation of our fiction-making impulses that Johnson sought to deny himself. But the belligerent, purist tone of his polemics on the novel is in fact deceptive. Johnson may sometimes have claimed that he was simply writing autobiography in the form of a novel, but then the novelist who swears with hand on heart that he is not a liar has put himself in a position of the famous person from Crete. The anecdotes with which Johnson ended his most important fictional manifesto, the Introduction to *Aren't You Rather Young to be Writing Your Memoirs?* (1973), suggest that he was well aware of this. The reader's incredulity mounts with each of the three tall stories he tells about the reception of his novels—ending with the claim that *Trawl* was found in the Angling section of an eminent bookshop. Truth may be stranger than fiction, and I do not claim to know whether or not this story was a hoax. The point lies in the inherent solipsism of an author's claims about 'fiction' and 'truth'. What relevance, after all, do such unverifiable assertions have for the reader?

Johnson's renunciation of fiction was, then, not so much a principle to guide the novel-reader as a standard against which to measure himself. Superficially he may have hoped to change contemporary fiction but deep down, it would seem, he was setting himself tests he did not believe he could pass. While the exploitation of self-conscious devices in his novels was often playful, it could also be anguished and hurt. The bilious emotional outburst which interrupts the narrative near the end of *Albert Angelo* (1964) is far removed from the suavity with which a practitioner such as John Fowles exploits the convention of the novel with a thwarted ending. Johnson's principles provide for many comic moments, but they also produce anguish when he cannot live up to them and guilt when he contravenes them without the reader knowing. In *Aren't You Rather Young* he expressed his private struggle in terms that any serious writer could understand: 'I feel myself fortunate sometimes that I can laugh at the joke that just as I was beginning to think I knew something about how to write a novel it is no longer of any use to me in attempting the next one' (p.17). If we see his aims as, in some senses, unattainable the joke here will seem rather precarious. Johnson's self-deprecation is compounded by the fact that, once he had declared in public that he hated telling lies, he had done his best to make the reader suspicious of every novel he wrote. Any success of his will seem hypocritical since he has substituted an impossible technical standard for the impossible moral standards of religious Puritanism.

*

Johnson's attempt to reconcile fiction and truth was explicit in his first novel, *Travelling People* (1963). Here he announced his intention to expose the mechanism of the novel, by means of interludes, jokes and stylistic variation, in order to eliminate deception between writer and reader. *Travelling People* was well received, but Johnson later called it a 'disaster' because it was 'part truth and part fiction' (*AY*, pp.22, 29). He refused to reprint the book, which evidently became abhorrent to him—rather like George Eliot's Bulstrode setting aside his own past. His next novel, *Albert Angelo*, contains an extraordinary exercise in self-abasement when the hero, a supply teacher, sets his secondary-modern class an essay on 'What I think of teacher'. The answers make a brilliant series of parodies, but then Johnson interrupts the narrative, denouncing his fictional structure as a sham and confessing that 'teacher' is himself. There followed *Trawl* and *The Unfortunates*, novels of mordant self-examination in which the narrator broods over his futile love-affairs and over a painful bereavement. In *House Mother Normal* (1971) and *Christie Malry*, by contrast, Johnson abandons the autobiographical mode and portrays masterful and self-confident main characters whose behaviour arouses outright revulsion or, at best, a guilty and sneaking admiration. These are novels which cauterise normal human reactions, and only on reflection does their moral purpose become apparent. Such purpose is hidden as if Johnson were ashamed to take credit for it, preferring to be allied with his protagonists as scapegoat-turned-villain. Finally there was to be the *Matrix* trilogy, announced as his major work—a double humiliation in that his determination not to tell lies seemed likely to reduce the narrative to a random montage,[4] and in that he did not live to complete it.

Johnson's suicide prompts the question whether the pattern that can now be discovered in his career could be found in the lives of most experimental artists. A reading of A. Alvarez' study of suicide, *The Savage God* (1971), is illuminating in Johnson's case. Alvarez points out that technical exploration implies psychic exploration and that the rejection of conventional art-forms is evidence of loss of the traditional sense of personal identity. The experimental writer, if he is serious, must be engaged in radical self-scrutiny, but art provides him with no magical protection against the possible consequences of this:

> for the artist himself art is not necessarily therapeutic; he is not automatically relieved of his fantasies by expressing them. Instead, by some perverse logic of creation, the act of formal expression may simply make the dredged-up material more readily available to him. The result of handling it in his work may well be that he finds himself living it out.[5]

What complicates Johnson's case is his determination to bear public witness to his own artistic development. Most writers in the habit of issuing manifestos are eventually led into embarrassed retractions. Wordsworth, pretending in old age that his preface to *Lyrical Ballads* was written only to pacify Coleridge, must be the classic case of this. Still earlier, Wordsworth had written the 1815 preface which implicitly contradicts most of what he had said in 1800. In this light, Johnson's failure could have been a consequence of his excruciating honesty. He lacked the resourcefulness that would have prompted a fresh start by joining in the chorus against his own 'doctrinaire attitudes'.

The correspondence between technical and psychic exploration is a working hypothesis which points us towards the real matter of Johnson's art. What was the 'dredged-up material' in his case? He himself wrote of his work as a systematic, rational struggle with technical problems, while I have initially approached it as a process of public self-humiliation. In fact it is the presence of a continuous moral vision that emerges from rereading the novels, although Johnson rarely spoke of that vision. Without such a vision, it would in any case be otiose to speak to him as a Puritan artist. I shall trace its embodiment in one novel, *House Mother Normal*, before proceeding to a fuller account of his development.

House Mother Normal, a 'geriatric comedy' set in an old people's home, is a technical *tour de force* consisting of nine interior monologues, each taking up twenty-one pages and covering exactly the same stretch of time. Every line in a given monologue corresponds to the same moment in each of the others. The strict scheme is handled with such ingenuity that we can identify with each of the inmates in turn, while putting together the complex jigsaw of events during the Social Evening which takes up the allotted time-span. The novel has a powerful *memento mori* effect, not least through Johnson's use of blank spaces to indicate periods of pain, mental confusion and unconsciousness. Here a typographical trick which was first exploited in *Travelling People* is put to serious and dignified use. The book is an intimate reminder that—in Johnson's final words—'worse times are a-coming, nothing is more sure' (p.204).

There are two aspects which seem to require some explanation. The first is the curiously sensational role played by House Mother, a role which ends with her stripping for the benefit of her senile charges and performing a sexual act with her dog. Then there is the correspondence of the novel with Johnson's principle that 'Telling stories is telling lies'. Admittedly, House Mother, like Albert Angelo, is finally exposed as an invented character:

> Thus you see I too am the
> puppet or concoction of a writer (you always knew
> there was a writer behind it all? Ah, there's
> no fooling you readers!)....
>
> So
> you see this is from his skull. It is a diagram
> of certain aspects of the inside of his skull! (p.204).

But, unlike the earlier novel, we are not told *why* she has been invented. At first reading her exhibitionism seems gratuitous and Johnson's purpose remains unclear. At the simplest level, he is no doubt using sexual titillation to sustain an air of suspense about actions which have to be reported nine times over. Beyond this House Mother is used to make a point about 'normality'. Johnson himself wrote that 'The idea was to say something about the things we call "normal" and "abnormal" (AY, p.26), but it is doubtful if the point needs such heavy underlining. There may be an error of judgment here, but at least House Mother will not seem the product of cynical sensationalism when we examine the attitudes contrasted in the novel more closely.

House Mother holds her position because society tries to ignore old age by calling its victims 'geriatric' and shutting them away in institutions. She is a petty tyrant with total control over the inmates, and has found how to derive a range of emotional satisfactions from her charge. These satisfactions must be perverse because a healthily sensual individual would not have taken on her job in the first place; this, at least, is what Johnson seems to imply. None the less she is an ordinary person and therefore combines various more or less understandable forms of corruption with an energetic habit of self-justification. We are put off from the beginning by her false, ingratiating tone of address; though ironically her voice introducing the narrative is also the authorial voice. This confusion is compounded later on when she answers the reader's objections to her behaviour:

How disgusting! you must be saying to yourself,
friend, and I cannot but agree. But think a bit
harder, friend: why do I disgust them?
I disgust them in order that they may not be
disgusted with themselves. I am disgusting to them
in order to objectify their disgust, to direct it to
something outside themselves, something harmless.
Some of them still believe in God: what would
happen if they were to turn their disgust on God
for taking away control over their own sphincter
muscles, for instance, and think, naturally enough,
that He must be vile to be responsible for such
a thing?   Far better for them to think
handling and smelling and seeing doggie's turd is
disgusting!   Do you not agree? (p.197)

Plausible though this may seem at first, the reasoning is in fact
very unpleasant. House Mother exerts maternal authority over
her patients, but the reality from which she wants to shield them
is that of disillusionment with God. Yet she is not a believer, only
a hypocrite who believes in maintaining the holy lies on which
respectable society is based.

Unlike her patients (whose self-absorption ranges from states
of reverie and self-admiration to heavy pain and extreme
catatonia) House Mother is always appealing to an audience. Her
monologue has a rhetorical purpose; she is an inveterate liar
because she is a deliberate story-teller using her fantasies as a
means of subduing and imposing on others. These fantasies have
become an adequate substitute for reciprocal human
relationships, so that she is content with her unenviable
profession and content also with a sexual partner who is her
dog. As individual psychology this may be fairly lurid, but
House Mother must be understood as a surrogate figure whom
Johnson invests with his own guilty compulsion to be a writer
and tell lies to command the attention of others. Yet the reader
who responds to the hints of moral condemnation in the way I
have done has himself been manoeuvred into the position of the
Puritan externalising his own guilts and finding a scapegoat for
them. The subtlety of the novel lies, I think, in Johnson's
realisation of the humanity that is fought over by these warring
ethical alternatives. House Mother may be seen as embodying

either misguided maternal protectiveness or a vile and perverted pretence of authority; but against her aggressive, fictionising potency there is set the unassuming naturalness and resignation of the old people, whose basic self-acceptance constitutes a true human dignity. The final irony of House Mother's attempts at protecting them is that she does not know these attempts are quite unnecessary.

In *Albert Angelo*, the hero prepares a homily to his class on 'the dignity of humankind'. They are unmoved and—in one of the novel's alternative endings—dump him unceremoniously in the Thames. The value of stoicism is sardonically affirmed throughout Johnson's novels. For him such an attitude was not abstract but was ingrained in his origins in the London working class. The experience of the Blitz is invoked at the beginning of an early story, written in a laconic neo-realist vein:

> That was the night a stick of landmines got the British Home Stores, the Salvation Army and the Surrey towpath just beside the bridge.
> 'Get your head down, mate,' said my grandmother, who believed bad luck came in threes, after we heard the first one....[6]

The story continues with a personal, not a generic reminder of death as seen through the eyes of the boy, who slashes his wrist in a history lesson at school. Suffering in Johnson's writing is both intensely personal and a general experience. The dignity of the old people in *House Mother Normal* is partly theirs as members of the generation that fought on the Somme, and who have survived only to face death again in the modern equivalent of the workhouse. As individuals they are not all very attractive, but their memories, whether of war or love or gaiety or bereavement, convey a fortitude which will enable them to meet whatever is in store for them just as they have done in the past. Unlike the reader they are simply unmoved by House Mother's exhibitionism and, whatever the causes of disgust that arise with the decay of the body, they are simply in need of material, and not of spiritual, help. In this novel Johnson has both dramatised the Puritan compulsions of bodily loathing, moral condemnation, guilty self-righteousness and keeping up appearances, and has transcended them by means of a more fundamental, non-rhetorical assertion of human dignity.

House Mother Normal, I believe, will stand as Johnson's finest work. I have argued that it makes subtle use of Puritan reactions, but it is in the middle-period novels *Trawl* and *The Unfortunates* that we find the more narrowly Puritan obsessions. *House Mother Normal* is a statement of the truth of non-rhetorical (and in this sense non-fictional) individual consciousness. Its interplay of nine interior monologues must be technically unique. In the two earlier novels the interior monologue is used in a much more traditional way, to convey the confessional meditations of a single character suffering from remorse of conscience. It was here that Johnson gave full rein to the solipsistic tendencies inherent in his hostility to 'fiction'.

Travelling People, set in the Stromboli Club in North Wales, had been a piece of extravagant farce; *Albert Angelo* combined the comic vitality with a much higher quota of realistic observation, until Johnson eventually kicked aside the facade of 'Angelo', supply teacher and failed architect: 'fuck all this lying what I'm really trying to write about is writing not all this stuff about architecture... im my hero ...' (p. 165). The same downrightness is echoed in *Trawl*, where 'one always starts with I......... And ends with I' (p. 205). The three-week voyage of an Arctic trawler provides both a naturalistic setting and a sustained metaphor for the narrator's exploration of his own past. He has chosen to go on the voyage, during which he is constantly and painfully seasick. The therapy afforded by this opportunity for uninterrupted meditation is thus shown as being willed and unpleasant; it is kind of dutiful self-punishment, as each humiliating fiasco or undigested meal is dragged to the surface in turn. *Trawl*, a monotonous book, is full of morbid, vulnerable sensibility, as if its author had renounced fancy and language-games for ever. His memories have an ungainly authenticity like those of an early Orwell hero; but the humiliations he encounters are not those of a social pilgrim but of an isolated egotist. While his introversion is traced back to the trauma of wartime evacuation, the narrator is mainly concerned with its results, a series of meagre sexual encounters in which his desires were sometimes assuaged, but never his emotional needs. Finally, the trawler returns to port with a sense of relief; he feels purged of his past and, having vomited the 'green bile' from the lowest level of the stomach, has gained his sea-legs. His new girlfriend may be waiting on the quay as the trawler comes in; but in his final words Johnson seems to draw back from the possibility that he is offering a statement of hope or an epiphany. What can have been established, after this long self-examination, except the writer's solipsism?

The gloomy, alienated viewpoint of *Trawl* is continued in *The Unfortunates*. This is a tribute to a friend who died of cancer (the beautiful cover design is a blown-up photograph of cancer cells). It introduces the theme which was continued in the later novels, written while his mother was dying of the same disease. The theme contrasts sharply with the whimsical randomness that results from putting the novel into a box. This is not a very successful device, and it must certainly have harmed the book's sales since any prospect of a 'paperback' reprint was ruled out. Johnson's idea is to allow the reader to participate in his own uncertainties about structuring the novel; but in fact the demonstration is pointless because it makes one feel that the structure does not matter. In my experience there is no way of re-ordering the twenty-seven different sections so as to introduce a previously hidden element of surprise. *The Unfortunates* is not a truly random work because we are never tempted to doubt the common source of the separate discourses constituted by each section. The author provides a 'First' and 'Last' episode, and the intervening sections are all interior monologues produced by a manifestly continuous first-person narrator, who is a journalist reporting a football match in a Midlands city. Given the uniformly confessional content of the novel, the fact that Johnson himself may have pieced it together from different episodes written at different times is really of no significance to the reader.

The one aspect in which Johnson's self-consciousness is triumphantly justified is the reporting of the match itself. Stuck to the bottom of the box is a facsimile of a football report signed 'B. S. Johnson' in the house-style of the *Observer* newspaper. The headline 'Sub inspires City triumph' is, of course, a Johnsonian pun calling attention to the drastically truncated form of the report as it appears 'in print'. The section which shows how this report is produced handles material which would have appealed to Balzac by means of the comic techniques of Joyce and Sterne. The narrator's interior monologue during the game is interspersed with the sentences he notes down in draft. There follows a transcript of his phone-call to the editorial desk during which he dictates his copy. The section combines the formal incongruities involved in the production of a 'text' with a highly authentic picture of a journalist at work; it could be seen as a portrayal of alienated labour with the journalist's professional skill balanced against his personal boredom and resentment. But his exposure of the mechanism of hack writing must make up for the absence of any real exposure of the process of writing *The Unfortunates* itself. The various forces that may have determined the latter text remain conjectural and implicit.

At his friend Tony's deathbed, the narrator ('Johnson') made a promise to 'get it all down'. The result, in all probability, is an exercise in literal truth-telling that failed to become significant fiction. If *The Unfortunates* was written out of a sense of duty, duty alone could not make Tony into an adequate foil for the narrator, or Tony's wife June into a tragic heroine. Only a full realisation of the magnitude and separateness of other people's experience could have done that. The narrator remains self-possessed, even remarking on his own achievement of sexual happiness at the very time when his friends are broken up with suffering. Life may be like that, but the rhetoric of the novel and indeed its *raison d'être* are falsified. Sitting in a pub he once visited with Tony, he reflects stoically that 'life goes on': 'bring on Fortinbras and cart the corpses off'.[7] The trouble is that Johnson's narrator cannot decide if he is meant to be Fortinbras or Horatio or even Hamlet. The clarity of an explicitly 'fictional' intention is lacking.

In his middle period Johnson failed to solve the conundrum of the non-fiction novel that he had set himself. Both *Trawl* and *The Unfortunates* have the form of a kind of pilgrimage, a successive discovery of the pain and nullity of the world of experience. The pilgrim has as his goal certain immanent truths but these must either be confined to the self (as in *Trawl*) or falsely objectified in terms of another (as in *The Unfortunates*). The effective result in either case is solipsistic—a dramatisation of the writing self which questions everything except its own justification. In *House Mother Normal* and *Christie Malry* Johnson broke away from this pattern, cauterising the 'I' of his fictions by creating characters who represent the anti-self and become scapegoats drawing upon themselves the weight of Puritanical loathing. The result is that the figure of the novelist comes under reflexive attack in these novels, but at the price of creating a fictional structure akin to traditional comedy, where the hero's bizarre and misguided modes of behaviour are in sharpest contrast to the implied securities of writer and reader. It follows that Johnson could no more escape the accusation that he is using a lie to root out a lie than could, say, Cervantes in *Don Quixote*.

Christie Malry is an urban guerrilla waging an isolated, solipsistic war with society. Trained as a bank clerk, he adapts the method of double-entry book-keeping to his own purposes; every debit entered by the outside world against his own name must be balanced by a corresponding credit. The idea of life as a vale of book-keeping, in which the account one can render of one's own life corresponds as exactly as possible to the balance that is written up in heaven, is one that is dear to the Puritan imagination. The difference between Christie and the 'Johnson' of the earlier novels is that the discharge of conscientious duty makes him not a novelist or a self-punishing solipsist but a Jacobean revenger. He reduces the debt that society owes him by expedients that range from pilfering stationery to blowing up a tax office and poisoning London's water supply. The result is an acrid little tale, written with tremendous verve and punctuated at intervals by the balance sheet which shows Christie's own reckoning of his 'current account'. Finally, with his debt-collection getting more megalomaniac and his methods of reckoning increasingly farcical Christie is struck down by cancer. The revenger has at last turned scapegoat, and before he dies he just has time to turn his dissatisfaction on the narrator: ' "In any case," he said, almost to himself, not looking at me, "you shouldn't be bloody writing novels about it, you should be out there bloody doing something about it" ' (p. 114). So we are back to the hideousness of cancer, and its unfairness—an unfairness which will not be wiped out when the doctors discover a cure. In *House Mother Normal* and *Christie Malry* Johnson has resolved the unfairness of cancer in the one (ineffectual and lying) way to which the novelist has access: by creating victims who for all their entertainment value are finally so monstrous that cancer is what they deserve.[8] The fiction of 'poetic justice' serves to bring home in a grim and farcical way the injustice—the lack of any balance-sheet—in life.

The creation of a scapegoat may be satisfying to the Puritan conscience, but what after all is it worth? Christie's sturdily anarchist values, his effortless success as a revenger and his capacity for uncomplicated erotic enjoyment may form the basis of the novel's comic exuberance, but the exuberance is superficial and behind it we sense the author's helpless and sardonic detachment. The idea that Christie ('Christ'?) deserves his fate does not compensate, except in the terms of his own dehumanised 'book-keeping' attitude to human relationships, for the pain and bewilderment that are present as surely as in *The Unfortunates* and *Trawl*. The book ends with the 'Final reckoning,' which is obviously a parody of the Last Judgment at which the entries in God's Book are to be revealed. Christie's account is closed with the balance due to him written off as a bad debt. One of the last items of compensation he demanded was because socialism had not been given a chance; a liability which the poisoning of '20,749 innocent west Londoners' had done almost nothing to expiate (p. 99). Christie's reasoning here is very like that of Christian sects through the ages who have been content to condemn the vast bulk of mankind to Hell.

B.S. Johnson may have seen *Christie Malry* as little more than a pot-boiler. His posthumous novel *See The Old Lady Decently* was the first volume of *Matrix* trilogy, a commemoration of his mother's death which in his more optimistic moments he may have envisaged as a cosmic celebration of life. *See The Old Lady Decently* makes manifold references to *Finnegans Wake* (especially in the figure of *uroboros*, the snake with its tail in its mouth) and ends in a final crescendo, complete with magisterial Johnsonian punning, describing the writer's own birth. Sadly and ironically, the novel which would have transformed his mother's funeral into a literary wake turned out to be stillborn.

*

Johnson was a conscious disciple of Beckett and Joyce, and his place in modern fiction may be best ascertained by invoking the category which Hugh Kenner has proposed for these novelists—that of the 'stoic comedians'. Kenner distinguishes between mythopoeic art of the Romantic tradition and an art of the 'closed field', sceptical, debunking and reductive, which has been the true home of the rational imagination since Flaubert. In a closed field, the number of permutations is finite and exhaustible, so that ultimately only repetition is possible. Beckett and Joyce, on this view, are novelists who lock themselves within a narrowing compass while employing the utmost cunning to avoid either silence or overt repetition. The activity of reduction itself gives birth in their work to a paradoxical fecundity.[9]

Johnson's principle that 'Telling stories is telling lies' is what makes the space available for his novels a confined one. In many ways he is a 'stoic comedian', a minor follower of one of the major modernist schools. But there is one crucial difference between Johnson and the giants who figure (whether rightly or wrongly) in Hugh Kenner's pantheon. Johnson's literary attitude, unlike theirs, is that of a humanist. In Beckett's fiction the tedium and sterility of life is experienced by a succession of fictional personae, behind whom their creator lurks, non-committal and unseen. Johnson is a confessional, not an impersonal artist, and the sterility and tedium are felt by him as a private burden or obsession. His first-person narrators are not distanced but transparently autobiographical, and the burden of inadequacy and guilt are his own. Against his occasional lugubriousness should be set the fact that he was able to be very direct about his reasons for writing:

> I think I write because I have something to say that I fail to say satisfactorily in conversation, in person. Then there are things like conceit, stubbornness, a desire to retaliate on those who have hurt me paralleled by a desire to repay those who have helped me, a need to try to create something which may live after me (which I take to be the detritus of the religious feeling), the sheer technical joy of forcing almost intractable words into patterns of meaning and form that are uniquely (for the moment at least) mine, a need to make people laugh with me in case they laugh at me, a desire to codify experience, to come to terms with things that have happened to me, and to try to tell the truth (to discover what is the truth) about them. And I write especially to exorcise, to remove from myself,

from my mind, the burden [of] having to bear some pain, the hurt of some experience; in order that it may be over there, in a book, and not in here in my mind. (*AY*, pp. 18-19)

This statement has an admirable simplicity, which not one of the great modernists would have managed. It may be modelled on Orwell's 'Why I write'. Perhaps so confidently discursive a tone speaks too much of the journalist-novelist, and throws into question Johnson's position as an experimental artist? Johnson himself would seem to have felt unhappy about it, since he went on to provide an alternative, more poetic but also much balder statement. The interest of this second statement lies in the last of the three motives which he lists for writing down an interior vision: 'so that I would not have to repeat it'. Even here, one would guess that the idea that he could exorcise his experiences, and avoid repeating them, may itself have come to seem a lie: one of life's unavoidable, and yet unjustifiable, fictions.

B.S. Johnson is like Bunyan's pilgrim, condemned always to go on writing in the hope of getting rid of the burden on his back. English seventeenth-century literature exemplifies two of the ways in which a writer may respond to the overwhelming presence of evil and death in the world. The first is the way of the Jacobean dramatists, with their farcical and morbid connoisseurship of evil, revenge and the suffering of the innocent; a way that is broached in *Christie Malry* and *House Mother Normal*. The second is the confessional impulse of the isolated soul searching for what is lasting among the ephemeral phantoms that assail him; this is what Johnson pursues in his middle-period novels. I would suggest that these are two sides of the lurid, isolated and self-punishing Puritan imagination. To see Johnson in these terms is to suggest that, for him, experimental writing was the authentic expression of a deep-rooted artistic individualism. Despite his anti-religious obsession Johnson succeeded in reviving the characteristic religious form which British individualist consciousness has taken. His Puritanism offered a standpoint from which—except in *Travelling People*—he could at all times attack merely fashionable or respectable values. A corresponding tendency to solipsism was most adequately countered in *House Mother Normal*, which exploits the forms of Puritan consciousness in such a way as to transcend and negate them. But if Johnson's reputation as a minor novelist continues to survive it will owe as much to his revival and exploration of the Puritan conscience as to his membership of the contemporary avant-garde.

(1977)

9

Descents into Hell:
The Later Novels of Doris Lessing

Doris Lessing is our leading contemporary novelist of ideas.
Readers throughout the world have followed her progress, in the
last three decades, from orthodox communism towards
feminism, irrationalism, Sufism, anti-psychiatry, and—most
recently—cosmic mysticism. Her always eclectic sense of
fictional forms has led her from social realism to postmodernism,
mythological fantasy, and what she calls 'space fiction'. *The Four-
Gated City* (1969) is the first of her later books in which she
appears (to quote one of her characters) as a 'nothing-but
Cassandra', a prophet of the doom she expects to overtake
Western Civilisation before the end of the twentieth century.
Lessing's position as a visionary novelist is now widely
recognised, although the comparatively pragmatic *Golden
Notebook* (1962) is still probably the most influential of her
novels. No assessment of her work can afford to overlook the
consistency and cosmic sweep of the vision she unfolds.

Rationalism and irrationalism are dialectical, rather than
merely logical, opposites in the Western mind. That is to say,
just as science has often provided a home for the perversions of
reason (culminating in the horror of impending nuclear
catastrophe), modern anti-scientific thinking is visibly a product
of the Enlightenment, being riddled with systematic theories of
man and of history, with appeals to observation and the evidence
of the senses. Doris Lessing's outlook is no exception. For all its
cosmological inventions, *Shikasta* (1979), the first of her 'space
fiction' sequence *Canopus in Argos: Archives*, contains nothing
incompatible with the view of modern history already familiar
from *The Four-Gated City* and its successors *Briefing for a*

Descent into Hell (1971) and *The Memoirs of a Survivor* (1974).
Indeed, the recurrence of Martha Hesse (Martha Quest) and
other characters from the *Four-Gated City* in minor roles in
Shikasta indicates the self-consciousness with which Lessing is
now striving towards a comprehensive philosophical, historical
and religious synthesis. Her later work should be seen as a whole
before we consider it, as its formal variety seems to demand, in
separate parts. Lessing takes her visionary system at least as
seriously as Yeats did his—perhaps still more so. Yet I do not see
how literary criticism can deal with it except as false (or partially
false) prophecy or as poetic invention. If Lessing were indeed the
seer that she claims to be, anything short of adulation or blind
faith would be an impertinence. In 1957, at the height of her
liberal ex-communist phase, she wrote an essay for Tom
Maschler's book *Declaration* in which she attributes the writer's
mission in society to his or her possession of 'The Small Personal
Voice'. Her voice is still personal and, beside the objects of her
hostility, it is small. Yet increasingly it has become a scriptural
voice, crying in a wilderness of her own choosing. My first object
will be to outline the nature of the prophecy that her recent
works deliver.

*

Human beings, Doris Lessing now maintains, are fallen creatures.
It is not merely that our twentieth-century history is one of
decadence and decline. The whole of recorded history, correctly
understood, is a chronicle of degeneration from the level of
culture achieved in early and supposedly barbaric times. The
prehistoric civilisation of the megalith-builders and others left its
traces in our 'collective unconscious' and can therefore be
recovered in the 'inner space' of hallucinations, visions and
dreams. Three kinds of imagery (drawn, we must believe, from
the collective unconscious) occur again and again in Lessing's
works. One is of the sea, of an arduous journey to or across the
sea; the second is of the earthly paradise, a land in which human
beings live hand in hand with the animal creation; and the third
image is that of the ideal city. Her autobiographical heroine

Martha Quest sees such a city, in a moment of vision during her girlhood on a Zambesian farm:

> She looked away over the ploughed land, across the veld to the Dumfries Hills, and refashioned that unused country to the scale of her imagination. There arose, glimmering whitely over the harsh scrub and the stunted trees, a noble city, set foursquare and colonnaded along its falling flower-bordered terraces. There were splashing fountains, and the sound of flutes; and its citizens moved, grave and beautiful, black and white and brown together; and these groups of elders paused, and smiled with pleasure at the sight of the children—the blue-eyed, fair-skinned children of the North playing hand in hand with the bronze-skinned, dark-eyed children of the South. Yes, they smiled and approved these many-fathered children, running and playing among the flowers and the terraces, through the white pillars and tall trees of this fabulous and ancient city...[1]

To its first readers this may have seemed a vision of the multiracial New Jerusalem, foreshadowing Martha's own conversion from white-settler values to those of socialism and communism. With hindsight we can identify the 'fabulous and ancient' city more accurately. It is the 'archetypal city', first realised in prehistoric times, which Lewis Mumford has identified as the foundation of the utopian idea.[2] This city is the visible expression of beauty and order—a symbolic representation of the order of the universe. Martha's vision is thus a race-memory of the ideal City of the Sun that was the inspiration for the legendary imperial capitals of Africa and the Near East. I would submit that such a reading, which would seem forced if we were concerned with *Martha Quest* alone, becomes inevitable once one has read such novels as *Briefing for a Descent into Hell* and *Shikasta*. In the latter book Lessing endows her prehistoric Earth with 'geometrical cities' in harmony with their natural surroundings and with the cosmos. 'Harmony' is not used here in a metaphorical sense. As with Plato's spheres, there is a literal harmony which bodies forth the perfection of transcendental reality.

The Earth, then, was once dotted with heavenly cities built around gardens, fountains, and (in *Shikasta*) the megalithic stone alignments which are the literal means of communication with the cosmos. (The Druidic cults surrounding the stones date not from this early period but from later, degenerate attempts to mimic a lost civilisation.) The countryside around the cities was a non-carnivorous paradise in which the animals were no more wild than was man himself. Even in our present fallen state, the ability to love and cherish animals—such as the seal of Kate's dreams in *The Summer Before the Dark* (1973), and Hugo, the mysterious cat-dog of *The Memoirs*—is a sign of grace. The earthly paradise itself can be fleetingly re-entered in moments of sexual ecstasy. Making love to Jack, the most expert of her long sequence of lovers in the *Children of Violence* series, Martha has a mystical experience in which

> she saw in front of her eyelids a picture of a man and a woman, walking in a high place under a blue sky holding children by the hand, and with them all kinds of wild animals, but they were not wild at all: a lion, a leopard, a tiger, deer, lambs, all as tame as house-pets walking with the man and the woman and the lovely children, and she wanted to cry out with loss; but it was a loss there was no focus to, there was no holding it.
>
> (*The Four-Gated City* p. 72)

Set against this vision of the golden age is the barren, polluted landscape of modern industrial civilisation, portrayed by Lessing in terms made familiar by forecasts of ecological catastrophe such as Rachel Carson's *Silent Spring* (1963). *Briefing for a Descent into Hell* (written, one suspects, under the immediate impact of Carson's work) contains a memorable vision of abandoned cities, stinking rivers, oily seas, and human offal mingled with dead birds and fishes. This is the Hell to which her title refers: a place (like Thulcandra in C.S. Lewis's *Out of the Silent Planet*) to be quarantined off from the rest of the universe.

Breakdown, the realisation of Hell on Earth, is at once an individual and a social process. At the individual level, the crack-up is a pervasive Lessing theme, treated already with great assurance in her first novel *The Grass is Singing* (1950). 'Every time one opens a door one is greeted by a shrill, desperate and inaudible scream', says Milt in *The Golden Notebook*; this is '"the dark secret of our time"' (p. 647). These rooms with their 'women going mad all by themselves' are often papered with newspaper cuttings, 'facts' about the Cold War, the arms race, the space race, and the treatment of mental illness; they are not so much realistic domestic interiors as the very landscape of claustrophobia. A striking example is that of Dr Kroll, the ex-Nazi psychiatrist who, during his annual sojourn as a patient in his own hospital, covers his walls with Goyaesque pictures of 'graveyards, and skulls and corpses, of war scenes, and bombed buildings and screaming women and houses on fire with people falling from burning windows like ants into flames' ('The eye of God in paradise' p. 241). Not infrequently the paranoia to which Lessing's characters are prone, as representative victims of the twentieth-century nightmare, has spilled over into the narrating consciousness. What else can account for the assertion, offered without a shred of evidence in at least three of her recent works, that much of the development of space flight has gone on in secret and that many of the 'flying saucers' sighted from Earth are in fact American or Russian spacecraft on military missions? Lessing's alertness to the frightful dangers of the arms race and of what E.P. Thompson has called 'the logic of exterminism' has not prevented her, unfortunately, from indulging at times in the paranoid assumption that every common-sense argument is false and every governmental statement a self-serving lie. Not only is her vision, or that of her narrators, occasionally tinged with paranoia; it is also largely fatalistic. Lessing's conviction of human impotence appears as the necessary component of a deep-rooted religious and philosophical system, rather than as an expression of transient despair. It is not that we have failed, but that we are fallen, and that fall took place before the beginning of recorded history.

Predestination, except of a wholly secular kind, is hardly a subject for realistic fiction. Yet the knowledge that her fate is being determined elsewhere comes to Martha as a consequence of the mystical experience during sexual intercourse to which we have already referred. Her vision of the golden age is followed by a premonition of the actual life she is to live in London as a member of the Coldridge household. As she lies in bed, recovering from this dual vision, she speaks to her partner in the wryly sceptical tones of a realistic heroine:

'Have you ever thought—we make decisions all the time; but how? it's always in reference to—we make them in obedience to something we don't know anything about?'

'No. *I* make decisions!'
'Ah, you're master of your fate.'
But one did not tease Jack, he could not be teased.
(The Four-Gated City, p. 84)

This bare hint (for it is no more than that) that our lives are not our own is startlingly developed in the later novels. In *Briefing*, Professor Charles Watkins undergoes a schizophrenic experience which includes a mystical vision of the Earth and its workings as seen by a traveller in the heavens:

> ...I watched how wars and famines, and earthquakes and disasters, floods and terrors, epidemics and plagues of insects and rats and flying things came and went according to the pressures from the combinations of the planets and the Sun—and the Moon. For a swarm of locusts, a spreading of viruses, like the life of humanity, is governed elsewhere. The life of man, that little crust of matter, which was not even visible until one swooped down close as a bird might sweep in and out for a quick survey of a glittering shoal of fish that puckered a wave's broad flank, that pulse's intensity and size and health was set by Mercury and Venus, Mars and Jupiter, Saturn, Neptune, Uranus and Pluto, and their movements, and the centre of light that fed them all. Man, that flicker of life, diminished in numbers and multiplied was peace-loving or murderous—in bondage. (p.101)

If astrology provides one aspect of the external control of human affairs, the other is the interest taken in this planet by extraterrestrial intelligences. At the end of *The Four-Gated City* Martha and some of her fellow-refugees on a Hebridean island take heart for the future of humanity as a result of their meetings with 'people from the sun'. Another fugitive from the coming catastrophe, the unnamed narrator of *The Memoirs*, experiences a serial vision of life in a dream country on the other side of her living-room wall. The coming and going of the vision is quite independent of her conscious will:

> After all, it was never myself who ordained that now I must interrupt my ordinary life, since it was time to step from one life into another; not I who thinned the sunlight wall; not I who set the stage behind it. I had never had a choice. Very strong was the feeling that I did as I

was bid and as I must; that I was being taken, was being led, was being shown, was held always in the hollow of a great hand which enclosed my life, and used me for purposes I was too much beetle or earthworm to understand. (p. 91)

We know this is not hallucination because, at the end of the story, the narrator is able to walk through the walls to safety under the protection of a woman from the other dimension. In *Briefing* Charles Watkins leaves the Earth in a crystalline spaceship. He listens in to the collective mind of the universe and attends a Briefing at which a race of benign aliens, the bringers of Cosmic Harmony, decide to reinforce their Permanent Staff on Earth. Once he has discharged himself from mental hospital, Watkins disowns this schizophrenic episode and returns to normal life. Other characters in the novel, however, remain true to the Briefing even if they do not consciously know themselves to be agents of an alien power. Far from curing himself of a megalomaniac delusion, Watkins is one of the 'chosen' who is running away from his portion of visionary truth.

In *Shikasta* Lessing's aliens are given a concrete identity. They are the emissaries of Canopus, benign imperialists who believe it is their mission to foster the growth of intelligence and co-operation throughout the galaxy. Their attempts and those of their Sirian allies (who have also established colonies on Earth) are frustrated both by unfortunate conjunctions of the stars and by the malign activities of Shammat, a rival galactic empire. The sustenance that Canopean agents bring to Earth is known as SOWF (the 'substance-of-we-feeling'). It will be seen that Lessing has now chosen what is known in the trade as 'space opera' as the appropriate metaphorical vehicle for the insights and intimations which, in *Briefing* and *The Memoirs*, she expressed largely in terms of mythological fantasy. This has not proved a happy choice. Ever since *The Four-Gated City*, she has been outspoken in her claims for 'space fiction' (I assume that her avoidance of the term 'science fiction' is deliberate and, given her ideological outlook, well-advised). In a foreward to *Shikasta* she calls this genre 'the most original branch of literature now'. To avoid misunderstanding, I should say that the clearest-sighted reviews of *Shikasta* that I have come across—those whose judgment was least clouded by the formidable reputation Doris

Lessing enjoys—were in the specialist science-fiction press. I shall
return to the failure of *Shikasta* later in the present chapter.
Perhaps we should say of Lessing's mysticism what G.K.
Chesterton once said of Dickens's plots: her secrecy (*The Four-
Gated City, Briefing, The Memoirs*) is sensational; but the secret
itself (*Shikasta*) is tame. Canopus is, among other things, an
idealised embodiment of the terrestrial imperialism which
Lessing attacks as scornfully in *Shikasta* as she has always done in
the past. Twenty years after being declared a prohibited
immigrant in her home country of Southern Rhodesia, she has
created an extraterrestrial civilisation which reminds us of
nothing so much as the official aims of the British Empire with
its 'civilising mission'. The activities of Canopean agents on
Earth sometimes make them sound like the best type of District
Officer in mufti.

The plan of *Canopus in Argos: Archives* is to unfold the history
of Canopean and Sirian interventions on Earth and its
surrounding Zones. A race of giants from another planet was
implanted on Earth, with responsibility for building the cities
with their stone alignments, and developing earthly civilisation to
the point where a Lock, or mental connection, could be
established with the rest of the Empire. Lessing's myth of human
origins—an extravagant substitute for the myth of 'primitive
communism' to which she must formerly have adhered—is based
on those archaeological theories which reveal the remarkable
astronomical, mathematical, and architectural feats of our Stone
Age ancestors. (One of the characters of *Briefing*, a character
whose sole function is to expound Lessing's ideas, is a
professional archaeologist.) Like Erich von Däniken and other
best-selling occultists, Lessing asserts that the truth about the
megaliths runs counter to the basic assumptions of Western
humanism. Far from representing a technological triumph of
which man can be proud, they were built by aliens (pictured in
the folk-memory as giants or gods) vastly superior to ourselves.
Hence the need for Canopus, Sirius and Shammat.

The failure of the Lock, and the passing of the golden age, are
mysterious occurrences. 'The main cause of the disaster was what
that word *dis-aster* implies: a fault in the stars', says the narrator
somewhat primly (p. 21). As a result, the name of the planet is
changed from Rohanda, the fruitful, to Shikasta, the stricken.

The shift in stellar alignments makes it necessary to evacuate the giants, but by now the forces of jealous Shammat, which can succeed only amid confusion and discord, have been at work. Some of the giants resist evacuation, while the native earthmen soon forget their allegiance to Canopean law and revert to a savage state. Soon the 'ancient mysteries' are forgotten, prehistory gives way to recorded history, and Shikasta's delinquency gets steadily worse. After several thousand years the crisis reaches its peak—a fact which can scarcely surprise the seasoned Lessing reader—in the second half of the twentieth century. Yet, in these dark days of neo-Fascist outrage, international anarchy, pollution disasters and a Third World War, the first signs of recovery from the long nightmare of so-called civilisation on Shikasta begin to appear. These indications emerge, as in *The Memoirs*, *Briefing*, and *The Four-Gated City*, from the instinctive and non-political coming-together of individuals who find that they share certain occult and visionary experiences which orthodox society conspires to suppress. Here we should remember that, in the *Children of Violence* series, Lessing's Marxism confers extreme importance on the activities of a tiny political clique, the Communist Party of Zambesia, on the grounds that they represent the vanguard of political consciousness under colonialism.[3] In her later novels Lessing replaces the small group of political militants with another type of avant-garde: a group of knowers or *illuminati*. Borrowing a label from a novelist of whom Lessing has written in terms of high admiration, I propose to call such a group a *karass*.

The *karass*, as Kurt Vonnegut Jr's narrator explains in *Cat's Cradle* (1963), is a kind of team to which, unknown to themselves, various scattered human individuals belong. The teams are organised by God to do His will without ever discovering what they are doing. One may, however, come to recognise the fellow-members of one's *karass*. Thus some members of the Coldridge family, in *The Four-Gated City*, find themselves instinctively working together in ways which enable them to survive the coming holocaust. Martha, unknown to herself, was one of their *karass*; hence the premonition which made her come to live with them. *Briefing* is a portrayal of another *karass*, and *The Memoirs* of another. In *Shikasta*, the Canopean envoy Johor seeks to exert conscious control over a *karass* whose members include the surviving Coldridges. The chief task of this *karass* is to foster the growth of a new generation of children with ESP capacities. In effect, these children are a new mutation of the species, to whom it is given to recover the mental outlook of the Shikastans of the golden age. Without written orders or plans, these new people begin to rebuild the old geometrical cities.

Doris Lessing's terrestrial history, then, consists of a golden age, a Fall, and the growth of an evil civilisation which must eventually destroy itself, to be succeeded by some kind of resurrection. The inherent Christianity of this scheme has scarcely escaped the author's notice, though she herself takes the more ecumenical position that 'there has never been more than one Book in the Middle East' (Foreword to *Shikasta*). If we discard her space-fictional machinery of rival empires, benign giants, and envoys-in-disguise, we are left with a Christian eschatology together with the role of the *karass* which no doubt reflects Lessing's adherence to the doctrines of Sufism. Emphasising spiritual intuition rather than dogma, and the uses of the parable rather than the textbook or catechism, Sufis tend to portray themselves as an élite, if not exactly a secret society (though one of the European institutions they claim to have fathered is that of freemasonry). Lessing quotes the Sufi doctrine of evolution as an epigraph in *The Four-Gated City*, and that is my excuse for quoting it here:

> Sufis believe that, expressed in one way, humanity is evolving to a certain destiny. We are all taking part in that evolution. Organs come into being as a result of the need for specific organs (Rumi). The human being's organism is producing a new complex of organs in response to such a need. In this age of the transcending of time and space, the complex of organs is concerned with the transcending of time and space. What ordinary people regard as sporadic and occasional bursts of telepathic or prophetic power are seen by the Sufi as nothing less than the first stirrings of these same organs. The difference between all evolution up to date and the present need for evolution is that for the past ten thousand years or so we have been given the possibility of a conscious evolution. So essential is this more rarefied evolution that our future depends upon it.[4]

Since Sufis believe in speaking in parables, we should be aware that this quote from Idries Shah's *The Sufis* is a parable for the benefit of Western rationalists. Having once been a member of the Communist Party, Doris Lessing has more recently lent her name to the propaganda of Sufism in Britain. *The Memoirs of a Survivor* was published and copyrighted by the Octagon Press, a house which specialises in Sufi texts and commentaries. Readers will draw their own conclusions as to the viability of Lessing's synthesis of Near East and West, and as to the gullibility or otherwise with which she endorses the claims of present-day occultists. My concern is with the artistic consequences of these beliefs, and is time to try to sort out the tangle of our author's fictional development.

*

For all its indebtedness to Lawrence and Conrad, *The Grass is Singing* (1950) is surely one of the most accomplished first novels by any writer since the Second World War. The title, taken a little self-consciously from *The Waste Land*, indicates that this is to be the first embodiment of the mythos of catastrophe in Lessing. It is also a novel of coherent political vision. The tragic breakdown of Mary Turner, a Rhodesian farmer's wife who is eventually murdered by her houseboy, serves to focus the dark undercurrents of the master-servant relationship on which colonial society is based, as well as the impossibility, within the white settler mentality, of telling the truth about that relationship. *The Grass is Singing* has stood the test of political change and the passing of time. It is notable not only for its powerfully dramatised themes—themes of colonialism, of emotional isolation, of racial and sexual obsession—but also for what I can only call Lessing's urbanity, her confident admixture of narrative tones. The author's range stretches from the intensely subjective, including the dreams and hallucinations so characteristic of her work, through the tone of political outrage to one of disenchanted objectivity. At this end of the scale we not only encounter a vivid use of metaphor (the heroine goes to work in 'one of those sleepy little towns scattered like raisins in a dry cake over the body of South Africa' p. 41), but the flat, generalised observations which have earned Lessing a deserved reputation for wisdom and penetration with regard to human relationships:

> Women have an extraordinary ability to withdraw from the sexual relationship, to immunize themselves against it, in such a way that their men can be left feeling let down and insulted without having anything tangible to complain of. (p. 66)

> Perhaps it was not such a bad marriage after all? There are innumerable marriages where two people, both twisted and wrong in their depths, are well matched, making each other miserable in the way they need, in the way the pattern of their lives demands. (p. 67)

Though these are observations which could hardly have been stated thus explicitly before Freud, there is no doubt about the tone of voice in which they are made. It is that of the secure nineteenth-century narrator—Tolstoy or George Eliot or Charlotte Brontë—and it is to this tradition that Lessing's fiction up to the end of *Children of Violence* belongs. Yet the realist tradition, to which she was drawn by her creative instincts as well as by Marxist doctrine, was to become increasingly problematic to her. *The Golden Notebook* is a confession that, faced with a 'fragmented society' and 'fragmented consciousness', the coherence and sweep of the nineteenth-century novel no longer seemed possible. A new departure was necessary.

The Golden Notebook, Lessing's most celebrated novel, is by now an almost legendary weapon in the armoury of 'consciousness-raising' about politics, psychoanalysis, feminism, and fictional structures. There is no lack of witnesses to the 'importance' of this novel, but I do find a strange absence of agreement, or even serious debate, about its artistic success. Too often this has been taken for granted, or asserted with the aid of basically circular arguments. The fact that it remains a mosaic of (sometimes) brilliant fragments is taken as evidence, not only of its idiosyncrasy, but of its superior authenticity to other contemporary novels, including the other novels in the Lessing canon. It is with some trepidation that one advances one's considered judgments over this. *The Golden Notebook* is undeniably a landmark in the spread of fictional self-consciousness in the modern British novel, an example of what might now be called creative deconstruction *avant la lettre*. Yet it is not a novel which tells the full truth about itself, any more than do the masterpieces of classical realism. Perhaps it is still more ripe for critical deconstruction than they are said to be. Most of the separate 'stories' the book tells, in the 'Free Women' sections and the variously-coloured notebooks, have obvious flaws. 'Free Women', in which Tommy shoots himself after reading Anna's notebooks, is a wry little domestic melodrama. The relationship of Ella and Paul at the centre of the 'Yellow Notebook' is tinged with (*Cosmopolitan*-or *Playgirl*-style) women's magazine fantasy. And so on. From time to time the narrator intervenes to deplore the failings of these various stories, reminding us of the untruthfulness of all fictionalised narrative. The idea that this *ensemble* of text and commentary somehow adds up to more than the sum of the parts is an attractive one, but after repeated readings I have come to feel that it is mainly an illusion. This is not to say that there are no moments of creative mastery in *The Golden Notebook*. The Mashopi Hotel sequences, set in wartime Zambesia—a reworking of material to be found in two of the *Children of Violence* novels, *A Ripple from the Storm* and *Landlocked*—are as fine as anything Doris Lessing has written. Concentrated in these sequences—it is present, though more diffusely, in *Children of Violence*—is an almost Chekhovian view of the decadence of white colonial society, a decadence which ironically finds its fullest expression in the small group of youthful communists to which the narrator herself belongs.

At the end of her first Mashopi sequence, Anna writes in her notebook that it is 'full of nostalgia' (p. 154). The sequence portrays political and moral futility—that of a group of revolutionaries who stick together out of mere comradeship, though they have largely lost faith in what they are doing—yet the nostalgia is justifiable because, waiting for the end of the war, they had no choice but to postpone the attempt to face up to their inner misgivings. For all the privileges they enjoy in Zambesia, their life is like that of the inhabitants of a very luxurious prison camp. Cynicism and play-acting are very much in order. Lessing's masterful evocation of the interactions of this ill-assorted group of people casts an unacknowledged shadow over the later episodes of *The Golden Notebook*, which show Anna, now in London, striving to rebuild her own identity in earnest. Do not her various experiences as a disillusioned communist, a fashionable author, a psychoanalytic patient, a 'welfare worker', and an unsuccessful lover and mistress, all culminating in the experience of therapeutic crack-up, represent so many more roles, each in its own way as unsatisfactory as the role of 'leader's girl-friend' that she played at the Mashopi Hotel? The whole of *The Golden Notebook* might be seen as an exploration of decadent consciousness, the fragmented life of a thwarted heroine unable to discover any integral meaning to her existence. Yet that is not how we are invited to read the book, which sets out to expound a positive (though tentative and painful) process of psychic evolution. Anna experiments with her life to some purpose, it is suggested, and that purpose is revealed in the culminating section, 'The Golden Notebook'.

'I have no time for people who haven't experimented with themselves, deliberately tried the frontiers', she writes in the 'Blue Notebook' (p. 532). Like membership of the Zambesian Communist Party in the 1940s, self-experimentation in the London of the 1950s marks her out as belonging to a vanguard, as inhabiting one of the growth-points of contemporary consciousness. As she sardonically remarks to her American lover Saul Green: 'You say, I am what I am because the United States is such and such politically, I am the United States. And I say, I am the position of women in our time' (p. 566). What is most striking about her self-experimenting is the energy of her repudiations, and above all (since she is a creative artist) her repudiation of her artistic creations. Anna runs through these on her internal projector, at the height of her 'madness':

The Mashopi film; the film about Paul and Ella; the film about Michael and Anna; the film about Ella and Julia; the film about Anna and Molly. They were all, so I saw now, conventionally, well-made films, as if they had been done in a studio; these films, which were everything I hated most, had been directed by me. The projectionist kept running these films very fast, and then pausing on the credits, and I could hear his jeering laugh at *Directed by Anna Wulf*. Then he would run another few scenes, every scene glossy with untruth, false and stupid. I shouted at the projectionist: 'But they aren't mine, I didn't make them'. At which the projectionist, almost bored with confidence, let the scenes vanish, and he waited for me to prove him wrong. And now it was terrible, because I was faced with the burden of recreating order out of the chaos that my life had become. Time had gone, and my memory did not exist, and I was unable to distinguish between what I had invented and what I had known, and I knew that what I had invented was all false. It was a whirl, an orderless dance, like the dance of the white butterflies in a shimmer of heat over the damp sandy vlei. (pp. 604–5)

The energy of negation is impressive, but it will not seem finally truthful unless the author has something better to put in the place of these discarded fictions. Can it be that that better thing is the fragmented, self-destructive form of *The Golden Notebook* itself? That is what some critics would have us believe. Yet we should not ignore that this novel concludes with a dramatised statement of values, in precisely the same way as the various earlier fictions that she convicts of falsity. Anna's experience of jointly going mad with Saul (or is it his 'double' Milt?) is represented as something which will change her life hereafter. It is a terrifying experience, a crack in the personality 'like a gap in a dam', and through which 'the future might pour in a different shape' (pp. 463–4). In her 'cocoon of madness' Anna, the political idealist and welfare-worker, is forced to acknowledge the destructiveness and egotism within her own personality. Violence is not merely external to her, since 'I knew that the cruelty and the spite and the I, I, I, I of Saul and of Anna were part of the logic of war' (p. 576). As a writer, we must assume it is Anna's business to explore that discovery, which is 'the dark secret of our time'. The idea of the secret book—whether the unpublished novel that every communist keeps in his bottom drawer, the anonymous cries for help that flood into women's magazines, the dreams that Anna notes down for her psychoanalyst, or the notebooks themselves—is a major theme of *The Golden Notebook*. The nineteenth-century novelists, Charlotte Brontë and George Eliot, consciously set out to expose silent and unspoken feelings, the 'secret agonies of the heart', to the public view. They did so within the context of a fully-structured vision of life. *The Golden Notebook* equally rolls back the frontiers of modern silence, but it does so in the name of an aesthetic of self-therapy, as if for Anna to explore and write about her problems were sufficient, and even tantamount to resolving them. *The Golden Notebook* is then an open-ended, transitional novel, incomplete because the experience to which it refers is not finally ordered or (one suspects) fully understood. Anna's sense that she has made progress in her self-explorations receives no independent confirmation. Lessing has subsequently re-arrived at an ordered and systematic way of understanding the world, so that the desperate self-searching that *The Golden Notebook* represents is now long past. Yet the formal incoherence of this novel, which has been so widely applauded for its own sake, recurs in some of her later books (and above all in *Shikasta*), where it begins to strike the reader as a cover for sheer uncertainty about the best way of telling the story.

After *The Golden Notebook*, Lessing returned to conventional realism for a while. Her next novel was *Landlocked*, the fourth in the Martha Quest sequence, which she now re-christened *Children of Violence*. (Its predecessors were *Martha Quest*, *A Proper Marriage*, and *A Ripple from the Storm*.) Four years after *Landlocked*, *Children of Violence* was concluded with *The Four-Gated City*, a blockbusting novel in which she brought her semi-autobiographical *Bildungsroman* up to the present time and beyond. The main narrative covers two decades (1950–1970), while the Appendix consists of a selection of documents from 'after the catastrophe', piecing together the collapse of European civilisation through the memories of those of her protagonists (including Martha herself) who managed to survive it.

The initial formal problem of *The Four-Gated City* is severe enough: how is it possible to maintain continuity while moving the scene of a *Bildungsroman* from one country to another? In Zambesia, Martha is defined by the conflict between her parents' comfortable social position and her allegiance to communism. In London, now a politically disillusioned and rootless 'colonial', she must create a social identity from scratch. As Lessing's narrative metaphors keep reminding us, she is socially and psychologically at sea. Halfway through the book, she is visited by her mother, who fails to re-establish contact with Martha and goes home to die. If this rounds off the mother-and-daughter conflict whch has been going on since childhood, it also underlines the extent to which Martha, in London, has found a new family circle which will carry her through the rest of *The Four-Gated City*. Finally, the Appendix contains a fourteen-page letter from Martha, telling of nearly two decades of exile on a

Hebridean island. (Perhaps Doris Lessing might still give us a more adequate account of Martha's experiences in old age?) There are numerous changes of focus and point of view in *The Four-Gated City*, and often they are clumsily handled. Yet the end-result is a *Bildungsroman* with a breadth of subject which no other contemporary British novelist has attempted.

Martha's new family circle are the Coldridges, for whom she performs the various roles of secretary, housekeeper, stepmother, collaborator, companion, and mistress. Mark and Lynda Coldridge belong to an extended family or clan which includes among its ranks a society hostess, a Labour minister, a left-wing MP, a TV interviewer, a nuclear physicist who defects to Moscow, and a homosexual publisher and cultural bureaucrat. Mark is a novelist and inventor of imaginary cities, Lynda a schizophrenic who, in *Shikasta*, will make contact with the envoy from Canopus. The realistic doctrine of dramatising typical individuals at the point of action of social development has been stretched to its limits here. The Coldridges are at once the personification of the progressive liberal intelligentsia and—if we eliminate a few black sheep—a *karass*, whose joint efforts will enable themselves and others to survive the coming holocaust.[5]

The Coldridges are a charmed circle; a circle of typical individuals whose characterisation is sometimes very thin. They are all too clearly intended to dramatise the recent social history of England, on which Lessing comments abundantly in her narrative. Yet they offer no more than a two-dimensional, colour-supplement view of English life. It is not simply that Lessing knows nothing of what goes on outside the metropolis (her narrators' forays into the provinces are perhaps summed up by Stella in 'A Man and Two Women', who 'left London at midday by train, armed with food unobtainable in Essex' (p. 90)—and who had no difficulty in tearing herself away from Essex again in time to catch the last train back to Liverpool Street). Her grasp on the British academic and political scene is shaky. Charles Watkins in *Briefing* is not a credible Cambridge professor. Phoebe Coldridge, a 'sub-Minister with various responsibilities in the new government', is shown collecting signatures for a letter to *The Times* on foreign affairs and for 'a statement or affirmation, designed for the *New Statesman*, about the behaviour of the police' (*The Four-Gated City*, p. 561). In real life a Minister who lent her name to a press campaign against the police would instantly be relegated to the back benches. Moreover, the narrowness of the social base of *The Four-Gated City* must be obvious. The working class, represented by a family who run a fish-and-chip shop, two elderly rural retainers, an actor on the make, and an ex-sailor turned brothel-owner, is as ludicrously travestied here as in any of the bourgeois novels of the mid-nineteenth century. Within the Coldridge family, it is a striking defect that there is no true representative of Tory England—not even at the level of male-chauvinist tycoonery personified by Richard in *The Golden Notebook*. Clearly the merits of *The Four-Gated City* are not those of social realism.

Nor is it satire, though at times Lessing is capable of almost Waugh-like thrusts. Sandra, we are told—one of the occultists with whom Lynda Coldrige tends to consort—'not only believed in flying saucers from other planets—after all, nearly everyone did—but corresponded telepathically with a demon lover who was captain of one of them' (p. 580). It would be an absurd mistake to read this isolated sally as expressing any general contempt for outlandish beliefs. By and large, Lessing earnestly sets out to convince her readers of the futility of politics, and as earnestly argues that schizophrenia and psychic phenomena provide the keys to salvation. The supreme manifestation of the futility of politics, as Martha sees it, is the Campaign for Nuclear Disarmament with its Aldermaston marches. She sums up these demonstrations (which incidentally provide a convenient fictional rendezvous-point for the various Coldridges) in the figure of a blonde woman with a baby, marching from Aldermaston to London with a placard reading 'Caroline Says No'. Caroline and her fellow-activists, Lessing more than once reminds us, make up a force weaker than the crowd at a First Division football match. Protest in our society is ignominiously dwarfed by the might of the institutions it sets out to challenge, such as the 'Defence Estimates for the United States in 1961—a figure so enormous that it was meaningless to the ordinary mind, like distance expressed in light-years' (p. 460). In the nature of things this sermon on political futility will not convince anyone who is not already of Lessing's persuasion. A hundred years earlier she would probably have moralised with equal fervour over the premature eclipse of socialism and communism.

Having convinced herself of the futility of politics, Martha is free to pursue her researches into what H.G. Wells once called the 'mental hinterland'. She hears voices and starts overhearing the thoughts of people around her. She has a breakdown, experiencing other human beings as utterly alien to her; she descends into Hell, struggles against the Demon of Self-Hatred, and follows the Stations of the Cross. Recovering, she recognises her kinship with Lynda, who has been classified as mentally sick since childhood. Both are sensitives with ESP powers (once the common possession of mankind), who thereby possess a far more effective and thoroughgoing way of saying No than ever Caroline had. Meanwhile Mark Coldridge pursues his own, more rationalistic, concern with survival. He invents the imaginary four-gated city—an image stored in the collective memory, though no one yet knows this—and describes it in a novel. He and his business partner, Jimmy Wood, begin to move in science-fiction circles. Jimmy, whose science fiction is beneath the notice of the liberal intelligentsia, becomes a bestselling author, drawing his plots from 'a kind of potted library representing everything rejected by official culture and scholarship' (p. 528). Reading these books, Martha has the sense of the fundamental unity of all occultist doctrines; it is as if she has obscurely found a key to all mythologies. Mark's concerns, however, are more practical. Convinced of the possibility of precognition, he devotes his efforts to a plan for survival and, thanks to the timely appearance of an American millionaire, starts up a series of settlements in the Tunisian desert. He remains sceptical to the end: 'I can't stand that nasty mixture of irony and St John of the Cross and the Arabian Nights that they all (Lynda, Martha, Francis) went in for', he dyspeptically reflects (p. 667). But his move to Tunisia was premature—bubonic plague killed off most of the settlers—and we are not to take his grumbling very seriously. He is the kind of man who takes brushed tweeds, an umbrella, and a shooting-stick on the Aldermaston march.

There is far more to it than this—quantitatively, at least—but we must now try to sum up *The Four-Gated City*, which is a clumsy, engrossing, ideas-filled melodrama. It has various precedents in English fiction, including the burningly topical reading of Victorian poets and prime ministers. Misleading alike as art and as social history, it is full of ingenious and one-sided dramatisations of contemporary ideology. Doris Lessing's artistic gifts do not stand or fall by this ramshackle edifice, a city of packing-cases held together with old bits of string. *The Four-Gated City* remains the source-book for her later novels, yet these continuing experiments in narrative form have taken her in directions which none of its early readers could have predicted.

Briefing for a Descent into Hell, her next book, was as radical a departure from her earlier fictional mode as *The Golden Notebook*. Described by the author as 'Inner-space fiction', this is a novel which is open to two alternative, and incompatible, modes of reading. As a psychological novel of the subject, it tells of the transitory mental aberration of Charles Watkins, who is found wandering on the Embankment suffering from loss of memory. Watkins's case-history is reconstructed by means of a succession of documents: letters, case-notes, 'autobiography', doctor-patient dialogues, and the recollections of his wife, friends, and acquaintances, all surrounding the interior monologue of a schizophrenic voyage (a likely source is R.D. Laing's account of 'A Ten-Day Voyage' in *The Politics of Experience*) with which the novel begins. Yet *Briefing* is also a science-fiction novel, incorporating a variation on the type of imaginary cosmic voyage to be found in some of Wells's short stories and in Stapledon's *Star Maker*. To some extent Lessing relies on literary pastiche, whether of the Shelleyan mode of cosmic rhapsody when the main character is carried off in the flying saucer, or of the twentieth-century 'space opera' in the actual Briefing of Watkins and his fellow-emissaries for their 'descent into Hell'. Watkins later disowns the Briefing and agrees to electric-shock treatment to remove the last traces of mental disturbance. There is no doubt that this is a spiritual defeat. *Briefing* is not a successful marriage of the psychological novel and the science-fictional mode. The portrayal of Watkins's family and social milieu is dutiful rather than inspired, and, though we are left with two individuals still in possession of the higher knowledge which Watkins has suppressed, their characterisation is wooden in the extreme.

The Summer Before the Dark was, until the mid-1980s, the last of Lessing's realistic reports on contemporary life. Kate Brown, a suburban housewife, lives through her last 'flowering', her last chance to explore and discover her own identity before 'the dark', which we may imagine as death, old age, or the catastrophic times which lie ahead. Her self-exploration includes a schizoid interlude and a serial dream, the dream of the seal in which Kate is able to use her maternal strength to conserve the life of a dying animal. This is a novel of social decadence—Lessing's evident distaste for most aspects of contemporary life leaves a somewhat acrid impression—with muted hints of the mental and spiritual reserves that mankind might still be able to draw upon in the event of disaster.

The Memoirs of a Survivor is a vividly-imagined account of disaster itself. The narrator, whose confined point of view dominates the novel, is a woman living isolated in an apartment block in North London. Her restrained and moving story makes a most salutary contrast with *The Summer Before the Dark*, since her experiences have the unbroken immediacy of a dream rather than being mixed in with the increasingly pontifical generalisations of Lessing's mode of social history. Exactly why law and order, the social fabric, and finally all civilised inhibitions and restraints are breaking down around the unnamed narrator we are not told; this alone is a striking innovation. The tale focusses on the narrator's struggle to bring up a stepdaughter, Emily, while at the same time pursuing her mysterious sequence of visions of life 'behind the wall'. Such visions belong, of course, to popular occultism, the 'potted library' of arcana and apocrypha that Martha devoured in *The Four-Gated City*. Another version of the contemporary myth that Lessing draws upon in *The Memoirs* may be found in Alan and Sally Landsburg's *In Search of Ancient Mysteries* (1974). The Landsburgs argue that there are 'short-cuts in space-time'—a notion that they offer to clarify by means of the following analogy. Two apartment buildings with entrances on different streets stand back-to-back in Manhattan. For the inhabitants of one of these apartments to visit the neighbours with whom they share a party wall involves two elevator rides and a walk around the block; they may even decide to hail a cab. This is the way in which we move in ordinary three-dimensional space. Travelling in a fourth dimension, however, would be the equivalent of simply stepping through the party wall without harming either themselves or the wall. Herein lies the real explanation—or so the Landsburgs assure their readers—of 'how so many great religious leaders just rose up and disappeared, as the legends have it; they went into other dimensions'.[6] This engagingly dotty scenario is remarkably similar to *The Memoirs of a Survivor*. A man appears in the narrator's apartment from nowhere, delivering Emily into her care. She both brings Emily up, and simultaneously watches her growing up in the other dimension beyond the wall. A pet animal, the cat-dog Hugo, appears on the scene to keep them company. As Emily grows to maturity she teams up with Gerald, a natural leader who collects around him a gang of abandoned children. Society is collapsing, but life on the other side of the wall continues serene. Finally, the walls dissolve; the 'one person [the narrator] had been looking for' is there on the other side (p. 190); and she, Emily, Hugo, and Gerald (a Pied Piper followed by his band of children) go through to their deliverance. That is all, though we may be entitled to guess that they have gone through, not to bare survival, but to an idyllic pastoral world like that which the narrator and Emily have earlier imagined together:

> And so we talked about the farm, our future, hers and mine, like a fable where we would walk hand in hand, together. And then 'life' would begin, life as it ought to be, as it had been promised—by whom? when? where?—to everybody on this earth. (p. 33)

The Memoirs is a deliberate romance, and it is essential to its quality that the questions 'by whom? when? where?' are not answered. Indeed, they cannot seriously be asked.

Lessing's second excursion into the field of the generically pure, self-conscious romance is *The Marriages Between Zones Three, Four, and Five* (1980). Once again this is a tale of a woman whose suffering and devotion to duty leads to a kind of salvation, but it is set in an archaic, mythological landscape, and the woman concerned is no *femme moyenne sensuelle* but a hereditary queen, Al·Ith. Zone Three, over which she rules, is a classic (and classically sterile) pastoral utopia. In order to relieve the blight which has fallen upon her land, she obeys a summons to marry the king of Zone Four, a sexual barbarian whose emotional and sensual education she takes in hand. He, in turn, reluctantly leaves her once he is summoned to marry the warrior queen of Zone Five. Zone Four is a centralised feudal tyranny in which women are held in subjection, Zone Five a land of farmers and merchants terrorised by marauding nomads. The marriages lead to cultural cross-fertilisation, releasing the inhabitants of Zone Three from their complacency and encouraging them to aspire onwards and upwards to Zone Two, known only as the 'realm of the storytellers' (the Zones are situated on a series of ascending plateaux). After a long process of purification, Al·Ith and her followers, roused from their sluggish contentment, are beginning to move on 'up the pass'—an ending which might be seen as a collectivist, and triumphant, rewriting of Ibsen's *Brand*. The whole system of imaginary countries is apparently in the care of benevolent overseers, known simply as 'The Providers'. As in *The Memoirs*, the questions 'by whom? when? where?' are not asked.

Yet the truth is that this time we know the answers. *The Marriages* being the second volume of *Canopus in Argos: Archives*, we must assume that the Providers are the rulers of the Canopean Empire. There are actually six Zones, ranged in concentric circles around the Earth, and Zone Six (not mentioned in *The Marriages*) is that inhabited by human souls while they wait for reincarnation. This, and much more, information is set out in the opening pages of *Shikasta*, a novel cast not in the genre of romance but of the science-fictional history, and a very dry one at that. *Shikasta* purports to be a 'compilation of documents selected to offer a very general picture of Shikasta for the use of first-year students of Canopean Colonial Rule' (p. 2). Like *The Golden Notebook*, *The Four-Gated City*, and *Briefing*, here is another instance of the novel not as utopian city but as shanty-town.

The idea that *Shikasta* is a sort of Canopean textbook does not invite suspension of disbelief for a moment. We get very little idea of the Canopeans, but the first-year students they have in mind are very obviously terrestrial, English-speaking, and born in the second half of the twentieth century. But to do justice to the preceding observation I must translate it into the language of Canopus. The subjects for whom this textbook has been compiled are members of the dominant native species on Shikasta, born somewhere towards the middle of the Century of

Destruction. They comprise citizens of the Isolated Northern Continent and of a certain country in the northwest fringes of the central landmass. (It may be said here that the importance of geography—that latchkey to the understanding of the basics of planetary development—completely escapes these benighted animals.) This country in the northwest fringes, a small island as it happens, has, because of its warlike and acquisitive qualities, overrun and dominated a good part of the globe, though more recently it has been driven back again. When not engaged in forming impersonal pairing bonds or in attending to a device which supplies identical indoctrinational material simultaneously into every living or working unit, great sub-armies of the youth of this species congregate in the country's institutions of higher instruction and mentation. It is at the novices in these institutions that this compilation is directed. (*History of Shikasta*, vol 4321. Summary Chapter. EXCERPT.)

A minor side-effect of the Century of Destruction, it must be said, is the devastation wrought by *Shikasta* and the conception of the all-wise, nearly-all-powerful Canopeans on Doris Lessing's prose. Can the *Canopus in Argos* sequence be some vast, bloated satire at the expense of the benevolently despotic aliens, one wonders hopefully? Will they turn out, after all, to be the phantasma of computerised human malignancy which their bureaucratic jargon would lead one to expect? Unfortunately, in *Shikasta* Lessing seems equally innocent of the artistic self-searching needed to make her aliens likeable, and of the narrative sleight-of-hand which a more professional science-fiction writer would use to confer some basic plausibility on them. Nor is this her first exercise in narrative from an extraterrestrial standpoint. Like so much in her later work, we may trace it back to *The Four-Gated City*, where Martha, during her schizophrenic episode, sees the streets of London as filled with bestial creatures with whom she has no common identity. She imagines herself writing a report which begins: 'This particular planet is inhabited thickly by defectively evolved animals who ...' (p. 521). Lessing continued that report in a short story in her 1975 collection *The Story of a Non-Marrying Man*, entitled 'Report on the Threatened City'. The city is San Francisco, which, the aliens have discovered, will almost certainly suffer a severe earthquake before 1976. They take it upon themselves to warn the earthmen of their peril. The city's inhabitants take no notice, although they have already experienced a devastating earthquake in 1906. What is the cause of their stupid insensibility? The answer is plain: unlike the dominant species on all other known planets, this species is incapable of rational action. One of the attributes that fatally incapacitates them is their recourse to so-called humour.

It is just possible, though not very plausible, to read 'Report on the Threatened City' as a satire poking fun at the absurdly arrogant pretensions of these 'alien intelligences'. *Shikasta*, with its lengthy account of the Canopean envoy George Sherban's experiences on Earth, and of his attempts to avert the process of social collapse, cannot conceivably be read in that way; its anthropological naivety is genuine. The author's combination of vitriolic attacks on earthly imperialism with the romantic fantasy of a benevolent and omniscient Empire 'out there' in space represents, to my mind, a self-deception which—after half a century of science fiction dealing with galactic empires—one can only regret. We may conclude with her Canopean narrator's explanation of how human life as we know it evolved on Shikasta. It was as a result of the decision to subject the planet to an 'all-out booster, Top-Level Priority, Forced-Growth Plan' (p. 15). To many of her readers such language is reminiscent of nothing so much as the American intervention in Vietnam.

*

Doris Lessing has had an extraordinary career, and English fiction since the Second World War would have been much poorer without her. Her reputation will surely survive, though whole areas of her writing may have to be evacuated in order for it to do so. Such intellectual and emotional *vade mecums* as *The Four-Gated City*, not to mention her attempts at 'space fiction', were more widely read at the time of their first appearance than they ever will be in the future. It is easy to focus on the shortcomings of so uneven a writer, but it is the profound contradictions in her outlook and talent which should stand out in a final assessment. Here is a born writer who rarely seems at ease with her medium, a born novelist whose penetration of social and individual defences has come to verge on general misanthropy. Though she has systematically adopted an irrationalist philosophy, her impatience with human beings, and her conviction that there is a meaningful standard against which they can be measured as 'immune to reason' or 'defectively evolved', are in fact those of an extreme rationalist. Some of her recent books resound with the exasperation of the prophet whose message is not being heard, no matter what fictional form it is clothed in. Yet her movement away from realism has highly positive as well as negative aspects. The romance form, in novels like *The Memoirs of a Survivor* and *The Marriages Between Zones Three, Four, and Five*, has released what Arnold would have called the 'natural magic' which is always at war, in her work, with her urge towards strident political and philosophical statement. In the domain of fantasy she had been able to bring together her concern with hallucinations and dream states, and the deep understanding of human relationships, those of husband and wife or parent and child, characteristic of the best of her realistic fiction. She may yet be revered, not for her clumsy, argumentative fictional sagas, but for the occasional well-wrought, harmonious romance which stands out among its compeers like a city in the desert.

POSTSCRIPT

'Descents into Hell' was first published in 1980. In the preface to her third *Canopus* novel, *The Sirian Experiments* (1981), Doris Lessing described her 'space fiction' series as a framework that enabled her to 'put questions' and to 'explore ideas and sociological possibilities', rather than offering a system of belief: 'if I have created a cosmology, then it is only for literary purposes!' The disclaimer is well taken—did not Yeats once say something similar?—but there is another strain in the preface which supports my diagnosis of irrationalism. UFOs in particular are resurrected. Since *The Sirian Experiments*, two subsequent *Canopus* novels have been published: *The Making of the Representative for Planet 8* (1982), a fable of survival on a cooling planet which belongs in the sequence of Lessing's well-wrought romances; and *The Sentimental Agents in the Volyen Empire* (1983) which, together with *The Sirian Experiments*, repeats in a more subdued way many of the faults of *Shikasta*. One curious feature of *The Sentimental Agents* is that the narrator recounts thinly disguised versions of the French Revolution, the Russian Revolution, and the history of communism in Western Europe in order to exemplify the pathology of 'Rhetorical Diseases' to which human beings are supposedly subject.

But another extraordinary twist in Lessing's career was in preparation: her return to realistic fiction. In 1984 it was revealed that 'Jane Somers', the author of a 'first novel', *The Diary of a Good Neighbour*, published the previous year, was a Lessing pseudonym. When *The Diaries of Jane Somers* (1984) were followed by *The Good Terrorist* (1985), critics and reviewers, always slow to catch up with this author, were at last ready to admit her to the category of 'novelists reborn on the Right'.[7] It is too soon to comment on these latest Lessing novels except to say that they have caught some of her most ardent admirers badly off balance. The present chapter turned out to be controversial when it first appeared.[8] I would claim, however, that my recourse to rational and mimetic standards in judging Lessing's writings (including her experimental and fantasy fiction) employs the only critical framework which can survive her latest change of direction. The point of appealing to rational and mimetic standards is not, of course, to elevate a work such as *The Good Terrorist* above its predecessors. In this, her latest novel at the time of writing, Lessing has abandoned her visionary system in order to produce an earth-bound right-wing political thriller. *The Good Terrorist* demonstrates Lessing's continuing ability to shock and stir up her readers, but her long odyssey as a novelist of ideas is far from completed.

10

Muriel Spark and Her Critics

How wonderful it feels to be an artist
and a woman in the twentieth century.
                    Fleur Talbot in *Loitering with Intent* (1981)[1]

In *Loitering with Intent* Muriel Spark created a heroine who was
able to look back on a successful career as a novelist with pride
and satisfaction. Fleur Talbot is at once a purely fictional
creation—as fictional as any character in the Sparkian
canon—and an autobiographical mouthpiece whose liberally-
expressed views on the novelist's craft are plainly those of her
author. 'I always hope the readers of my novels are of good
quality. I wouldn't like to think of anyone cheap reading my
books', says Fleur. Reviewers, as everyone knows, are not always
of good quality, but at least they can be relied upon to warn off
the rest. Ruth Whittaker, in her excellent study of *The Faith
and Fiction of Muriel Spark*, cites a *TLS* reviewer who
complained of *The Driver's Seat* (1970) that it 'will take you 60
minutes to read and cost you sixpence a minute'.[2] Clearly this
comment cannot have been as damaging as it was meant to be.
Spark has found her readers, and has given them great pleasure
over the years. In the quality of her reception she has been
peculiarly fortunate.

The earliest novels were welcomed by Evelyn Waugh and
Graham Greene, while their successors won the approval of the
most influential group of British critics in the 1960s and 1970s.
As early as 1963 Frank Kermode wrote of her (in an article
reprinted in *Modern Essays*) as a 'strong imagination', a
'remarkable virtuoso ... in her prime' (pp. 281, 267). *The Prime*

of Miss Jean Brodie (1961) became the subject both of a major film and of a much-cited formal analysis by David Lodge. Malcolm Bradbury, in an essay entitled 'Muriel Spark's fingernails', recommended her as a 'very high stylist indeed' (p. 247). More recently Gabriel Josipovici in *Writing and the Body* (1982) has described the author of *Territorial Rights* (1979) as 'one of the few major living writers still producing work worthy of her best', and as one who can be discussed without incongruity beside T.S. Eliot (pp. 83–4). These are serious claims. *The Faith and Fiction of Muriel Spark* does not attempt placing or comparative judgments of this sort, but it does provide a most lucid, convincing and detailed account of what Henry James would have called the Sparkian 'case'.

The case is that of a witty, graceful and highly intelligent writer who often fails to provide the emotional satisfactions and to produce the sort of intellectual conviction traditionally associated with novel-reading. As Whittaker points out, the most influential critic of Muriel Spark has been Frank Kermode, who tends to approach her as a pure formalist. Kermode's influence has been several times acknowledged; for example, Malcolm Bradbury wrote in a 1972 article in *Critical Quarterly* that 'the closeness between an important novelist and an important critic one senses here has itself an exciting cultural significance' (p. 250n). Other critics who write in her praise have frequently done so with an air of apology, of stilling doubts or making amends. David Lodge described his essay on *Jean Brodie*, reprinted in *The Novelist at the Crossroads*, as a 'personal act of amends' for a hostile review of the same novel (p. 124). Bradbury conceded that he had 'not always' thought of Spark as a 'particularly distinguished' writer (p. 241). Peter Kemp, in his *Muriel Spark* (1974), gave vent to a number of paragraph-long tirades against various aspects of her work, only to follow them up with still more eloquent and dexterous paragraphs in her defence. It is, perhaps, unusual for such a divided critical response to be acknowledged by a novelist's most ardent defenders. What it suggests, I believe, is that Spark is a genuinely disturbing writer—one who disturbs our deepest convictions and prejudices about novel-writing, and about more fundamental matters as well—and that her case is by no means easy to judge.

Two inescapable themes of any criticism of this novelist are the formal self-consciousness of her art, and her Catholicism. Kermode described the early books as 'an inquiry into the way fictions work' (p. 269). In the 1970s she produced a series of 'estranged' fictions which seemed deliberately experimental and designed to tear up the contract she had earlier established with her readers. In these books she used present-tense narration, and abandoned any explicit pointers to narrative significance in favour of a teasing reliance on hidden or understated allegory. The *nouveau roman* was an obvious influence—especially on *The Driver's Seat*—yet these novels (or novellas) were never wholly without some form of meta-discourse; it was just that the 'moral', once the reader had found it, tended to negate the story. *The Driver's Seat*, for example, ended with the traditional formula of 'pity and fear' suggesting a tragic spectacle; but what was tragic about a wholly external and dispassionate account of a woman who (apparently) set out to find someone to rape and murder her? Similarly, *The Abbess of Crewe* (1974) was at some level a moral satire on the downfall of President Nixon; but what claimed the reader's attention was a fantastic, skittish and lavishly self-referential account of nunnish megalomania. In these books the dislocation of the moral from the story was thrust into the foreground, as a problem for which, the narrative implied, the reader had best find his own solution. Yet a dislocation of story and moral is not unusual in fiction—which after all abounds in cardboard heroes and enjoyable villains—and it is certainly to be found in Spark's other books as well.

Looking at her whole career, it would be a travesty to describe Muriel Spark as a major experimental novelist. For one thing, the novels that followed *The Abbess of Crewe*—*The Takeover* (1976) and *Territorial Rights*—are not experimental at all. (My own view is that they are among her weakest books.) For another, popularity of a rather modish sort has continued to be a feature of Spark's work. Not only was *Jean Brodie* a successful film, but *The Girls of Slender Means* (1963), one of her most distinguished books, was originally serialised in the London *Evening Standard*. She sells widely in paperback and library copies of her books are much in demand. She has the profile of a very astute and sophisticated novelist, but not of an avant-gardist.

Ruth Whittaker is not the first reader to be concerned less with Muriel Spark as pure aesthetician than with Muriel Spark as a Catholic. Her earlier novels, as Whittaker reminds us, are 'demonstrations of faith with an implied QED at the end of each one' (p. 72). She is a notoriously anti-humanist novelist, who ultimately puts down a large proportion of the manifestations of human nature that she portrays to the ragings of the devil: as Joanna Childe in *The Girls of Slender Means* says (using a quotation that is scarcely understood by her fellow-inmates in the girls' hostel), 'He rageth, and again he rageth, because he knows his time is short' (p. 196). Now, not every novelist can be or should be a George Eliot committed to the democratic and materialistic extension of the reader's sympathies; but there is a peculiar Sparkian attitude to these matters which both awes, and grates upon, at least a proportion of her readers. Kermode has called her 'an unremittingly Catholic novelist committed to immutable truths' (p. 268), and Ruth Whittaker endorses this; but one must, however tactlessly, insist that such a commitment does not in itself convey aesthetic value.

I believe the 'Catholic novel' in general to be a suspect category—Catholicism is large and contains multitudes—but the Sparkian Catholic novel does admit of fairly precise delimitation. A Catholic novelist in this country is likely to get a good press, and a communist novelist probably would not; yet it is helpful to consider Spark's novels in relation to their antithesis, which is surely the novel of socialist realism. Spark is self-consciously fictive, playful and cynical; she is wryly despairing about the social world in which we live and anything to which this world seems likely to lead; and in every novel she invites us to contemplate characters who are, as Fleur in *Loitering with Intent* says, 'pure evil'. She is resolute in destroying utopian illusions, and romantic only in the extent of her negations. Yet, like socialist realist novels, her plots tend to be propaganda vehicles manipulating her characters' destinies for a dogmatic purpose. She is, in fact, a reactionary allegorist. Critics have often implied that this does not matter, even where it leads to shallow and implausible characterisation—the play (of style and fictive self-consciousness) is the thing. But the problem of the dislocation of moral and story is not solved by simply denying the relevance of the moral. If Spark's novels are expressive of 'immutable truths' one would expect these to be translated into sensible truths of representation. And so, at times, they have been.

It is doubtful if there is any such animal as a pure socialist realist artist; at any rate, history shows very few who could feel absolutely safe within the walls of any of the modern successors to Plato's Republic. Nor, despite the propaganda in her novels, do I believe Muriel Spark is a 'pure' Catholic artist. She has her own strongly-felt opinions. Some of these concern matters and attitudes within the Catholic Church, some those outside it. Usually, it is true, her overt hostility is directed at contemporary liberalism. The author of *The Bachelors* (1960) was plainly no friend to practitioners of abortion, contraception or homosexuality. *The Driver's Seat*, with its 'liberated' heroine contriving her own sexual murder, seems like a slap in the face to feminists and anti-rape campaigners. In *The Takeover*, a novel set among the Anglo-Italian smart set, the narrator offers a quite hysterical outburst on the economic effects of the 1973 oil crisis: this has caused, she informs us, 'such a sea-change in the nature of reality as could not have been envisaged by Karl Marx or Sigmund Freud' (p. 127). Anyone dissatisfied by the received view of Spark's works should, in a manner of speaking, take heart from these manifestations of human weakness on her part. They do not seem to belong either to the devotional writer, whose imagination is safely *sub specie aeternitatis*, or to the self-conscious fabulator and artistic manicurist whose virtue resides in her detachment and poise. Such outbursts suggest, perhaps, that the *sensational* quality of her novels—a quality I shall seek to define—is not wholly unconnected with worldly sensationalism and polemic. (And why should it be?) Muriel Spark's novels express not only formalism and Catholicism but a controlling personal vision; a vision which reveals itself through the manipulation and, as it were, the anaesthetisation of strongly emotive aspects of reality. We must approach this matter through a consideration of their plots.

Her novels are said to be 'heavily-plotted'[3]—a term which conceals as much as it explains. What is the ground of this heavy plotting? I think Ruth Whittaker is mistaken when she refers to the earlier novels as 'basically realistic' (p. 12). True, there is a surface verisimilitude—the evocation of post-war London, or of a pre-war Edinburgh childhood—which gives them a strongly picturesque appeal. She is also a master of strictly contemporary settings (the telephone call, the aeroplane trip). But if this is what realism means, then a James Bond novel is realistic because of its accuracy in naming the hero's brand of Scotch. Ruth Whittaker offers a rather trite little chronology of contemporary fiction since the 1950s—a tale of realism leading via the *nouveau roman* and postmodernism to something called 'criction' (pp. 6-8). Even if, charitably, we re-christen 'criction' as self-conscious fiction or meta-fiction, it will be clear that this apostolic succession of movements (which stinks of the graduate school) is quite inadequate as a critical history of the novel in the last three decades. There was plenty of self-conscious fiction around in the 1950s—only it was slightly less fashionable then. In Muriel Spark's first novel *The Comforters* (1957)—supposedly belonging to her 'realist' period—the heroine is a novelist and academic student of the novel who is trying to write a book on *Form in the Modern Novel* but is 'having difficulty with the chapter on realism' (p. 57). There is little that Muriel Spark can have learned about realism since the 1950s—and still less that academic critics can have taught her—that she did not already know. The heroine of *The Comforters* is rumoured to have taken up science fiction as a new religion (p. 163). In fact, Spark has always been a fantasy novelist whose deepest allegiance has been to the fictional sub-genres—and especially to the Gothic—rather than to realism and its apparent successors. To take some examples, *Robinson* (1958) is as one would expect a Robinsonade or desert-island adventure; *The Ballad of Peckham Rye* (1960) an urban pastoral verging on the supernatural; *The Prime of Miss Jean Brodie* a girls'-school story stood on its head; *The Hothouse by the East River* (1973) a concealed ghost story; *The Abbess of Crewe* a political allegory; *The Only Problem* (1984) a moral fable based on the Book of Job. Running through all her books, including those just named, are elements of the Gothic thriller and the supernatural fantasy. All of her books, from *The Comforters* (1957) with its diamond-smuggling plot to *The Only Problem* with its background of terrorism and *Loitering with Intent* which hinges on the theft of a manuscript, are at one level crime novels. Supernatural occurrences include the mysterious telephone calls in *Memento Mori* (1959) and the demonic bumps on Dougal Douglas's head in *The Ballad of Peckham Rye*. The mediumistic feats of Patrick Seton in *The Bachelors*, and the ability of Fleur Talbot's novel to foretell and influence events—including a fatal car crash—in *Loitering with Intent*, are supernatural or at least uncanny.

To some readers this may sound like a foolishly reductive emphasis; but what are we to make of Spark's heavy use of the fantasy, the Gothic, and the thriller? Only one of her novels has the *amplitude* of conventional realistic fiction—is this merely a preference for economy? (And that one novel, *The Mandelbaum Gate*, has flaws which almost every critic has identified.) Peter Kemp, in a typical ploy, writes that the early *Robinson* 'presents itself, at first sight, as a sophisticated exercise in desert-island writing' (p. 30). The implication—not really borne out by the critical treatment that follows—is that *Robinson*, for the experienced reader, becomes something quite different and much more sophisticated still. Ruth Whittaker speaks of the sub-genres as 'fictional stereotypes' informing the novels (p. 94). Again, their reality is said to be different; she reads *Robinson*, for example, as a distorted fictional autobiography. I suspect that we have returned, here, to another version of the problem I mentioned earlier; that of the dislocation of moral and story. Our critics, in the tradition of E.M. Forster's *Aspects of the Novel*, are not really interested in the story. They prefer a theoretical notion of fictiveness somehow abstracted from the telling of stories. For such critics, the sub-genres of fiction are intrinsically crass. (Recently, another crass sub-genre, the so-called 'realist text', has been added to the list.) Yet to give a critical account of a novel minus its plot is to run into extreme artificiality. The modern sub-genres did not exist until created, for the most part, by writers of genius (Defoe for the desert-island adventure, Poe for the detective story). Since then, it is cross-fertilisation and generic incorporation—rather than averting one's attention or cultivating a high style *in vacuo*—which has kept the plots of novels novel. In *Loitering with Intent* Fleur Talbot writes that 'I think that ordinary readers would be astonished to know what troubles fell on my head because of the sinister side [of her novel *Warrender Chase*], and that is part of this story of mine; and that's what I think makes it worth the telling' (p. 46). Just a lure for the naive reader, perhaps? On the contrary, I am convinced that without this it would not be 'worth the telling'. From Muriel Spark's point of view, I suggest, self-consciousness in fiction is quite inextricably bound up with the promise of a story worth telling. And that story is, time and again, defined within recognisable generic limits.

It has, first of all, an artificially circumscribed social setting. A Muriel Spark novel is set on an island, in a school, a convent or a country house, among expatriates or foreign tourists, or in some arbitrarily isolated London community: a working-class suburb, a girls' hostel, a coterie of amateur authors or Hampstead and Kensington bachelors. These closed and allegorical communities never, to my mind, possess the sort of typicality and focal validity demanded by the realist tradition. (One could contrast *The Driver's Seat*, for example, with V.S. Naipaul's *In a Free State* and *Guerrillas* in this respect.) The communities are much more akin to those found in (say) Agatha Christie. Still more telling is what happens when the author breaks out of her closed community. At the end of *The Girls of Slender Means* she takes us away from the May of Teck Club to the revelling crowds assembled in front of Buckingham Palace in 1945 on V.J. night. Notice how ruthlessly she denies any historical significance to the scene:

> The public swelled on V.J. night of August as riotously as on the victory night of May. The little figures appeared duly on the balcony every half-hour, waved for a space and disappeared.
>
> Jane, Nicholas, and Rudi were suddenly in difficulties, being pressed by the crowd from all sides. 'Keep your elbows out if possible,' Jane and Nicholas said to each other, almost simultaneously; but this was useless advice.
>
> A seaman, pressing on Jane, kissed her passionately on the mouth; nothing whatsoever could be done about it. She was at the mercy of his wet beery mouth until the crowd gave way, and then the three pressed a path to a slightly healthier spot, with access to the park.
>
> Here, another seaman, observed only by Nicholas, slid a knife silently between the ribs of a woman who was with him. The lights went up on the balcony, and a hush anticipated the Royal appearance. The stabbed woman did not scream, but sagged

immediately. Someone else screamed through the hush, a woman, many yards away, some other victim. Or perhaps that screamer had only had her toes trodden upon. (p. 286).

The author's attention settles on a meaningless, barbarous, private moment. Like the episode in Flaubert's *Sentimental Education* where the hero takes advantage of the 1848 Revolution to slip away to the country for a dirty weekend, it is a statement of social disconnection verging on existential absurdity. This is a *coup de théâtre*, designed to leave the reader unsatisfied (if gloomily aware of human nullity). And it is typical of Spark's sensationalist vision that the beery kiss had to be counterbalanced by a murder.

The high style of Muriel Spark is lavished on a brutal and disillusioning world. Nicholas Farrington in *The Girls of Slender Means* has a brief vision of the May of Teck Club as a 'microcosmic ideal society' (p. 233), a kind of utopia. His vision, like the girls' hostel itself, is razed to the ground by the end of the story. Saintly Joanna Childe, a lover of poetry and especially Hopkins, is the one victim of the fire, which is caused by an unexploded bomb in the hostel ground. Value, it is implied, is not to be found in this world, and Nicholas casts aside his utopian dreams to become a Catholic missionary and eventually a martyr. Apart from that decision, the only other source of value is embodied in the cool, sardonic, tight-lipped narration. Society is a predatory arena in which the successful are also the sensationally crooked—cold-blooded plotters like the unnamed sailor and like Selina Redwood, Nicholas's beautiful girlfriend, who goes back into the blazing building in which her companions of less slender proportions are still trapped in order to loot a piece of shared property, the Schiaparelli dress.

Nicholas, not until then a Catholic, responds to Selina's act of rapacious selfishness by making the sign of the cross. He himself is eventually murdered in Haiti. *The Girls of Slender Means* is set 'long ago in 1945', when 'all the nice people in England were poor, allowing for exceptions' (p. 193); one of several hints that suggest an illusive earthly paradise. The same determination to discredit utopian illusions appears in *Robinson*, where the desert island is quickly despoiled. Death, present as we have seen amid the 'general pandemonium' of V.J. night, is the mysterious caller in *Memento Mori*, which is perhaps Spark's best-known moral fable. *The Hothouse by the East River* takes the *Et in arcadia ego* theme a shade further, being largely concerned with the doings of characters who are already dead. Pandemonium, in this and other recent novels, is apt to break out at the slightest excuse. A new character, a maidservant, is introduced to us in *The Hothouse* as 'neat, orderly Delia'; there are no prizes for guessing that within the space of two paragraphs she will have gone berserk, dropped her teatray on the floor, and done her best to throw herself out of the window into the East River. (Nor are we very surprised when the narrator foils her efforts; being modern windows they won't open.)

Murder and violent death are so commonplace in her novels that a spate of Muriel Spark films would be good news for the tomato-ketchup manufacturers. Among these bloody and unnatural acts are the stabbing of Lise (who has carefully chosen a non-stain-resistant dress for the occasion) in *The Driver's Seat*; the slicing of a victim's body in half by two jealous women in *Territorial Rights*; the murder of a secretary by her boss in *The Ballad of Peckham Rye*, the murder weapon being a corkscrew stabbed nine times into her neck; and the trail of goat's blood stretching halfway across the island in *Robinson*. Apart from these murders, it would be true to say that blackmail and desecration provide the small change of Spark's version of a loveless, treacherous modern world. It is hard to think of a Spark plot which does not hinge on blackmail, while literal images of desecration—the idea of dancing on somebody's grave—are a recurrent device. At the official narrative level both activities are clearly condemned. Spark's 'positive' characters are usually the blackmailed, her villains the blackmailers. There is the odious Wells in *Robinson*, the murderous little medium Patrick Seton in *The Bachelors*, and the creepy Sir Quentin Oliver in *Loitering with Intent*. Nevertheless I suspect there are deep connections between the themes of blackmail and desecration and the portrait of the artist that emerges in her fiction. She sometimes uses the word 'blackmail' in an unusually wide sense; for example, Lady Edwina (a sympathetic character) in *Loitering with Intent* is described as 'holding up the proceedings [of the Autobiographical Association] with the blackmail of her very great age and of her newly revealed charm'

(p. 33). If Lady Edwina is a sort of blackmailer then so is Fleur Talbot and so, by extension, is the author herself. The blackmailer, as Ruth Whittaker points out, is a manipulator, and so pre-eminently is the Sparkian artist. Desecration, too, is a relevant image for a writer who shows the vanity, hollowness and deadness of the world in which we live by means of scintillating and shocking comedies which dance on that world's tomb. Her blend of artistic desecration and artistic blackmail may, ultimately, induce some of her readers to share her own refuge of Catholic piety; but it is the sensationalism and inherently anti-utopian bent of her imagination that stand out.

Spark's villains tend to be purveyors of fictions, and she is far from the only novelist to have portrayed fiction-making at its lowest as a thoroughly disreputable activity. 'The expert self-faker', she explains in *The Takeover*, 'usually succeeds by means of a manifest self-confidence which is itself by no means a faked confidence. On the contrary, it is one of the few authentic elements in a character which is successfully fraudulent' (p. 147). Clearly she is aware that novel-writing is, by this definition, a fraudulent pursuit. The novelist, understood as a sort of self-faker, may be expected to raise her art on foundations of guilt; a guilt caused, insofar as it is a matter of art, by the disjunction between her stories and their morals. There is, here, a possible explanation of an interesting biographical fact pointed out by her critics: that she did not become a novelist until after her conversion to Catholicism. In *Loitering with Intent*, as we have seen, she has produced a serene and self-confident reprise of her novelistic career. In this novel Fleur Talbot sees Sir Quentin Oliver and some of his friends as the bearers of pure evil, and they turn the same accusation back on her. But Sir Quentin and his friends are also identified, at an occult level, with the characters of the novel she is writing. While they try to manipulate her, she triumphs through her double power to outwit them in 'real life' *and* to exploit them in art. The joy that shines through the novel is, in part, that of dancing on their graves. All this is offered to the reader as an allegory of artisthood and also a distorted confession: 'Although in reality I wasn't yet rid of Sir Quentin and his little sect, they were morally outside of myself, they were objectified, I would write about them one day. In fact, under one form or another, I have written about them ever since, the straws from

171

which I have made my bricks' (p. 142). Seen in the context of the themes of blackmail and desecration, here is a statement of the conditions of Muriel Spark's own art.

She is, in Ruth Whittaker's words, a novelist who 'brilliantly utilises her own limitations'—and, one might add, the limitations of the sub-genres out of which she makes her bricks. Will future readers be more aware of these limitations, or of the impact of her explorations in self-conscious fiction and her uncompromising moral attitudes? I remain troubled by her sensationalism, and her lack of compassion, and were I Fleur Talbot I should doubtless go on to say that some of her most enthusiastic critics (though not Ruth Whittaker) 'were out to justify themselves, and were generally up to no good' (p. 49). But then Fleur Talbot was also justifying herself.

11

Orwell and Burgess:
Two Versions of Cacotopia

Cacotopia. *nonce-wd*. A place where all is evil; opp. by Bentham to *Utopia* 'nowhere', taken as *Eutopia* 'a place where all is well'. (*OED*)

Dystopia has been opposed to eutopia, but both terms come under the utopian heading. I prefer to call Orwell's imaginary society a cacotopia—on the lines of cacophony or cacodemon. It sounds worse than dystopia. (Anthony Burgess, *1985*, p. 52)[1]

Time, which made George Orwell's novel one of the principal talking-points of 1984, has not been so kind to Anthony Burgess's *1985*. Published in 1978, this composite mixture of essay, dialogue, self-interview, satire on 'workers' Britain' and anti-Orwellian pastiche began to seem misconceived the moment that Mrs Thatcher, and not the Labour Party, won the 1979 General Election. Nevertheless, it remains of interest for two reasons. Firstly, its critique of *Nineteen Eighty-Four* from a conservative and Catholic standpoint is one of the most penetrating and provocative commentaries on Orwell in recent years. Secondly, unlike the vast majority of critics, Burgess has put his theories to the test by writing a novella to express his own vision of the 'Worst of All Imaginary Worlds' in the near future. The task that he set himself in *1985* was as follows:

To understand the waking origins of Orwell's bad dream—in himself and in the phase of history that helped to make him. To see where he went wrong and where he seems likely to have been right. To contrive an alternative picture—using his own fictional technique—of the condition to which the seventies seem to be moving and which may well subsist in a real 1984—or, to avoid plagiarism, 1985. (p. 19)

The 'alternative picture' was a let-down by Burgess's best standards, and today it mainly stands out as an example of the fallacy of predicting the future by extrapolating from the most obvious of existing trends. But the novella at the centre of *1985* has the virtue of sending us back to two much earlier Burgess novels, *A Clockwork Orange* and *The Wanting Seed*, both first published in 1962. All three books share a similar understanding of the nature of evil, though it was in *A Clockwork Orange* that Burgess made his most forceful contribution to the genre of the cacotopian vision.

1985 traces the adventures of Bev (= Beveridge, Bevan, or Bevin) Jones, a successor to Winston Smith who is pitted not against Big Brother but against the bullying brethren of strikebound Tucland (England under the heel of the Trades Union Congress). Having torn up his union card in an act of desperate rebellion, Bev is made homeless and eventually finds himself sent to a Rehabilitation Centre. Here he is browbeaten by a bespectacled academic, physically beaten by two working-class bruisers, and pleasured on the house by Mavis, a former history teacher. Unrepentant, he next joins an armed opposition group led by the self-styled Colonel Lawrence and financed by a consortium of Arab princes, one of whom debauches his daughter. Finally, Bev is committed to an insane asylum, where he takes his life, as much from boredom as anything else. 'History was a record of the long slow trek from Eden towards the land of Nod, with nothing but the deserts of injustice on the way', he reflects (p. 219). Tucland, meanwhile, muddles on.

As a satirical exposé of Britain in the 1970s this is feeble stuff, the work of an expatriate novelist with a stereotyped notion of the targets he is attacking. Its inspiration is perhaps largely literary, since it burlesques not only *Nineteen Eighty-Four* but *The Road to Wigan Pier* with its injunctions to the middle classes to drop their pretensions and throw in their lot with the workers. Orwell is remembered as a minor social critic ('"You have nothing to lose but your aitches", he said') who died fighting in the Spanish Civil War (p. 164). The lost aitch is one of the principal features of the new Workers' English—a dialect which Burgess outlines in an epilogue carefully modelled on Orwell's appendix on Newspeak. The serio-comic tale of Bev Jones reflects Burgess's ingenious and liberating conviction that

Two Versions of Cacotopia

Nineteen Eighty-Four is 'essentially a comic book'—a compound
of music-hall grotesqueries and self-lacerating private jokes
meant to keep a personal horror at bay. Room 101 in Broadcasting House was the studio from which Orwell broadcast
propaganda to India. Hatred of the Enemy was taught to
National Servicemen, and Big Brother, Burgess recalls, featured
in the advertisements for a pre-war correspondence college. The
clocks striking thirteen come from the same stable of humour as
Wigan Pier. In *The Road to Wigan Pier* itself, Orwell accused
H.G. Wells of populating one of his future cities with armies of
debased industrial workers in order to 'make your flesh creep.'
There is an inordinate amount of flesh-creeping in *Nineteen
Eighty-Four*, but very little in Burgess's fictive 'sequel', which
never for one moment persuades us that it is tragedy rather than
farce. Not even *A Clockwork Orange*, despite the reputation of
Kubrick's film, haunts us in the way that Orwell's nightmare
does. There are, of course, manifest differences of talent and
temperament (and arguably Orwell's book is not really as funny
as Burgess makes out). Yet Burgess's inability or unwillingness
to profoundly disturb our sensibilities also points to the literary
and ideological differences between the two writers.

There is, in Burgess's view, something deficient in Orwell's
understanding of the nature of freedom. *Nineteen Eighty-Four* is
an 'allegory of the eternal conflict between any individual and
any collective' (*1985*, p. 82), but it misstates that conflict, since
Orwell 'could see the possibility of evil only in the State. Evil
was not for the individual: original sin was a doctrine to be
derided' (p. 60). Against Orwell's secular, liberal-humanist view
of man, Burgess sets his own conservative and Christian position
based on a synthesis of the Pelagian doctrine of free will and the
Augustinian doctrine of original sin. Readers will recognise this
position from his previous works: in *The Wanting Seed*, for
example, the cacotopian bureaucracy oscillates between
extremes of liberal paternalism ('Pelphase') and martial
repression ('Gusphase'). The agony of *Nineteen Eighty-Four*
results, in his view, from Orwell's dilemma as an 'inveterate
proponent of free will' (p. 87) and thus of human perfectibility.
It is, in fact, proportionate to the depth of its author's
commitment to socialism.

At this level the opposition between Orwell and Burgess is

175

that of the radical liable to shattering disillusionment and the conservative immune to political hopes; and these positions are familiar enough. One can answer Burgess by saying that the renunciation of any vision of political progress and change is a genuine impoverishment. Burgess counters the generalisations of socialism by preaching the virtue of individual Christian love. He does not say how we can love our neighbours without wishing to help those of them who are victims of injustice. He suggests Orwell's Pelagianism was a comforting illusion, but it is no less comforting for Burgess to regard this Old Etonian who sought to join the proletariat as a thwarted human being, who would eventually find himself trapped by "a personal despair of being able to love" (p. 102). However, I wish to get beyond the *impasse* of this kind of debate by arguing that Burgess's reading of the text of *Nineteen Eighty-Four* has not been close enough. He has manifestly overlooked some of the sources of its universality and power.

He correctly identifies the weakness of Winston's love for Julia, when invoked as a principle on which to base his opposition to the state:

> The main fictional weakness of *Nineteen Eighty-Four* lies here. There is an insufficiency of conflict between the individual's view of love and the State's. Winston and Julia do not oppose to Big Brother the strength of a true marital union and, by extension, the values of the family. They have fornicated clandestinely and been caught naked in the act. There is a sad moment when Julia, whose sole notion of freedom is the right to be sexually promiscuous, gives Winston a potted history of her love affairs. Winston rejoices in her corruption, and Orwell seems to abet the false antithesis—oppose to the moral evils of the State the moral evils of the individual. (p. 98)

It is impossible that Orwell could have been unaware that the Winston-Julia relationship had, as Burgess puts it, 'death in it from the start.' Who is not shocked by Winston's insistence that, the more corrupt Julia is, the more he loves her? (It is even possible that Julia was shocked.) There are many incidents in the book which refute the allegation that Orwell could see the possibility of evil only in the state. Both as a child and as an adult Winston is capable of evil. As a child he steals his sister's chocolate ration. As an adult he joins (or thinks he is joining) the

Brotherhood, promising O'Brien that he will do whatever he is ordered to do, even if it means throwing acid in a child's face. This degrading oath cannot be redeemed by his refusal to betray Julia if asked to—a refusal which, in any case, is initiated by Julia and not by Winston. Winston is certainly not shown as being untainted by evil. But the question of the source of that evil—whether it is innate, or the result of the subtle corruptions of his environment, or even (just possibly) something that has been programmed into him—remains obscure.

In *Nineteen Eighty-Four*, Burgess claims, 'we hear very little about the scientific takeover of the free mind' (p. 84). It is true that O'Brien requires a *voluntary* submission from Winston. Yet, earlier, Winston experiences dreams and premonitions which help to undermine the idea that he is a free agent. He dreams of O'Brien saying 'We shall meet in the place where there is no darkness'; he dreams of Julia throwing off her clothes in the Golden Country. Is it possible that these premonitions were implanted by the (aptly named?) Thought Police? Where else could they have come from? If not from the Thought Police, how is it that O'Brien gets to know about them? Despite the mass of criticism on *Nineteen Eighty-Four* (much of it devoted not to the fiction itself but to the ideas or supposed ideas behind it) the question of Winston's dreams is scarcely ever addressed. A common-sense view might presumably regard them as mere sinister coincidences, or as the unheeded warnings of Winston's unconscious, or as devices to whip up the haunted atmosphere of the Orwellian nightmare. None of these explanations is satisfactory; though it should be remembered that at least one critic has argued that Winston is a textbook case of paranoid schizophrenia,[2] in which case his mind would be playing tricks on him throughout. And then there is the question of Julia herself. Who is she?

Is she really just a 'rebel from the waist down', a sexual adventurer, as we are told? Until she seduces him Winston hates and fears Julia as an agent of the Thought Police or at least an amateur spy. Once we start to question the mutual frankness of Julia and Winston[3] it is hard not to think of Julia as a possible spy, or, better, as a decoy; in other words, as someone who might have been 'turned' by O'Brien or another of the members of the Inner Party with whom she has been intimate. (Winston, for his

177

part, is surely dishonest with himself about the source of the excitement he feels when he learns of these intimacies.) Julia, apparently, grows genuinely fond of Winston, which is why she shares his eventual downfall. Her role as temptress, together with her knowledge of the Inner Party, suggests a Mata Hari rather than a wholesome example of the liberated woman. Perhaps, like the history teacher in *1985*, she is both. It is true that Julia is eventually tortured to the point of losing her sexual attractiveness, but on Oceania there is no reason to suppose that a police spy would be safer than a minor official like Winston. Orwell often pokes fun at Winston's paranoia, of which his initial hatred of Julia is an example. Yet in yielding to her advances, as well as to the fascination of O'Brien and to the intoxicating freedom of the room above Mr Charrington's shop, he almost knowingly co-operates in his own betrayal. His behaviour is less that of a rebel than of a helpless victim, and his moments of lucidity occur between extremes of self-pity and paranoid rage.

It is here that we must locate the *modernity* (in Matthew Arnold's sense) of Orwell's nightmare; that is, its adequacy as an expression of the human dilemma in an age of guns, bombs, and concentration camps. It is also this feature, leading to Room 101 and to O'Brien's revelation that he knows the content of Winston's dreams, which has led many readers to view *Nineteen Eighty-Four* as a sick book, the product of a distraught mind. The ambiguity with which Orwell invests Winston and Julia extends to the one oppositional force in the state, the so-called Brotherhood, into which they are inducted by O'Brien. The oath they take degrades them to a level indistinguishable from the Inner Party or the Thought Police, and, indeed, if it were not so far-fetched, one might suppose that the privilege it brings—that of the opportunity to read *The Theory and Practice of Oligarchical Collectivism* by Emmanual Goldstein—is a privilege of Inner Party Membership. Julia's and Winston's refusal to promise to betray one another constitutes disloyalty to the Brotherhood, but, of course, they are later tortured for it by the Party.

In this moment of belated and selfish affirmation of human love (what value can it have when one has promised to throw acid at a child?), Julia prompts Winston to declare the sexual 'weakness' that compromises him both as Party member and as the Brotherhood's potential recruit. There is nothing, except the literal terms of the oath—and we know, in Oceania, what they are worth—to contradict the supposition that the mythical Brotherhood *is* the Inner Party. In this case, Winston has narrowly but decisively failed a test which would have made him a potential secret agent for the Party—whether from conviction or from fear of exposure would have made little difference—rather than one of its tortured victims. The point of such conjectures is to highlight the book's appalling ambiguities; my own conclusion is that no explanation which has yet been proposed will cover all the relevant facts.

When writing his diary, or in his spontaneous life in the room above Mr Charrington's shop, Winston does momentarily transcend the status of addicted, self-deluded victim which governs so many of his actions. But it is his masochistic weakness which finally enables him to love Big Brother. Burgess argues that a man with a more robust conscience would have been able to discount his enforced betrayal of Julia in Room 101. Between them 'an even stronger fidelity—reinforced by renewed hatred of the manipulators'—could have ensued. Whether this is true or not, Winston's defences are sapped as much from within as they are from without. Critics such as Alan Sandison and Christopher Small have examined *Nineteen Eighty-Four*'s unresolved ambiguities—the products of a tortured imagination which, apparently, eluded Orwell's own rational control—in specifically theological terms.[4] What emerges from any such examination is that Orwell's theme of self-delusion and inner betrayal states the problem of the individual and the collectivity in a far more disturbing way than do the traditional concepts of 'evil' and 'original sin' invoked by Burgess. The 'free individual' whom Winston sees in O'Brien's mirror—the 'inner heart' symbolised by his cherished glass paperweight—can only be a delusion. Winston's inner freedom has been violated at the moment the novel begins.

Yet, though Winston is trapped and internally corrupt from the start, *Nineteen Eighty-Four* still prompts a powerful reaction in favour of human freedom in the minds of its readers. This is the paradox of the naturalistic novel, where a portrayal of men as the helpless victims of their social environment frequently stimulates the reader to outrage rather than despair. Zola distinguished between determinism, which leaves open the possibility that social conditions could be altered by human action, and fatalism which holds that they cannot. Yet it is perhaps the fictionality of the naturalistic cacotopia that is at issue, rather than Zola's somewhat dubious distinction. We do not identify with Winston's self-delusions, which at times are clearly intended as shocking. We identify rather with his suffering. The fictional form both subjects us to, and insulates us against, the full impact of Orwell's nightmare. No subsequent reading of *Nineteen Eighty-Four* is likely to be as rawly emotional an experience as one's first reading of the book. Yet, after a first reading, Winston and Julia linger in many minds as relatively uncomplicated figures, true lovers and brave rebels.

*

Beside Winston Smith, the heroes of Anthony Burgess's cacotopias are much more straightforward specimens of Bourgeois Man. Tristram Foxe in *The Wanting Seed* and Bev Jones in *1985* are both ex-history teachers whose refusal to conform lands them in a series of picaresque adventures. There is something desultory about their wanderings, so that they strike us more as fictive devices to enable Burgess to unfold their respective societies than as genuine or would-be free spirits. Neither has much life of his own. Since everything they do is 'in character', their function is to propagandise for the free individual without ever forcing us to consider what such freedom might mean. Their gestures of independence satisfy the formal demands of the narrative without deeply engaging the reader's imagination.

It is different with Alex, the teenage gang-leader and narrator of *A Clockwork Orange*, who at first glance would appear to represent anything but Bourgeois Man. Yet, though Burgess now looks back on this most celebrated of his novels with some slight embarrassment, the lesson of *A Clockwork Orange* is still central for him:

> It is better to have our streets infested with murderous young
> hoodlums than to deny individual freedom of choice.... The evil, or
> merely wrong, products of free will may be punished or held off with
> deterrents, but the faculty itself may not be removed.
>
> *(1985*, p. 93)

Alex, it will be remembered, is imprisoned for manslaughter and
then lured into undergoing an experimental Reclamation
Treatment by the prospect of an early release. The Treatment
consists of aversion therapy which destroys his enjoyment of
thuggery, and, as an unforeseen side-effect, of music, literature,
and sex. He makes an unsuccessful suicide attempt, after which
the effects of the therapy wear off. Subsequently Alex, who has
become the leader of another gang, gives up violence of his own
accord; he has turned eighteen, nature has taken its course and he
is ready to 'go straight.'[5]

'*Alex* is a rich and noble name, and I intended its possessor to
be sympathetic, pitiable, and insidiously identifiable with us',
Burgess writes in *1985* (p. 92). One of its meanings is *a lex*: without
a law. Alex is, of necessity, a literary creation, a transformation of
the teenage hoodlum into 'your little droog', 'your Humble [and
highly articulate] Narrator.' Among Burgess's battery of devices
for making him sympathetic are his linguistic command, his love
of classical music, and his sense of belonging in the same league of
precocious youths as Mozart and Rimbaud. He is one of
'Bakunin's Children', the spokesmen of intergenerational warfare
to whom Burgess devotes a surprisingly sympathetic chapter in
1985. In addition, *A Clockwork Orange* suggests its kinship with
such novels of the 1950s as J.D. Salinger's *The Catcher in the Rye*
and Colin MacInnes's *Absolute Beginners*. Like Salinger's and
MacInnes's teenage heroes, Alex has seen it all before he should
even have begun. 'That was everything. I'd done the lot, now.
And me still only fifteen' (p. 60), he reflects in prison. Burgess's
characteristic linguistic virtuosity is here deployed in the creation
of *nadsat*, a teenage argot based on Russian vocabulary with
some added bits of Romany. (The Russian is said to have entered
their heads by 'subliminal penetration.') Another significant trait,
which contributes to our sense that we have here a
romanticisation of the bandit or ruffian no less blatant than the
left-wing romanticisation of the urban guerrilla, is Alex's obvious

attraction towards the bookish types whom he delights in mugging. He has no difficulty in grasping the meanings of the title of the book one of them is writing—*A Clockwork Orange*. After this, it is no surprise that he is able to expound Burgess's own theory of original sin:

> Badness is of the self, the one, the you or me on our oddy knockies, and that self is made by old Bog or God and is his great pride and radosty. But the not-self cannot have the bad, meaning they of the government and the judges and the schools cannot allow the bad because they cannot allow the self. And is not our modern history, my brothers, the story of brave malenky selves fighting these big machines? I am serious with you, brothers, over this. (p. 34)

Scratch the most unlikely of Burgess's heroes and he is liable to turn into a history teacher. One can see why its author now describes *A Clockwork Orange* as 'too didactic, too linguistically exhibitionist' (*1985*, p. 91).

*

Alex's counterparts in *1985* are the still more improbable 'kumina youths', bands of Robin Hood-style Blacks who have started an Underground University—staffed by unemployed history teachers!—to keep alive the outlawed traditional culture. They are philosophers of violence, taking their cue from Shakespeare ('Literature teaches revenge') among others. They talk and chant in Latin while engaging in multiple pederastic rape. These amateurs of the *vie de bohème*, late twentieth-century style, do not have to be taken seriously; but Alex, who uses Beethoven and Mozart as background music for his private theatre of pornographic violence, evidently does. ('I am serious with you, brothers.') How is it that Alex can indulge his sadistic fantasies to the accompaniment, not of the 'hideous, grinding' sounds of Orwell's Two Minutes' Hate, but of the Ode to Joy in Beethoven's Ninth, without internal conflict? Should not such a response to Beethoven be regarded, not merely as startling and brutal, but as psychopathic and perverse? This would seem to be the real problem with *A Clockwork Orange*, though it is one that Burgess would dismiss, apparently, as of no more than secondary interest.

'Oh bliss, bliss and heaven', Alex exclaims, listening to a violin concerto and imagining an orgy of indiscriminate violence against men, women and girls (p. 29). When he loses his enjoyment of music as a result of the Treatment, the reader is moved to indignation at this destruction of his personality. Yet what Burgess is portraying here is surely a type of mental derangement. It is a bit tame to suggest that this is something Alex will simply grow out of. (Possibly the only thing he can grow up into is a novelist!) At issue here is the idea of the moral neutrality of art, which Burgess asserts in a passage in *1985* where he discusses George Steiner's example of the camp commandant in Nazi Germany, who, having supervised the killing of a thousand Jews, went home to hear his daughter play a Schubert sonata and cried with 'holy joy.' Burgess argues that there is no real mystery in this:

> The answer is that the good of music has nothing to do with ethics. Art does not elevate us into beneficence. It is morally neutral, like the taste of an apple. (p. 58)

This is scarcely convincing. The camp commandant's achievement, perhaps, was to show how efficient a machine the human brain can be when it is determined, at all costs, to play out a particular role. His impressions are kept in rigidly separate compartments. Art, unlike apples, is man-made and we are right to recognise something perverse in this. Alex's achievement, by contrast, is one of yoking heterogeneous impressions violently together. His is a much more difficult, unlikely, and (it might be argued) insane feat than the camp commandant's, since the latter does not find that his holy joy at Schubert's sonata consists in fantasies of killing Jews. If this is correct, we can only consider it a gross sentimentality when, in the final chapter which is missing from some editions of the novel, Burgess shows Alex growing up into 'normality.'

Our little droog, it turns out, has unconsciously, as it were, cut out a newspaper photograph of a baby and put it in his pocket! Boys will be boys—with, alas, a little of the old ultra-violence—but one day they grow up, and you can tell by the fact that they start dreaming of a son. The truth is that Alex's path to normality can only be miraculous or unreliable (he is, let it be remembered, a first-person narrator). The suggestion that nature, by an unexplained miracle, could do the job bungled by therapy seems confused, and perhaps even dishonest; this is not the sort of ambiguity that enriches a novelist's portrayal of character. Both *A Clockwork Orange* and *The Wanting Seed* have upbeat endings, invoking a philoprogenitiveness which seems to owe as much to divine grace as to biology. The nightmare of cacotopian perversity and sterility has lifted. The fictional part of *1985* does not end in this manner. Bev Jones, having utterly failed in his mission of protest—a mission conferred upon him by the last, unforgiving words of his dying wife—has no choice left but to commit suicide. His is a thoroughly honourable suicide, but is not one that makes our flesh creep or interferes, even in the smallest way, with our enjoyment. In artistic terms, does Bev Jones amount to much more than his cardboard adversary, the Tucland emblem of Bill the Symbolic Worker? *1985*'s portrayal of a Last Bourgeois Man so sure of his own identity, so free of traumas, so innocent of any complicity with the forces that have defeated him, belongs to the entertainment industry rather than to that future time to which, 'from the age of doublethink', Winston Smith sent his greetings.

12

A Novel for Our Time:
V.S. Naipaul's *Guerrillas*

I

I think there's an element of nostalgia in reading Hardy, and even in reading Dickens or George Eliot. There is narrative there, the slow development of character, and people are longing for this vanished, ordered world. Today, every man's experience of dislocation is so private that unless a writer absolutely matches that particular man's experience the writer seems very private and obscure. So I think the art of fiction is becoming a curious, shattered thing....I think it may be that the world now requires another kind of imaginative interpretation.[1]

An autobiography can distort; facts can be realigned. But fiction never lies: it reveals the writer totally.[2]

Of the five contemporary novelists considered in Part II of this book, Anthony Burgess, Muriel Spark and Doris Lessing were born in 1917, 1918, and 1919 respectively. V.S.Naipaul and B.S.Johnson belong to a younger generation, having been born in 1932 and 1933. These novelists are 'English' in the sense that their life and work has been centred in Britain and the Commonwealth rather than the United States. For all that, two are resident in Mediterranean countries, one (Muriel Spark) is of Scottish-Jewish descent, and both Muriel Spark and Doris Lessing spent much of their childhood in Southern Africa. V.S.Naipaul is a Trinidad East Indian. Several of the five (like most successful English writers of the century) probably derive a large proportion of their income from the United States. Only Johnson, a Londoner and a London novelist, satisfies *all* the standard criteria of 'Englishness'—or did so, that is, at the time of his suicide in 1973.

V.S.Naipaul's characters are, as often as not, homeless expatriates. Like them, their creator has no fixed audience or close-knit community to which he belongs. He is not even a 'novelist's novelist' in the Jamesian or Conradian sense, having shown himself to be as uneasy about the inherited traditions of the novel as any of his contemporaries. His novels do not seem to have been written according to predetermined patterns or preconceived theories, and they have appeared at irregular and increasingly lengthy intervals. He has spoken of writing as an instinctive, unconscious process: 'The world abrades one, one comes to certain resolutions and then one devises by instinct and through dreams and all kinds of senses a story that is a symbol for all this'.[3] Novels and stories are offered to him (as he once put it)[4] from time to time, though in the last dozen years he has published only two of them, *Guerrillas* (1975) and *A Bend in the River* (1979). Meanwhile, his writing and his occasional interviews have emphasised the contemporary novelist's idiosyncrasy, his determined isolation and cherished independence of his fellow-writers, groups and movements.

The belief that a writer's identity lies in his or her unpredictability and independence is a defining characteristic of the culture in which Lessing, Spark and Burgess, as well as Naipaul, are significant names. B.S.Johnson was another dedicated individualist, the leader, as it were, of a literary movement that was never permitted to attract more than one member. Almost any other contemporary English novelist of repute could be chosen to illustrate the same qualities of pluralism and idiosyncrasy. Literary theory would argue, however, that the individualism of these writers is simply one of the delusions of bourgeois liberalism.

It is curious that two of the opposing literary dogmas of the age—the creed of authorial independence and the structuralist theory of the 'death of the author'—should particularly attach themselves to the writing of novels. (Roland Barthes' seminal essay 'The Death of the Author', for instance, begins and ends with the question of whether Balzac was an 'Author').[5] Naipaul has described the novel as a literary form 'born at the same time as the spirit of rebellion', which 'expresses, on the aesthetic plane, the same ambition'.⁶ The concept of 'rebellion', which Naipaul derives from Albert Camus' *The Rebel*, refers in the first instance not to collective upheaval but to the action of an individual, which is 'representative' to the extent that it comes to be seen as focal and symbolic. The novel also is an act of individual, not of collective, creation. Unlike works for the cinema, the theatre and the concert hall, it is not dependent on the dynamics of group performance for its realisation. At the same time, novels are composed of time-honoured structures and devices whose function it is to disguise and dissipate their origins in the work of named individual producers. These devices, such as the fictitious narrator, the multiplication of internal discourses and the artificiality of the narrative situation have understandably been emphasised by formalist and poststructuralist criticism.

In the past, many novels not only had a fictitious narrator but remained anonymous or pseudonymous on their first appearance. Yet the novel as Naipaul has defined it—as an expression of the spirit of rebellion—cannot forever remain anonymous. The fact that anonymous or pseudonymous novels have often been presented as 'authentic' and 'non-fictional' documents before their authorship was revealed suggests that a novel, like an act of rebellion, may be constituted as such at the moment when somebody claims the responsibility for it. A hold-up or a bomb explosion requires the signature of an individual or an organisation in order to be construed as an act of rebellion or sabotage; and much the same may be said of the way that we recognise a novel. But the author remains invisible, 'underground', even though he has put his name to the text; all we know for certain is that the visible fictive structure is his handiwork. To recognise the author behind the fiction requires an inductive leap comparable to the leap we make when we come to see a crime or a display of intransigence as an intelligible act of rebellion.

This argument suggests that, if the 'death of the author' proclaimed by literary theory had indeed taken place, the novel could survive only as a 'curious, shattered thing', a feeble anachronism. On the other hand, if the novel remains healthy it is surely because the inductive leap which converts literary structures into forms of individual expression is still everywhere capable of being made. The two epigraphs to this chapter (which both date from the early 1970s) show how Naipaul, for one, has oscillated between the paralysis of doubt and the energy of faith. Both the moment of doubt and the moment of renewed energy are implicit in the dialectics of the novel as an act of self-assertive rebellion. As for Naipaul's expressed belief that fiction 'never lies', that it 'reveals the writer totally'—these statements are no less true for being, on the face of it, outrageous paradoxes. It is as if he were calmly declaring that the ideal of a morally transparent art of fiction—the ideal towards which B.S.Johnson had so valiantly and yet so laboriously striven—was attainable, as it were, by default: that fiction always reveals the author (just as the deed reveals its perpetrator) whether he likes it or not. This belief bespeaks a confidence in liberal humanism which Johnson, for one, could not feel. But Naipaul's liberalism is not of a traditional sort, any more than his fiction belongs to such crude theoretical categories as 'classic realism' or the 'conventional novel'. To make this case we must turn to *Guerrillas*, a major novel which I shall interpret as Naipaul's answer, given in the mid-1970s, to the question of the 'kind of imaginative interpretation' which the world now requires.

II

Does fiction 'never lie'? Does it 'reveal the writer totally'? The cliché of 'imaginative interpretation' is a reminder that the novel occupies a middle ground between journalism (which almost inevitably lies as it attempts to tell the truth) and fantasy (which reveals the writer even in the act of concealing him). The plot of *Guerrillas* shows marked similarities with a series of actual events in Naipaul's native Trinidad in 1971–2—events which he has outlined in a penetrating journalistic essay, 'Michael X and the Black Power Killings in Trinidad' (1980). When *Guerrillas* first appeared some reviewers, aware of these events, mistook it for a documentary novel rather than a work of imaginative invention. It is not a documentary, as comparison with Naipaul's essay makes clear. Yet the essay also argues that the 'actual events' in Trinidad represented a horrifying and revealing acting-out of the fantasies of those responsible for them; and

Naipaul in turn has fantasised about the events and has used his fantasy to explore the revelatory relations of the real and the fantastic. If the result is to be classed as fictional 'realism' then it is the realistic fiction of a fantasy age.

Even the title is a fantasy, for in *Guerrillas* no one is a guerrilla (though there is one disillusioned ex-guerrilla) and yet everyone fantasises about guerrillas. On the unnamed Caribbean island in which the novel is set 'the newspaper, the radio and the television spoke of guerrillas'[7], but nobody really knows why they do so. The crimes and acts of violence that occur could be the manifestations of an organised revolutionary group, but it seems far more likely that they are the work of isolated bandits, fanatical sects, and criminal gangs. The government, however, has an interest in proving that the 'guerrillas' exist, and can be defeated, once it is confident of putting an end to the disturbances. The world-wide cult of the guerrilla which has inflamed the imaginations of many people on the island is responsible both for the spread of this collective fantasy and for the possibility of exploiting it.

A guerrilla is an irregular soldier. However, there are many other activities which overlap with guerrilla warfare to some extent, so that bandits, outlaws, terrorists, assassins, rebellious peasants, and agrarian revolutionaries all came to be associated with the cult of the guerrilla (which reached its height at the time of the killing of Che Guevara in Bolivia in 1967). *Guerrillas* is constructed around the figure of Jimmy Ahmed, a would-be revolutionary leader whose 'agricultural commune' on a disused colonial plantation is looked upon by the authorities as a 'cover for the guerrillas' (p.213). Although some parallels could be drawn with events in Jamaica and Grenada as well as Trinidad, the model for Jimmy Ahmed is Michael Abdul Malik, the former Black Power leader known as 'Michael X' who was hanged in Trinidad in 1975. Four years earlier, Michael X had returned to his and Naipaul's native island, where he started a commune on a suburban plot near Port of Spain. The produce of the $1\frac{1}{2}$-acre strip of land was to be sold at a 'People's Store'. Far from becoming a base for agrarian reform, the commune was soon torn apart by the murder of two of its own members.

It is a reflection of the well-publicised spread of guerrilla and terrorist activities in the last twenty years that there has grown up a genre of 'terrorist novels', comparable perhaps to the industrial novels of the 1840s and to the anarchist novels of the 1880s and '90s. In addition to *Guerrillas*, Doris Lessing's *The Good Terrorist*, Muriel Spark's *The Only Problem*, Brian Moore's *The Revolution Script*, Angus Wilson's *Setting the World on Fire*, and Raymond Williams's *The Volunteers* may be mentioned as examples of the form. Closely related to it are novels of violent social revolution, such as Nadine Gordimer's *July's People*, and novels of state terrorism and social upheaval such as Margaret Atwood's *Bodily Harm* and Naipaul's own *In a Free State*. Many of these novels portray political violence from a 'middle-class' standpoint, but its handling in *Guerrillas* is unusually indirect: we do not even get an eye-witness account of the riots in which Jimmy Ahmed briefly emerges as a popular leader. Naipaul's most distinctive contribution to the 'terrorist novel', however, is his exploration of the symbiotic relations between revolutionary violence and literary fantasy. He has quoted a witness of the urban guerrillas in Argentina in the early 1970s as saying that 'They see themselves as a kind of comic-book hero. Clark Kent in the office by day, Superman at night, with a gun' (*REP*, p.98). Of the murder of the Englishwoman Gale Benson, planned by Michael Abdul Malik and Hakim Jamal (an American Black Power campaigner) in Trinidad in 1971, Naipaul has written as follows:

> This was a literary murder, if ever there was one. Writing led both men there: for both of them, uneducated, but clever, hustlers with the black cause always to hand, operating always among the converted or half-converted, writing had for too long been a public relations exercise, a form of applauded lie, fantasy. And in Arima it was a fantasy of power that led both men to contemplate, from their different standpoints, the act of murder....Benson, English and middle class, was just the victim Malik needed: his novel began to come to life. (*REP*, p.76)

Naipaul is probably unique among commentators on the Malik case in focussing on Michael X's unfinished novel, a primitive narrative which nevertheless serves as a 'pattern book, a guide to later events' (*REP*, p.67). In it he was 'settling scores with the English middle class' (p.76). *Guerrillas*, like 'Michael X and the

Black Power Killings in Trinidad', tells the story of a literary murder, and in a certain sense both works are extended pieces of literary criticism.

Jimmy Ahmed's public statements, such as his '*Communique No 1*' (*G*, pp.16–17) and his noticeboard advertising the 'PEOPLE'S COMMUNE/ FOR THE LAND AND THE REVOLUTION' (p.12), are themselves a species of fiction. In addition, *Guerrillas* offers lengthy extracts from Ahmed's correspondence and from the novel he is trying to write. Both Naipaul's novel and his essay on Michael X can be read as the work of a genuine novelist relentlessly exposing a bad and bogus one. In the essay, Michael X is portrayed as the creator of an elaborate murder plot: 'When he transferred his fantasy to real life', Naipaul observes, ' he went to work like the kind of novelist he would have liked to be' (*REP*, p.89). Whether or not Jimmy Ahmed's involvement in murder is premeditated to this extent is hard to determine; on the whole it seems unlikely. The murder in *Guerrillas* is felt as inevitable and is the outcome of a powerful literary logic—but the 'author' of this particular plot is V.S.Naipaul, not one of his characters.

Jimmy Ahmed has named his commune 'Thrushcross Grange'. In the opening paragraphs Jane, an Englishwoman, and Roche, a politically exiled white South African, are on their way to visit the Grange. Jimmy, Roche explains, 'took a writing course', and *Wuthering Heights* was one of the books he had to read. 'I think he just likes the name', Roche adds (p.10). But Jimmy, a half-breed who claims to have been born in a Chinese grocery, identifies with Heathcliff, to whom Catherine Earnshaw once said that 'Your mother was an Indian princess and your father was the Emperor of China' (p.62). Jimmy's self-projection as Heathcliff makes him one of the line of literary fantasists—including Ganesh Ransumair, the mystic masseur, B. (for Black) Wordsworth, the poet of Miguel Street, and Mr Biswas, sign-painter and journalist[8]—who had been the central figures of Naipaul's early fictions. The comic innocence of those earlier books is summed up in the figure of Elias, the slum boy in *Miguel Street* (1959) who pronounces 'literature' as 'litricher' ('it sounded like something to eat, something rich like chocolate'[9]). But Jimmy's mispronunciations, such as 'T'rush-cross Grange' and 'Wur-thering Heights' (p.10), have a more sinister sound.

Guerrillas makes other references to the Victorian novel. Naipaul has mentioned Jean Rhys as the pioneer of West Indian fiction,[10] and *Guerrillas*, like Rhys's *Wide Sargasso Sea*, has some crucial echoes of *Jane Eyre*. The heroine is called Jane, she is English, and she is associated with air travel, flying in near the beginning of the novel and being on the verge of using her return air ticket to the end; finally the fiction of her departure by air is used to cover up the fact of her murder. Jane, whose mind is a morass of borrowed notions and half-baked radical opinions, might be called Jane Air (she has no other surname). She is torn between two lovers—Roche, who has come to the island to work in public relations for one of the old colonial trading companies, and Jimmy—a choice faintly reminiscent of Jane Eyre's choice between St John Rivers and Mr Rochester, especially as Jimmy has a prior commitment in the form of his homosexual relationship with the psychopathic slum-boy Bryant. Socially the situations of Jane and her Mr Rochester have been reversed: he is the orphan, she is the 'blanche' or white lady. Yet her status cannot protect her from the series of violations foreshadowed when Bryant, aware that she is beginning her liaison with Jimmy, calls her the 'white rat' (*G*, p.90). (Jane Eyre, it will be remembered, was called a 'rat' by her arch-enemy John Reed.)[11]

The tragedy of *Guerrillas* takes the form it does because Jimmy's affair with Jane arouses Bryant's latent fury. Jimmy has been described as a 'succubus', a word that Jane is forced to look up (pp.31, 60); this may mean that he has a demonic nature like Heathcliff, or it may be a codeword for homosexuality. Jimmy's ambitions are not confined to being the leader of an agricultural commune, 'buggering a couple of slum boys' in the bush (p.142). But despite the bravado of his public statements, in private he is a lost and disillusioned man in whose eyes the 'revolution' has become devalued to endless, anarchic and pointless struggle. As he writes to an English friend,

Things are desperate Roy, when the leader himself begins to yield to despair, things are bad. The whole place is going to blow up, I cannot see how I can control the revolution now. When everybody wants to fight there's nothing to fight for. Everybody wants to fight his own little war, everbody is a guerrilla. (p.87)

V.S. Naipaul's *Guerrillas*

(The last two sentences here supply Naipaul with his title and epigraph.) Many strands in Jimmy's make-up, including fear and something one can only describe as generosity, go into the promise he makes, immediately after writing these words, to pacify Bryant (who has just seen the 'white rat'):

> He went and put his hands on Bryant's shoulders. His fingers pressed against the gritty jersey and the damp skin below. He took his face close to Bryant's and said, 'I'll give her to you'. (p.90)

The 'gift' of Jane to Bryant cannot be paralleled in *Jane Eyre* or *Wuthering Heights*; on the contrary, love is fiercely possessive in the Brontë novels. We are in the presence of an older literary stereotype, to which a slender clue may be given by Jane's reading-matter shortly before she is murdered. For why should Jane, a representative of a section of the middle class which Naipaul has described as 'the people who keep up with "revolution" as with the theatre, the revolutionaries who visit centres of revolution, but with return air tickets, the people for whom Malik's kind of Black Power was an exotic but safe brothel' (*REP*, p.35)—why should Jane with her fate hanging over her be found indulging in such 'safe' reading as a copy of Hardy's *The Woodlanders* (G, pp.222, 252)? Is it coincidence that the idea of the greenwood—the forest in which men struggle to maintain their independence and comradeship in defiance of the state apparatus—is subtly connected with Jimmy's 'agricultural commune'?

The Thrushcross Grange communiqué, a 'fairy story, a school composition, ungrammatical and confused, about life in the forest', begins as follows:

> *All revolutions begin with the land. Men are born on the earth, every man has his one spot, it is his birth right, and men must claim their portion of the earth in brotherhood and harmony. In this spirit we came an intrepid band to virgin forest, it is the life style and philosophy of Thrushcross Grange. (p.17)*

Thrushcross Grange is not 'virgin forest' but an abandoned plantation originally developed in the days of slavery. Jimmy, whose personal slogan is *'I'm Nobody's Slave or Stallion, I'm a*

Warrior and Torch Bearer' (p.17), ironically refers to Roche, the agent of the trading company which helps him with supplies, as 'Massa'. Fear of Jimmy and the power he might exert over the dispossessed has caused the leading capitalists of the island to subsidise the commune, which is ostensibly serving a useful purpose by rescuing slum-boys from a life of unemployment and gang warfare. Jimmy's description of his commune as an 'intrepid band' makes him a Robin Hood figure, and, since his threats have produced a small amount of charitable redistribution, he might actually claim to be robbing the rich and giving to the poor. The historian E.J.Hobsbawm has described Robin Hood as 'the quintessence of bandit legend',[12] and Jimmy Ahmed's self-image corresponds, at most points, with Hobsbawm's analysis of the image of the Noble Robber which forms part of the world-wide mythology of peasant societies. Jimmy, that is, sees himself as a victim of injustice and persecution whose mission it is to right wrongs, to take from the rich and give to the poor, and to kill only in self-defence or just revenge ('I have no gun, I'm no guerrilla', he says (p.28)). Jimmy relies on getting popular support, and for a brief moment when the poor quarters of the city erupt into rioting he becomes their leader. In all this he seems to be a twentieth-century radical intellectual playing at the role of Noble Robber or primitive rebel.[13] At the end he is waiting to be hunted down by the authorities. Naipaul certainly does not glamorise the Noble Robber, but he takes this figure seriously, in a way that (for example) Muriel Spark in her recent novel *The Only Problem* singularly refuses to do. (To the extent that *The Only Problem* contains a subsidiary Robin Hood theme, Spark's sympathies lie unambiguously with the Sheriff of Nottingham.) Spark's international terrorist and bank robber, Effie, embarks on her career as a result of stealing two bars of chocolate from a petrol station. Her rich travelling companions are merely embarrassed by this woman who 'ate her chocolate inveighing, meanwhile against the capitalist system'.[14] It is the companions, not Effie, who arouse Spark's curiosity and interest. *The Only Problem* is the work of a novelist who can only caricature and trivialise the issue which is fundamental to any prospect of real social justice and equality: the issue of forcible redistribution.

In Naipaul, redistribution and the circulation of commodities become the subject of a profoundly disturbing series of actions. Jane, the revolutionary tourist, is theoretically committed to political, economic and sexual redistribution. Politically, she has come to the Caribbean because she had subscribed, in London, to the theory that 'the future of the world was being shaped in places like this, by people like these'. But she has learned instead that 'she had come to a place at the end of the world, to a place that had exhausted its possibilities' (*G*, p.50)—and she hangs on to her return air ticket. Sexually, Jane has a history of mild promiscuity and she measures up every new man as a 'candidate' or competitor for her sexual favours. In a novel in which sexual relations can be construed as commodity relations she is herself a prime example of the fetishism of commodities. When she arrives at the all-male commune of Thrushcross Grange she fails to respond when Bryant first addresses her, calling her 'sister'. The name to which she does respond, however, is 'white lady'—and she responds by giving Bryant a dollar (Ch.1). At the Grange, partly through her own choice, she becomes a priced and labelled commodity—first the 'white lady', later the 'white rat'. On two occasions Jimmy will lure her back to the Grange with the claim that Bryant wants to give her back her dollar. Bryant, however, actually spends the dollar on going to see a Sidney Poitier movie, which merely intensifies his sense of deprivation. Money in the novel circulates within a closed system: the advanced countries exploiting the Third World by holding out the lure of consumer gratifications. With sex, however, it is different. By telling the story of Jane, Naipaul means to bring home to his readers that redistribution can only be accomplished with violence, and that redistribution involves violation.

The central image of violation in the novel is sexual: rape and sexual degradation leading to murder. The sexual politics of *Guerrillas* will probably not meet with universal approval: both men and women are shown as being complicit in the sexual violence and commodification. Men are the consumers of pornography, the sexual aggressors, and the projectors of an agrarian communism in which (apparently) there is no place for women. Jimmy treats Jane as if she were a commodity, although his fantasies—revealed in the Mills-and-Boon style romance he is writing—convert her image into a fetish. Jane's sex life, however, has always been a process of violation, with which she has more or less willingly complied. It is she who reaches out for her neighbour's pornographic book in order to while away the time during her flight from London (p.45). When Jimmy goes to bed with her he perceives that 'without knowing it, she had developed the bad temper, and the manners of a prostitute' (p.81). And with Jimmy she realises that she is 'playing with fire' (p.83), and yet she goes on playing with it, just as Jimmy himself goes on playing with the idea of revolution. Both seem destined to die in the knowledge that they have been fooling themselves.

Guerrillas is the most sexually explicit of Naipaul's novels, with an explicitness which only the social currency of pornography in today's world has made possible for the writer. The meaning of the sexual acts Naipaul describes is that, through them, his protagonists find themselves working out the symbolic conflicts inscribed in the history of the Caribbean—a history of slavery. The men reading pornography on the plane are executives of the American bauxite company which, as Roche puts it, 'owns the island'; in earlier days they would have got their kicks from exploiting the 'niggers'. Both Jimmy and Bryant, as Jane's murderers, are acting out fantasies based on the role of the rebellious slave—the slave who cannot get at his real aggressors, such as the bauxite company's shareholders or the American soldiers whose arrival at the airfield is sufficient to quell the city riots. The circuit of sexual redistribution is thus not only violent but wholly ineffectual, symbolic; but this is the case with almost all the actions of primitive rebels.

Of Jane we are told that 'she was indifferent, perhaps blind, to the contradiction between what she said and what she was so secure of being' (p.25); and this faculty of saying one thing and being another is, according to Naipaul, a characteristic of European duplicity.[15] Nevertheless, every figure in *Guerrillas* has a split personality, and each of them is guilty to a greater or lesser extent of Orwellian 'doublethink'. On several occasions we see one person inflicting humiliation by exposing the contradictions of another; yet Jane, having been humiliated by Jimmy, is eventually killed by the one character who is more helpless and vulnerable than she is. The split in Bryant is represented by the irreconcilable dualism of his taste in films: on the one hand, Sidney Poitier movies, and, on the other, 'interracial-sex films with Negro men as star-boys' (p.36), which he comes to believe are wicked. Bryant's split personality gives rise to an intense self-hatred, which can only find an outlet in spasms of uncontrollable symbolic hatred of others. Together with Jimmy he kills Jane, and (if the authorities do not get there first) he will probably end up by killing Jimmy as well.

Jane's sexual value as a 'white lady' and Bryant's murderousness are, in a sense, the givens of the novel, the barbarous and unexamined results of a history of colonialism and slavery. Jimmy's behaviour and emotions are more elaborately fantastic, more of a deliberate narcissistic creation. He writes a novel in which Jane is the narrator, and in which Jane sees him as the incarnation of the Noble Robber:

> He lives in his own rare world, his head is full of big things, he is carrying the burden of all the suffering people in the world, all the people who live in shacks and grow up in dirty little back rooms....He is an enemy to all privilege and I am middle class born and bred and I know that in spite of his great civility and urbane charm he must hate people like me. I only have to look in his eyes to understand the meaning of hate. (p.40)

The extent to which Jimmy's self-consciousness is a fictional artifice is revealed when we learn that, in England, a female journalist had written of him that to look into his eyes was to understand the meaning of hate (p.140). In Jimmy's novel, in Mills-and-Boon style, 'Jane' reflects that *'he's the man who controls this hate I see around me and he's the only man who can turn this hate into love'* (p.89). In place of self-reflection Jimmy has substituted the fetishisation of a fetishisation.

The presence of Jimmy's debased romantic narrative within Naipaul's novel is an exemplification of Harry Levin's view of the realist novel as a dialectic of 'fabulation and debunking', a synthesis of the 'imposition of reality upon romance' and the 'transposition of reality into romance'.[16] Unusually, we see the progress of Jimmy's fictionalisation of Jane and of his actual attempt to start an affair with her side by side. The fictionalisation feeds his behaviour; at one moment early in the seduction he even tells Jane that 'I thought my imagination might have been playing tricks' (p.73). Jane is aware of what this might mean, but she is trapped because she 'yet allowed herself to play with the images he had set floating in her mind' (p.74).

III

We say that Jane is trapped *because*...—and in that judgment, and in judgments of a similar kind that we might make about many other characters and incidents, lies the whole force of *Guerrillas*. In other words, Naipaul's novel stands or falls by its mimetic evocation of the Aristotelian processes of probability and necessity. The novel for Naipaul is a supremely rational imaginative medium, an inquiry into human action and the reciprocal relationships of fantasy and action. Like a juridical process, the inquiry itself is open to inquiry, and that is why Naipaul could later claim that 'fiction never lies': to the extent that it did lie, it would be found out. Perhaps it is inevitable that fiction of this sort would come down harshly on the spectacle of the imagination playing tricks on itself. Finally—as in a law-court—'truth' and 'fantasy' have to be distinguished from one another. If my reading of *Guerrillas* is found to be persuasive, then Naipaul's fundamental opposition to the sort of nihilism which is endemic in deconstructionist thinking will be evident; indeed, I would say that *Guerrillas* poses a challenge to contemporary literary theory of a kind that theory, as at present constituted, could only meet by misreading or belittling Naipaul's work. After all, to a rigorous conventionalist the idea that there is some external moral standard against which hallucination, or the imagination 'playing tricks', could be weighed and found wanting is meaningless. All that matters to the conventionalist is, so to speak, winning tricks in the game that the imagination plays. And this is why poststructuralist 'textuality' tends to exalt comic fiction, with its self-delighting virtuosity and witty reflexivity, and (by the same token) to call in question the gravity of tragic fictions which, so often, turn on what we must call the 'fact' of murder. Tragic novels cannot *force* our acceptance of the deaths or murders, with which they conclude, as 'facts'—for they are after all fictions—but unless we accept these deaths as truths in the Aristotelian sense (that is, as probable and necessary outcomes) tragic gravity will seem to be no more than a device and the impact of the fiction will be much diminished.

Jane views her sex life as a form of compulsive play; but play that is a 'continuing violation'. 'She spoke as though she had never exercised choice. Events, society, the nature of men, her own needs as a woman, had sent her out into the sexual jungle, to play perilously with the unknown' (p.97). Her 'needs as a woman', as she sees them, are principally a need for the 'little delirium' (p.75), the adventure of sexual excitement. Naipaul views this need without compassion, revealing it rather as one of the phenomena of cultural decadence: his characters are conscious of decay and corruption all around them, of a sense of desolation learnt in England but enhanced by the squalor of the Third World and the tropics. This shared vision of a 'world running down' (p.56) and coming to an end stands in the novel for a version of truth; a truth against which the characters' addiction to various forms of play is to be judged. But there seem to be other forms of truth in *Guerrillas*, manifestations more specific and local, and perhaps more absolute. These are truths that appear in the form of momentary insights or pronouncements, 'sentences' which are unforeseen, involuntary, and apprehended privately. In *Guerrillas*, then, we find a contrast between the discourse of imaginative play and literary invention—a poetic mode of perception, moulded by fantasy, whether in the narrative voice or attributed to a particular character—and a discourse of revelation or annunciation: a perception, later to be authenticated by the unravelling of probability and necessity, which is said to be visited on the individual from an unknown source.

Jimmy Ahmed, for example, finds his equivalent to Jane's 'little delirium' in the act of writing sub-pornographic fiction; but once he has lost the 'writing excitement' he sees that 'The words on the page were again just like words, false' (p.41). The words are a screen intended to blot out his 'vision of darkness, of the world lost forever, and his own life ending on that bit of waste land' (p.38)—a prophetic vision which by the end of *Guerrillas* seems very likely to be fulfilled. Jane's momentary intimation of danger after she lets Jimmy seduce her is more explicitly invested with prophetic authority:

She looked at the driver's mirror: his red eyes were considering her, and they held her return stare. She looked out at the fields; the junked motor-cars beside the road; the men far away, small and busy, stuffing grass into the boots of motor-cars to take home to their animals; the smoking hills, yellow in the mid-afternoon light. But she was aware of the driver's intermittent stare; and whenever she looked at the mirror she saw his red, assessing eyes. A whole sentence ran through her head, at first meaningless, and then, as she examined it, alarming. She thought: I've been playing with fire. Strange words, to have come so suddenly and so completely to her: something given, unasked for, like an intimation of the truth, breaking into the sense of safety, of distance being put between her and the desolation of that house. (p.83)

We can, of course, discount this if we wish: the taxi-driver's eyes are a familiar figure for the Protestant conscience—Big Brother is watching—and, the 'little delirium' over, Jane feels as if she has been naughty and has been found out. But the narrative will confirm that this was indeed an intimation of the truth. Roche, arriving at Thrushcross just after the murder and also aware of someone else's gaze, has a comparable moment of insight:

He thought: This place has become a slaughter-ground. The words seemed to have been given to him, and he thought: I've just done the bravest thing in my life. He concentrated on Jimmy and addressed him mentally: You wouldn't do anything to me. You wouldn't dare. (p.249)

The moment is not without its irony: Roche's 'courage' does not consist in denouncing the crime that has been brought home to him, but in saving his skin by turning his back on it and walking away. The words which are 'given to him' and which convey an intuitive knowledge do not in any way guarantee a proper or heroic response. If language in Naipaul sometimes acquires a mysterious authority—as if it were the very voice of reality—his characters are destined to be judged by the reader not to have listened to it. But the novel itself does not enact such a judgment—it is left entirely to the reader. Where the modern tragic novel such as *Guerrillas* differs from its nineteenth-century predecessors is chiefly in the narrative restraint that it shows, presenting a delicate and arduous case and inviting the reader to serve as juror.

The central difficulty of moral judgment in *Guerrillas* is provided by the figure of Roche. At first sight he seems something of a cliché, an embodiment of the pathos of the defeated liberal. He seems to attract more narrative sympathy than either Jane or Jimmy, and his perceptions are made to seem more authoritative than theirs. Roche is a former guerrilla fighter who was involved in amateurish acts of sabotage in South Africa, and was subsequently imprisoned and tortured. He was exiled to England, wrote a book, and acquired something of a martyr's halo. But, like Jimmy's, his English reputation was bogus: he had lost his political vision, and left England for the Caribbean not under the sway of idealism but because he had been frightened away by the South African secret police. Torture and humiliation have entered his soul; to what extent, we do not fully realise until after the riots when official disapproval has descended on Thrushcross Grange, and Meredith Herbert, a politician and media personality, subjects Roche to a devastating radio interview. Roche has a propensity for walking into traps: in South Africa, in his Caribbean job of organising support for a commune which could not conceivably have fulfilled its promises, and in the interview—given when the government is in need of a scapegoat—which effectively undermines his position on the island. He does not fight back against the people who trap him, preferring to escape from their clutches and move somewhere else. There is something abject and sterile about his passivity, which Meredith (who would have made a passable torturer) cunningly exposes on the radio. Roche's intelligence and rationality are made to seem futile. Like Winston Smith, though much less sensationally, he bears an unacknowledged responsibility for his own victimisation. None of this, however, prepares us for the ending which robs him of the last vestige of moral heroism.

It is Jane's intuitions about Roche which add up to a different story. In the opening chapter, we read that 'Roche laughed, and Jane saw his molars: widely spaced, black at the roots, the gums high: like a glimpse of the skull' (p.13). No explanation is offered for this detail, but we later become accustomed to Jane's perception of Roche as a split personality, divided between his 'saint's manner' (p.160) and the 'satyr's smile' which appears when he reveals the roots of his molars. What is Jane, and what are we, to make of these glimpses of a 'grotesque stranger' (p.50)? 'In these relationships some warning, some little hint, always was given, some little sign that foreshadowed the future' (p.50), the narrator tells us (we are not quite sure whether or not to attribute this superstitious awareness to Jane). If we follow the logic of intimations such as these, we shall come to see all three of Naipaul's main characters as based on primitive archetypes: Jimmy the succubus, Jane the prostitute, and Roche the satyr. But Jane cannot deal with the 'little sign', and neither for the time being can the reader. The narrative foreshadowing is not obtrusive, and the ending, which shows Roche to be a personality as crippled as Jimmy or Jane, comes to us like a new and shocking revaluation.

Guerrillas is formally open-ended: Jimmy, Bryant and Roche are still apparently free agents, even if Jane is dead. There is not even the likelihood of the discovery of the murdered body and of a trial and a hanging such as closed the case of Michael Abdul Malik. Nevertheless, a burden of judgment is, as we have seen, laid upon the reader (though a poststructuralist interpreter would doubtless emphasise, not the nature of this judgment, but its deferral). The imagined evidence that Naipaul puts before us—though a good deal more complex than a necessarily simplifying and foreshortened account such as the present one can indicate—is not 'undecidable': it admits of a verdict. The narrative is one of circulation, a redistributive cycle in which a human being is violated by being turned into a commodity, but finally the circulation comes to a stop: Jane's violation is terminal. At this point we can pass moral judgments on those who took part in it. But the judgments are of a different sort from those implied or stated by more traditional 'liberal-humanist' fictions.

In an essay on 'Character Change and the Drama', Harold Rosenberg draws a distinction between the 'biological/historical' and the 'legal' views of character. According to the biological or historical view, character is the expression of a psychological condition, a developing organic identity. Action or behaviour, in this view, is 'a mere attribute of, and clue to, a being who can be known only through an intuition'.[17] The organic view of personality as based on 'continuity of being' is expressed in biography and, for the most part, in the modern novel; and this is the view which is normally associated with liberal humanism. The legal view, by contrast, defines the human individual as an actor, whose identity arises from the 'coherence of his acts with a fact in which they have terminated (the crime or the contract) and by nothing else'. Individuals are 'conceived as identities in systems whose subject matter is action and the judgement of actions. In this realm the multiple incidents in the life of an individual may be synthesised, by the choice of the individual himself or by the decision of others, into a scheme that pivots on a single fact central to the individual's existence and which, controlling his behaviour and deciding his fate, becomes his visible definition' (p.138). This mode of identity is represented in tragic drama, even though, from a traditional liberal-humanist perspective, the identification of a person with a single, terminal act (say, as a murderer or an accomplice after the fact of murder) may be no more than a 'legal fiction'. The legal identity of the individual is determined not solely by his own actions but by the judgment that is passed upon them.

The contrast between 'organic personality' and 'legal identity' is likely to be present in all major novels and plays: Rosenberg himself applies it to the analysis of *Hamlet*. My claim is that in *Guerrillas* Naipaul exploits it in a way that is quite different from nineteenth-century fiction, where a delayed revelation of legal identity is normally used to endorse organic identity. In his interview with Meredith Herbert, Roche is trying desperately to preserve and justify his own sense of organic identity in the face of Meredith's indictment of his actions. Roche is, in effect, arguing for forgiveness, for the right to make mistakes, the right to be judged on the purity of his intentions. He would like to plead that he is someone apart from his actions. Meredith, a harsh prosecuting counsel, denies this, mocking what he takes as Roche's self-indulgence: 'what a nice world you inhabit, Peter. You have so much room for error' (p.207). Inhabiting such a 'nice world' is, Meredith implies, one of the privileges reserved for 'white people'. The interview, however, is not fought to a finish, and the question of its moral outcome is something Naipaul is careful to leave suspended.

In nineteenth-century novels the commonest way of uncovering a character's organic identity is to look into his or her face: the face serving as a window allowing us to read off what is written in the soul, or the heart.[18] Jane, we have noted, has moments of recognition in which, looking at Roche's sinister smile, she intuits the 'inner man' (p.50). But the value of these moments is left uncertain, and what is revealed is so shockingly different from Roche's own sense of his 'inner man' that the intuition can only be taken as a parody of comparable moments in nineteenth-century novels. Jane does not see anything that liberal individualism would recognise as an organic identity. Instead, she sees a satyr, a being that is irreducible and inhuman: an alien. (In this, *Guerrillas* perhaps resembles *Wuthering Heights*, where the protagonists also invest one another with non-human characteristics. Both novels break with liberal individualism by invoking archaic and demonic notions of identity.) The significance of Jane's vision is that, arguably, it foreshadows the true 'legal identity' of Roche, as it appears from his terminal actions at the end of the novel. But we can scarcely maintain that Roche 'is' the satyr—we see him in all his complexity as a represented character—a character, however, who eludes our attempts to reduce him to organic coherence.

We can ask: who or what are Roche, Jimmy, Jane?—but finally our questions will turn to the novelist who animates these fictions with such originality and truth of observation. In *Guerrillas* Naipaul has furthered a technique of impartiality which is, more or less, constitutive of serious modern fiction. It is the technique of 'perpetual shifting of the standpoint' and of the 'artifice of seeing through the eyes of characters' which, as long ago as 1895, H.G.Wells observed in the novels of George Meredith. What Wells added on that occasion is also relevant: 'It may be that Mr Meredith sometimes carries his indirect method to excess, and puzzles a decent public, nourished on good healthy straightforward marionettes'.[19] There is no 'revolutionary' break between the fiction of writers such as Meredith and Conrad and that of Naipaul, but the degree of indirection achieved by the latter would, surely, have puzzled Meredith's most ardent readers. Naipaul's ostentatious, even fastidious, detachment is the most difficult element in the novel that we must unravel: a detachment which implies disinterestedness, but scarcely impartiality, for it 'reveals the writer totally'. Our sense of Naipaul's detachment comprehends a number of factors. There is, for example, a tension between the novelist's almost vindictive exposure of his characters' inadequacies and self-contradictions, and his shafts of surprising sympathy and generosity towards the least lovable of them. There is Naipaul's palpable irritation with the more rootless of his characters (those uncommitted to life on the island), and his, or the narrator's, rather unquestioning respect for the 'authorities' who have the task of making a continuing orderly life possible there. There is the curious and disturbing feature that, in such a mordant study of contemporary racial and sexual confusions, Naipaul has eliminated characters of his own race and has tied his characters' 'revolutionary' hopes to the success of a homosexual commune, a foundation on which (by definition) the future cannot be built.

The quality of detachment in *Guerrillas* is linked to the fact that, alone among Naipaul's novels, it does not contain a single character of Indian descent. (In real life Michael X's entourage included two Trinidad Indians, one of whom gave himself up to the police and was eventually sentenced to life imprisonment.) Naipaul's early novels, *The Mystic Masseur* and *A House for Mr Biswas*, portrayed the Trinidad Hindu as comic epic hero. His two other major novels, *The Mimic Men* and *A Bend in the River*, are first-person narratives told by Indian settlers (the former in London and the Caribbean, the latter in East and Central Africa). Even 'In a Free State', his novella-length study of Europeans in a politically turbulent African state, includes the image of an ordinary, 'decent' Hindu trader. In these books detachment coexists with an open warmth and partisanship; the characters' success in engaging our attention is also the author's, even when he mocks them. *Guerrillas*, however, is set not in Trinidad but on a fictional Caribbean island inhabited by Negroes, creoles, Europeans, and Chinese, but not apparently by East Indians. Is that why the island is so unremittingly condemned as a lost and fallen world, in which—though good order and restraint are still felt as virtues—'When everybody wants to fight there's nothing to fight for'? Can it be that in *Guerrillas* Naipaul has constructed for himself a way of playing with fire without getting burnt?

If so, that is his privilege. The weaknesses so fully exposed in Roche, Jane, and Jimmy, are human weaknesses, which in some way must reflect the weaknesses of their creator. If the figure of Jane, the murdered and violated woman, is offered as the embodiment of circulation as violation, the novelist is a circulator who can share the viewpoints of all his characters and yet remain inviolable. For example, in an unforgettable passage, Naipaul allows us to enter into Bryant's consciousness. Bryant, stunted, poverty-stricken and starved of affection, symbolises the moral injustice of the distribution of the world's resources which leads to the perennial, and misleading, legend of the Noble Robber. Bryant is doomed: whatever charitable gifts are made to him—his place in the commune, his dollar, his 'rat'—are only aids to his destruction. Bryant is rooted on the island, while the novelist, like his principal characters, is free of such roots: the slum-boy is, so to speak, the human material which Naipaul, as traveller and journalist, goes to investigate. And from this we may conclude that Naipaul, like Roche (his 'satyr') is an escape-artist, and that his art is the art of the survivor who pieces together a tale which could only be 'authentically' voiced by people who have been silenced, who have suffered violent deaths or who languish imprisoned by their own inarticulacy, if not by the law. Naipaul's art is, inevitably, fabricated, speaking not through revealed truths but through the constructions of fantasy and the 'legal fictions' of probability and necessity. Its significance lies not only in its intricate construction and imaginative play but in its wisdom. Writers, whom Naipaul has rather wistfully compared to tribal wise men, must, he has said, 'know more, have felt more and thought more than others, offering us some point of rest'.[20] They must also address the tribe on matters on which the rest of the tribe is silent.

Notes

PART I

1. The Failure of Theory

1. T.S.Eliot, quoted by Daniel G. Hoffman in *American Poetry and Poetics*, ed. Hoffman, Garden City, N.Y.(Anchor Books) 1962, p.277.
2. *Ibid.*, p.287. Subsequent quotations from 'The Philosophy of Composition' are from the text as printed by Hoffman.
3. Modern biographical evidence points to a very different conclusion. See e.g. J.R.Hammond, *An Edgar Allan Poe Companion*, London (Macmillan) 1981, p.157.
4. Daniel Hoffman, *Poe Poe Poe Poe Poe Poe Poe*, London (Robson Books) 1973, pp.82-8.
5. Howard Felperin, *Beyond Deconstruction: The Uses and Abuses of Literary Theory*, Oxford (Clarendon Press) 1985, pp.221-2.
6. Toril Moi, *Sexual/Textual Politics: Feminist Literary Theory*, London and New York (Methuen) 1985, p.15.
7. R.G.Collingwood, *An Autobiography*, Oxford (Oxford University Press) 1939, p.62.
8. See e.g. Richard Rorty, *Consequences of Pragmatism (essays 1972-1980)*, Brighton (Harvester Press) 1982, pp.150-1.
9. The article is by Antony Easthope. *Poetry Nation Review*, 48 (1985), pp.36-8.
10. Walter Benjamin, 'Conversations with Brecht', in Ernst Bloch *et al.*, *Aesthetics and Politics*, London (New Left Books) 1977, p. 97.
11. Jürgen Habermas, *Knowledge and Human Interests*, trans. Jeremy J. Shapiro, London (Heinemann) 1972, p.301.
12. See the definition given in the *Concise Oxford Dictionary*. This meaning is not, however, recorded in editions of the *Oxford English Dictionary* that I have consulted. The whole topic would benefit from much fuller investigation.
13. Max Raphael, *The Demands of Art*, trans. Norbert Guterman, London (Routledge & Kegan Paul) 1968, p.190.
14. See Christopher Norris, *The Contest of Faculties: Philosophy and Theory after Deconstruction*, London and New York (Methuen) 1985, pp.1-18.

2. Two Case-Studies

(i) Catherine Belsey and Classic Realism

1. Catherine Belsey, *Critical Practice*, London and New York (Methuen) 1980 ('New Accents' series). All page references in the text of this chapter refer to this book.
2. George Steiner, 'Viewpoint: A New Meaning of Meaning', *Times Literary Supplement*, 8 November 1985, p.1262.
3. In this spirit Belsey, seizing on the phrase 'relative human values' in Leavis's criticism, has accused him of promoting the sort of thinking that led to the concentration camp. Catherine Belsey, 'Re-reading the Great Tradition', in *Re-Reading English*, ed. Peter Widdowson, London and New York (Methuen) 1982, p.128. However, it is fair to add that the French for 'call in question' is *mettre en question*, so there is at least a prepositional difference between questioning and torture.
4. Quoted by Stephen Heath, *The Nouveau Roman*, London (Elek) 1972, p.89.
5. Terry Lovell, *Pictures of Reality: Aesthetics, Politics, Pleasure*, London (BFI Publishing) 1980, p.83.
6. Karl Marx, 'The English Middle Class', in Karl Marx and Frederick Engels, *On Literature and Art*, Moscow (Progress Publishers) 1976, p.339.
7. Stephen Heath's study of *The Nouveau Roman* provides some choice examples of this. Heath condemns the whole project of realistic fiction as epistemologically naive but, virtually in the same breath, he demands that we attend to the 'reality of language' (p.36), the 'reality' of Joyce's work (p.35), the 'reality of the work of the nouveau roman' and the 'reality of the experience of reading it proposes' (p.42). At no point does he show a moment's hesitation in assuming that these various 'realities' are directly accessible to himself as a literary theorist. At the same time he detects a campaign to suppress these realities on the part of rival interpreters and, on occasion, the novelists themselves.
8. Belsey, in *Re-reading English*, pp.125–8.
9. Leavis's work is part of the conspiracy of capitalist ideology, Belsey argues, because his discourse 'helps to guarantee relations of inequality by the endless production of discriminations between subjectivities'. A few lines later she proceeds as follows:

> What are the implications of a refusal of the Leavisian critical discourse? Does it follow that we reject both the institution of English and the great tradition in their entirety? Not necessarily, I want to argue. A case can be made, of course, for abandoning the whole bag of tricks, but it is finally, I think, a bad case. (*Re-reading English*, pp.129–30)

The style of authority here is less than Leavisian, but the show of appealing to rational argument is purely rhetorical. Belsey's 'I think' and 'I want to argue' are, precisely, a way of producing 'discriminations between subjectivities'. It is only on humanist grounds that a mode of address such as this could be justified. To a deconstructionist it is just hot air.

10. Cf. Richard Johnson, 'What is Cultural Studies Anyway?', in *Anglistica*, 26 Nos. 1-2 (1983), pp.69-70.

11. Belsey's attempt to disclaim any evaluative intention (p.103) is not, I think, very convincing. It is significant that she does not seem widely read in the realist tradition, and shows very little enthusiasm for it.

12. Belsey, *Re-reading English*, p.134.

13. For example, Belsey's account of *What Maisie Knew* in *Critical Practice* relies on the assertion that 'Maisie's subjectivity is given. She becomes sharper, more acute in the course of the novel, but her radical innocence, integrity and sensitivity are understood to be simply there and unalterable' (p.82). The moment we retort (as many readers would) that we are never exactly sure what Maisie knows or how she is changed by what she learns, *What Maisie Knew* becomes an 'interrogative' text and is redeemed from its status as 'classic realism'. A similar argument applies to Belsey's discussion of *Bleak House*.

14. Johnson, 'What is Cultural Studies Anyway?', p.70.

15. Harry Levin, *The Gates of Horn: A Study of Five French Realists*, New York (Oxford University Press) 1963, p.55.

(ii) The Myth of Terry Eagleton

1. Terry Eagleton, *Criticism and Ideology*, London (New Left Books) 1976, p.43; and *Walter Benjamin or Towards a Revolutionary Criticism*, London (Verso) 1981, p.96. The other books by Terry Eagleton referred to in this section are as follows: *The New Left Church*, London (Sheed & Ward) 1966; *From Culture to Revolution: The Slant Symposium 1967*, ed. Eagleton and Brian Wicker, London (Sheed & Ward) 1968; *Literary Theory: An Introduction*, Oxford (Basil Blackwell) 1983; and *The Function of Criticism: From 'The Spectator' to Post-Structuralism*, London (Verso) 1984. Page references are given in the text.

2. 'Art under Plutocracy' (1884), in *Political Writings of William Morris*, ed. A.L.Morton, London (Lawrence & Wishart) 1973, p.61.

3. T.S.Eliot, *Selected Essays*, London (Faber & Faber) 1951, pp.24-5.

3. On Disagreement and the Public Domain

1. Eliot, *Selected Essays*, pp.24-5.

2. See, for example, Tony Bennett, 'Text and History', in *Re-Reading English*, p.235.

3. Stanley Fish, *Is There a Text in This Class? The Authority of Interpretive Communities*, Cambridge and London (Harvard University Press) 1980, p.16. Subsequent page references are given in the text.

4. Walter Pater, *Plato and Platonism*, London (Macmillan) 1928, p.172.

5. *Ibid.*, p.159

6. The wording is from Jowett's translation. Benjamin Jowett and Thomas Arnold were the most prominent of the Victorian educators who consciously modelled their teaching on the 'Socratic method'.

Their significance for Matthew Arnold hardly needs underlining. See Richard Jenkyns, *The Victorians and Ancient Greece*, Oxford (Basil Blackwell) 1980, pp.248–9.

7. Matthew Arnold, *Culture and Anarchy* in *Complete Prose Works*. ed. R.H.Super, Ann Arbor (University of Michigan Press) 1965, V, pp.228–9.

8. From a recent article in the *Guardian* newspaper. Juliet Steyn and Brian Sedgemore, 'A Socialist Policy for the Arts', *Guardian*, 16 December 1985, p.18.

9. Pater, *Plato and Platonism*, p.166.

10. Jürgen Habermas, 'The Public Sphere: An Encyclopaedia Article' (1964), in *New German Critique*, 1 No.3 (Fall 1974), p.49. Subsequent page references are given in the text.

11. *Ibid.*, p.54

12. Peter Uwe Hohendahl, *The Institution of Criticism*, Ithaca (Cornell University Press) 1982, p.165. I have substituted the words 'public domain' for 'public sphere'.

13. Herbert Marcuse, *Negations: Essays in Critical Theory*, trans. Jeremy J.Shapiro, London (Allen Lane) 1968, p.95. Subsequent page references are given in the text.

14. Habermas, 'The Public Sphere', p.52.

15. Hohendahl, *The Institution of Criticism*, p.26.

16. *Ibid.*, pp.165, 243–4.

17. Jürgen Habermas, *Knowledge and Human Interests, op.cit.*, p.314. For a comment see Christopher Prendergast, *The Order of Mimesis*, Cambridge (Cambridge University Press) 1986, p.239.

18. Cf. Richard Johnson, 'What is Cultural Studies Anyway?', *Anglistica*, *loc.cit.*, pp.36–7.

19. Hohendahl, *The Institution of Criticism*, pp. 265–7.

20. *Ibid.*, p.179, citing Hans Magnus Enzensberger.

4. Culture and Society in the 1980s

1. Richard Hoggart and Raymond Williams, 'Working Class Attitudes', *New Left Review* 1 (January-February 1960), p.26.

2. Raymond Williams, *Culture and Society 1780–1950*, Harmondsworth (Penguin Books) 1961, p.13. Referred to as *C & S*. Subsequent page references in the text are to this edition.

3. Logan Pearsall Smith, *Words and Idioms*, 5th edn., London (Constable) 1943, pp.82–3.

4. William Empson, *The Structure of Complex Words*, London (Chatto & Windus) 1951, p.174.

5. Raymond Williams, *Keywords: A Vocabulary of Culture and Society*, London (Fontana/Croom Helm) 1976, pp.9–10. Referred to as *KW*. Subsequent page references are given in the text.

6. Williams does, however, comment on the arbitrariness of 'standard' or 'correct' English (*C & S*, pp.309–10). See also Chapter 4 in Part II of *The Long Revolution*, London (Chatto & Windus) 1961.

7. Quentin Skinner, 'Language and Social Change', in *The State of the*

Language, ed. Leonard Michaels and Christopher Ricks, Berkeley (University of California Press) 1980, p.563.

8. See Williams, *Towards 2000* (U.S. title *The Year 2000*), New York (Pantheon Books) 1983.
9. Raymond Williams, *The Long Revolution*, p.38.
10. On Althusser and Althusserians see E.P.Thompson, *The Poverty of Theory and other essays*, London (Merlin Press) 1978.
11. Raymond Williams, 'Preface to the American Edition', *The Year 2000*, p.ix.
12. A passage Williams has frequently quoted. See, eg., his *Orwell*, London (Fontana/Collins) 1971, p.21.

5. Utopia and Negativity in Raymond Williams
1. Raymond Williams, 'Beyond Cambridge English', in *Writing in Society*, London (Verso) 1984, pp.218, 220 and 212 respectively. The other books and articles by Raymond Williams quoted in this chapter are as follows: *Reading and Criticism*, London (Frederick Muller) 1950 (referred to as *R & C*); 'Film and the Dramatic Tradition' in *Preface to Film* by Williams and Michael Orrom, London (Film Drama) 1954, pp.1–55; *Culture and Society*, op.cit.; 'Culture is Ordinary', in *Conviction*, ed. Norman Mackenzie, London (MacGibbon & Kee) 1958, pp.74–92; *The Long Revolution, op. cit.; Modern Tragedy*, London (Chatto & Windus) 1966; *The Country and the City*, London (Chatto & Windus) 1973 (referred to as *C & C*); *Keywords, op.cit.; Marxism and Literature*, Oxford (Oxford University Press) 1977 (referred to as *M & L*); *Politics and Letters: Interviews with New Left Review*, London (New Left Books) 1979 (referred to as *P & L*); *Culture*, London (Fontana) 1981 (referred to as *C*); 'Marxism, Structuralism and Literary Analysis', in *New Left Review*, 129 (September-October 1981), pp. 51–66 (referred to as *NLR* 129).
2. J.P.Ward, *Raymond Williams*, Cardiff (University of Wales Press) 1981.
3. *Ibid.*, p.55.
4. E.P. Thompson, 'The Long Revolution', in *New Left Review*, 9 (May-June 1961), p.29.
5. *P & L*, pp.105–6.
6. See for example the controversy in *Critical Quarterly*, 6 (1964).
7. In 1984 Williams produced a revised and expanded version of his *Orwell* (1971), and took part in a public debate on Orwell at the Barbican in London.
8. Williams's revision of *Drama in Performance* (first publ. London (Frederick Muller) 1954; new edn. London (Watts) 1968) makes this particularly clear.
9. Terry Eagleton, *Criticism and Ideology*, p.43.

6. Revolutionising the Canon: From Proletarian Literature to Literary Theory
1. 'Attack on literature'—see eg. René Wellek, *The Attack on Literature and Other Essays*, Brighton (Harvester Press) 1982, pp.3–18. The phrase

'terrorist-critics' is from Alastair Fowler, *Kinds of Literature*, Oxford (Clarendon Press) 1982, p.2.

2. Quoted by Boris M. Ejxenbaum, 'The Theory of the Formal Method', in *Readings in Russian Poetics*, ed. Ladislav Matejka and Krystyna Pomorska, Cambridge, Mass. (MIT Press) 1971, p.8.
3. See eg. I.A.Richards, *Science and Poetry*, reissued as *Poetries and Sciences*, London (Routledge & Kegan Paul) 1970.
4. Jurij Tynjanov, 'On Literary Evolution', in *Readings in Russian Poetics*, op.cit., pp.66–78.
5. Wellek, *The Attack on Literature*, p.13 (citing Tertullian and Cassian).
6. *The Critical Writings of James Joyce*, ed. Ellsworth Mason and Richard Ellmann, New York (Viking Press) 1964, pp.39–40.
7. William Hazlitt, 'Coriolanus', in *Liber Amoris and Dramatic Criticisms*, London (Peter Nevill) 1948, p.222.
8. George Orwell, *Collected Essays, Journalism and Letters*, ed. Sonia Orwell and Ian Angus, London (Secker & Warburg) 1968, I. p.413.
9. Tynjanov, 'On Literary Evolution', p.72.
10. I.A.Richards, *Coleridge on Imagination*, London (Kegan Paul, Trench, Trubner) 1934, p.72.
11. Cf. Tynjanov, 'On Literary Evolution', p. 77. See also Dominique Lecourt, *Proletarian Science? The Case of Lysenko*, trans. Ben Brewster, London (New Left Books) 1977, p.158.
12. Ejxenbaum, 'The Theory of the Formal Method', p.35 (quoting Tynjanov).
13. William Empson, 'Proletarian Literature' in *Some Versions of Pastoral*, Harmondsworth (Penguin Books) 1966, pp.9–25. Referred to as *SVP*. Subsequent page references are given in the text. Empson's essay was first published in Japan in 1933, and then (slightly abridged) in *Scrutiny* (March 1935).
14. Karl Marx and Frederick Engels, *On Literature and Art*, ed. Lee Baxandall and Stefan Morawski, New York (International General) 1974, p.71.
15. [Irwin Granich], 'Towards Proletarian Art', reprinted in *Mike Gold: A Literary Anthology*, ed. Michael Folsom, New York (International Publishers) 1972, pp.62–70; Eden and Cedar Paul, *Proletcult*, London (Leonard Parsons) 1921.
16. See Victor Serge, *Littérature et révolution*, Paris (Maspero) 1976.
17. *Mike Gold*, ed. Folsom, p.204.
18. *Ibid.*
19. Lecourt, *Proletarian Science?*, op.cit., p.158.
20. Edward J. Brown, *The Proletarian Episode in Russian Literature 1928-1932*, New York (Octagon Books) 1971, p.219.
21. *Ibid.*, p.9
22. Leon Trotsky, *Literature and Revolution*, Ann Arbor (University of Michigan Press) 1968, pp.11–12. Subsequent page references are given in the text.
23. The Socialist Academy, later the Communist Academy, was the scientific counterpart of the Association of Proletarian Writers (RAPP).

Just as RAPP was disbanded in 1932 and superseded by the Union of Soviet Writers, the Communist Academy was incorporated into the Soviet Academy of Sciences as one of its specialised sections in 1936. Lecourt, *Proletarian Science?*, p.160.

24. Brown, *Proletarian Episode*, p.39; Serge, *Littérature et révolution*, p.120.

25. Max Raphael, *Proudhon, Marx, Picasso: Three Essays in Marxist Aesthetics*, ed. John Tagg, London (Lawrence & Wishart) 1981, p.42. Referred to as *PMP*. Subsequent page references are given in the text.

26. Brown, *Proletarian Episode*, p.213.

27. *Ibid.*, p.82.

28. E. and C. Paul, *Proletcult*, p.22.

29. *Mike Gold*, ed. Folsom, *op.cit.*, p.14.

30. My discussion of proletarian literature in America, and of the general history of the movement, owes more than I can easily record to Eric Homberger's encouragement and guidance. See especially Chapter 5 of his study of *American Writers and Radical Politics, 1900–39*, London (Macmillan) 1986.

31. *Mike Gold*, ed. Folsom, p.68.

32. *Ibid.*, pp.66–7.

33. Gold's article is quoted in Daniel Aaron, *Writers on the Left*, New York (Avon Books) 1969, pp.107–8.

34. Edmund Wilson, 'Marxism and Literature' in *The Triple Thinkers*, Harmondsworth (Penguin Books) 1962, pp.238–9.

35. Max Raphael, *Prehistoric Cave Paintings*, trans. Norbert Guterman, Washington (Pantheon Books) 1945, p.2. Subsequent page references are given in the text.

36. William Empson, *Collected Poems*, London (Chatto & Windus) 1962, p.63.

37. Empson's definition—*SVP*, p.13.

38. The first quotation is from the blurb of *PMP*. The second is from Herbert Read, 'Introduction' to Max Raphael, *The Demands of Art*, *op.cit.*, p.xx. (Referred to as *DOA*. Subsequent page references are given in the text.)

39. Raphael wrote extensively on philosophy and aesthetics as well as on art history. For a full bibliography, including a list of unpublished writings compiled by John Tagg, see *PMP*, pp.147–67.

40. *PMP*, pp.104–8.

41. Roger Fry, 'The Art of the Bushmen', in *Vision and Design*, London (Chatto & Windus) 1923, pp.85–98.

42. It could indeed be argued that Raphael's refusal of a literal reading of the paintings belongs essentially to the age of semiotics, and that it results in an early version of structuralist Marxism. However, my analysis will have shown that crucial aspects of Raphael's approach are incompatible with any form of dogmatic structuralism.

43. John Berger, 'Past Seen from a Possible Future', in *Selected Essays and Articles: The Look of Things*, Harmondsworth (Penguin Books) 1972, p.213.

44. Among the early visitors to the French caves was T.S.Eliot, who saw

them in 1919. Hugh Kenner, *The Pound Era*, London (Faber & Faber) 1975, pp.333–5. Soon afterwards Eliot expounded his conception of the 'mind of Europe', which included everything from 'the rock drawing of the Magdalenian draughtsmen' onwards, in 'Tradition and the Individual Talent'. Eliot, *Selected Essays*, *op.cit.*, p.16. The sculptor Gaudier-Brzeska was the first major modern artist to be inspired by paleolithic art.

45. Jonathan Culler, *On Deconstruction*, Ithaca (Cornell University Press) 1982, p.7.
46. Carole Snee, 'Working-Class Literature or Proletarian Writing?', in *Culture and Crisis in Britain in the Thirties*, ed. Jon Clark, Margot Heinemann, David Margolies and Carole Snee, London (Lawrence & Wishart) 1979, p.166.

PART II

7. The Age of Fantasy
1. Herbert Spencer, 'Use and Beauty' (1852), in *Literary Style and Music*, London (Watts) 1950, pp.115–16.
2. Christopher Lasch, *The Culture of Narcissism*, New York (W.W.Norton) 1978.
3. Christine Brooke-Rose, *A Rhetoric of the Unreal*, Cambridge (Cambridge University Press) 1981, pp.63–4. A subsequent page reference is given in the text.
4. Lasch, *The Culture of Narcissism*, p. 42.
5. Angela Carter, *Heroes and Villians*, Harmondsworth (Penguin Books) 1981, p.137.

8. Pilgrim's Progress: The Novels of B.S. Johnson
1. See B.S.Johnson, *Aren't You Rather Young to be Writing Your Memoirs?*, London (Hutchinson) 1973, pp.13–14 (referred to as *AY*). Other books by B.S.Johnson are cited in this chapter in the following editions: *Travelling People*, London (Panther Books) 1967; *Statements against Corpses: Short Stories* by B.S.Johnson and Zulfikar Ghose, London (Constable) 1964 (referred to as *Statement*); 'You're Human Like the Rest of Them', in *New English Dramatists 14*, Harmondsworth (Penguin Books) 1970, pp.221–31; *Albert Angelo*, London (Panther Books) 1967; *Trawl*, London (Panther Books) 1968; *The Unfortunates*, London (Panther/Secker & Warburg) 1969; *House Mother Normal*, Newcastle (Bloodaxe Books) 1984; *Christie Malry's Own Double-Entry*, London (Quartet Books) 1974; *See the Old Lady Decently*, London (Hutchinson) 1975.
2. Edmund Gosse, *Father and Son*, (1907) London (Heinemann) 1933, pp.22–3.
3. 'Only the Stones', in *Statement*, p.102.
4. Charles Clark of Hutchinson rejected the manuscript of the first volume, *See The Old Lady Decently*, as it stood and suggested it should

be reconstructed as a 'visual novel' on the analogy of *Wisconsin Death Trip*. There was some logic in this idea, but it must have seemed catastrophic to so essentially verbal an artist as Johnson. See Michael Bakewell, foreword to *See the Old Lady*, p.14.

5. A.Alvarez, *The Savage God*, Harmondsworth (Penguin Books) 1974, pp.53–4.
6. 'Clean Living is the Real Safeguard', in *Statement*, p.13.
7. 'Away from the ground', p.2, in *The Unfortunates*. The phrase is repeated in *Christie Malry*, p.113.
8. The list of House Mother's clinical symptoms in the earlier book concludes with 'malignant cerebral carcinoma (dormant)' (p.183).
9. Hugh Kenner, *The Stoic Comedians: Flaubert, Joyce, Beckett*, London (W.H.Allen) 1964.

9. Descents into Hell: The Later Novels of Doris Lessing

1. Doris Lessing, *Martha Quest*, London (Panther Books) 1966, p.17. Other books and stories by Doris Lessing are cited in this chapter in the following editions: *The Grass is Singing*, London (Heinemann) 1973; 'The eye of God in paradise' in *The Habit of Loving*, London (Panther Books) 1966, pp.191–252; *The Golden Notebook*, Harmondsworth (Penguin Books) 1964; 'A Man and Two Women', in *A Man and Two Women*, London (Panther Books) 1965, pp.88–107; *The Four-Gated City*, London (Panther Books) 1972; *Briefing for a Descent into Hell*, London (Panther Books) 1973; 'Report on the Threatened City', in *The Story of a Non-Marrying Man and Other Stories*, Harmondsworth (Penguin Books) 1975, pp.133–66; *The Summer Before the Dark*, London (Jonathan Cape) 1973; *The Memoirs of a Survivor*, Picador edn., London (Pan Books) 1976; *Re: Colonised Planet 5: Shikasta*, London (Jonathan Cape) 1979; *The Marriages Between Zones Three, Four, and Five*, London (Jonathan Cape) 1980; *The Sirian Experiments*, London (Granada) 1982.
2. Lewis Mumford, 'Utopia, the City and the Machine', in *Utopias and Utopian Thought*, ed. Frank E. Manuel, London (Souvenir Press) 1973, pp.3–24.
3. The *Children of Violence* series consists of *Martha Quest, A Proper Marriage, A Ripple from the Storm, Landlocked*, and *The Four-Gated City*. The third and fourth novels in the sequence recount Martha's membership of the Communist Party of Zambesia.
4. Idries Shah, *The Sufis*, London (W.H.Allen) 1977, p.54.
5. The origins of Doris Lessing's fictional portrait of the Coldridges should doubtless be sought in her acquaintance with the extended family of the novelist Naomi Mitchison. Mitchison's article 'Cold War—Then and Now', *New Edinburgh Review*, 52 (November 1980), pp.25–7, briefly recalls her association with Doris Lessing in the Communist Party in the early 1950s.
6. Alan and Sally Landsburg, *In Search of Ancient Mysteries*, New York (Bantam Books) 1974, pp.185–6.
7. This phrase is used in a review of *The Good Terrorist* by Amanda

Sebestyen, *New Socialist* 32 (November 1985), p.43.

8. See Carol Hayes, 'British Progress', *Doris Lessing Newsletter*, VIII No.1 (Spring 1984), pp.10–11.

10. Muriel Spark and Her Critics

1. Muriel Spark, *Loitering with Intent*, London (Triad/Granada) 1982, pp.19–20. Other novels by Muriel Spark are cited in this chapter in the following editions: *The Comforters*, Harmondsworth (Penguin Books) 1963; *Memento Mori and The Girls of Slender Means*, London (Reprint Society) 1965; *The Takeover*, London (Macmillan) 1976. Page references are given in the text.

2. Ruth Whittaker, *The Faith and Fiction of Muriel Spark*, London (Macmillan) 1982, p.129. Other works of criticism discussed in this chapter are: Frank Kermode, 'Muriel Spark', in *Modern Essays*, London (Collins/Fontana) 1971, pp.267–83; David Lodge, 'The Uses and Abuses of Omniscience', in *The Novelist at the Crossroads*, London (Routledge & Kegan Paul) 1971, pp.119–44; Malcolm Bradbury, 'Muriel Spark's Fingernails', in *Critical Quarterly* 14 (1972), pp.241–50, reprinted in *Possibilities*, London (Oxford University Press) 1973, pp.247–55; Gabriel Josipovici, *Writing and the Body*, Brighton (Harvester Press) 1982, pp.83–4; and Peter Kemp, *Muriel Spark*, London (Elek) 1974. Page references are given in the text. In the case of Malcolm Bradbury's essay, the *Critical Quarterly* version is quoted, except for the phrase 'a very high stylist indeed' which comes from the revised version in *Possibilities*.

3. The phrase is used by Kermode, *Modern Essays*, p.270.

11. Orwell and Burgess: Two Versions of Cacotopia

1. Anthony Burgess, *1985*, London (Arrow Books). The other books by Anthony Burgess to which reference is made in this chapter are: *A Clockwork Orange*, Harmondsworth (Penguin Books) 1979; and *The Wanting Seed*, London (Pan Books) 1965. *NB*. The 1972 Penguin edition of *A Clockwork Orange* is not authoritative, for reasons given in note 5 below.

2. Robert Currie, 'The "Big Truth" in *Nineteen Eighty-Four*', in *Essays in Criticism*, 34 No.1 (January 1984), pp.56–69.

3. Here I must respectfully disagree with Bernard Crick, whose searching introduction to the Clarendon Press edition of the novel argues that Winston and Julia 'trusted each other and they even trusted together Mr Charrington and O'Brien'. But Crick and I would both read *Nineteen Eighty-Four* as a 'Swiftian satire'; and as such it surely offers as many traps for the unwary reader as does *Gulliver's Travels*. Introduction to George Orwell, *Nineteen Eighty-Four*, ed. Bernard Crick, Oxford (Clarendon Press) 1984, pp.35, 15.

4. Alan Sandison, *The Last Man in Europe: An Essay on George Orwell*, London (Macmillan) 1974; Christopher Small, *The Road to Miniluv*, London (Gollancz) 1975.

5. Curiously enough, the final chapter in which this happens has been

omitted from at least two editions of the book, including that on which Kubrick's film was based. For Burgess's account of how he 'weakly agreed' to this excision, see his letter in the *Times Literary Supplement*, 11 January 1980, p.38.

12. A Novel for Our Time: V.S.Naipaul's 'Guerrillas'

1. V.S.Naipaul, interview with Ronald Bryden, *Listener*, 22 March 1973, p.368.
2. V.S.Naipaul, 'Michael X and the Black Power Killings in Trinidad', in *The Return of Eva Peron with The Killings in Trinidad*, Harmondsworth (Penguin Books) 1981, p.67. Referred to as *REP*. Subsequent page references are given in the text.
3. See Note 1.
4. 'From the end of 1970 to the end of 1973 no novel offered itself to me'. 'Author's Note' to *REP*.
5. Roland Barthes, 'The Death of the Author', in *Image-Music-Text*, ed. Stephen Heath, London (Fontana/Collins) 1977, pp.142–8.
6. V.S.Naipaul, *An Area of Darkness*, Harmondsworth (Penguin Books) 1968, p.216n.
7. V.S.Naipaul, *Guerrillas*, Harmondsworth (Penguin Books) 1976, p.32. Referred to as *G*. Subsequent page references are given in the text.
8. In *The Mystic Masseur* (1959), *Miguel Street* (1959) and *A House for Mr Biswas* (1961) respectively.
9. V.S.Naipaul, *Miguel Street*, Harmondsworth (Penguin Books) 1971, p.34.
10. V.S.Naipaul, interview with Ronald Bryden, *loc.cit.*, p.370.
11. To readers unfamiliar with Naipaul these literary parallels might seem far-fetched. However, there is a similar network of submerged contrasts and resemblances with Conrad's *Heart of Darkness* in his next novel, *A Bend in the River*.
12. E.J.Hobsbawm, *Bandits*, Harmondsworth (Penguin Books) 1972, p.127.
13. Cf. *ibid.*, pp.42–3.
14. Muriel Spark, *The Only Problem*, London (Bodley Head) 1984, p.16.
15. Compare Salim's analysis of European duplicity in V.S.Naipaul, *A Bend in the River*, New York (Knopf) 1979, p.17.
16. Harry Levin, *The Gates of Horn*, *op.cit.*, p.55.
17. Harold Rosenberg, 'Character Change and the Drama', in *The Tradition of the New*, London (Paladin) 1970, p.126. Subsequent page references are given in the text.
18. See my essay 'The Look of Sympathy', in *Novel*, 5 (Winter 1972), pp.135–47.
19. H.G.Wells, 'The Method of Mr George Meredith', in *H.G.Wells's Literary Criticism*, ed. Patrick Parrinder and Robert M. Philmus, Brighton (Harvester Press) and New Jersey (Barnes & Noble) 1980, pp.63–5.
20. William Drozdiak, 'Writer Without a Country', *Time*, 27 February 1978, p.9.

Index

218

Index